Third Voice: Preaching Resurrection

"Having been well-instructed by Michael Knowles in his previous books (like *We Preach Not Ourselves*), I expected that *Third Voice* would be a feast. I was not disappointed. Knowles is a master at working from biblical texts, particularly Paul's letters, weaving in theological insights, bringing in a wide array of conversation partners, and thereby giving preachers a robust, theological rationale for our preaching. There's not much wrong with contemporary preaching that can't be cured by Knowles' energetic invitation to preach as if God matters. He is so right: the 'third voice' in preaching is the voice that makes all the difference."
—Will Willimon, Professor of the Practice of Christian Ministry, Duke Divinity School, and author of *Accidental Preacher: A Memoir*

"Michael Knowles' homiletics trilogy culminates in this penetrating and eloquent account of preaching as a resurrectional, life-giving practice. He demonstrates that God's resurrection power—displayed in the resurrected life of Jesus—is the source, substance, focus, and hope of preaching. At the same time, Knowles reminds us that resurrectional preaching is cruciform, the words of dependent, inadequate human witnesses to a *crucified* resurrected Lord. This is a much-needed biblical, theocentric theology and spirituality of preaching."
—Michael J. Gorman, Raymond E. Brown Professor of Biblical Studies and Theology, St. Mary's Seminary & University, Baltimore

"How I wish that this book had been available in my juvenile study of homiletics and ordination to ministry. How certain I am to revisit it before returning to a pulpit. In exegetical acuity, capacious learning, careful reasoning, mature judgment, and eloquent clarity, *Third Voice* is one of the finest theologies of preaching I have ever read. 'We are not the ones who make sense of Jesus' resurrection; it is Jesus' resurrection that makes sense of us, fashioning us into witnesses by virtue of its ability to create a coherence and vitality that we would otherwise lack.' Amen."
—C. Clifton Black, Otto A. Piper Professor of Biblical Theology, Princeton Theological Seminary

"This is a smart and bold book. For Michael Knowles, preaching the resurrection is not merely a matter of exploring a theological topic or dissecting a doctrine. It is about being drawn so fully into the life of God that preachers, their sermons, and their hearers are carried up into the great hurricane wind of God's willingness and ability to raise dead hearers to life. Savor this book!"

—Thomas G. Long, Bandy Professor Emeritus of Preaching, Candler School of Theology, Emory University

Third Voice

PREACHING
RESURRECTION

Michael P. Knowles

CASCADE *Books* • Eugene, Oregon

THIRD VOICE
Preaching Resurrection

Copyright © 2021 Michael P. Knowles. All rights reserved. Except for brief quotations in critical publications or reviews, no part of this book may be reproduced in any manner without prior written permission from the publisher. Write: Permissions, Wipf and Stock Publishers, 199 W. 8th Ave., Suite 3, Eugene, OR 97401.

Cascade Books
An Imprint of Wipf and Stock Publishers
199 W. 8th Ave., Suite 3
Eugene, OR 97401

www.wipfandstock.com

PAPERBACK ISBN: 978-1-7252-6579-0
HARDCOVER ISBN: 978-1-7252-6580-6
EBOOK ISBN: 978-1-7252-6581-3

Cataloguing-in-Publication data:

Names: Knowles, Michael P.

Title: Third voice : preaching resurrection / Michael P. Knowles.

Description: Eugene, OR: Cascade Books, 2021 | Series: if applicable | Includes bibliographical references and index.

Identifiers: ISBN 978-1-7252-6579-0 (paperback) | ISBN 978-1-7252-6580-6 (hardcover) | ISBN 978-1-7252-6581-3 (ebook)

Subjects: LCSH: Jesus Christ—Resurrection. | Jesus Christ—Resurrection—Sermons. | Preaching.

Classification: BT482 .K50 2021 (print) | BT482 (ebook)

Manufactured in the U.S.A.   JANUARY 11, 2021

Copyright Notices

The ESV® Bible (*The Holy Bible, English Standard Version®*) copyright © 2001 by Crossway Bibles, a publishing ministry of Good News Publishers. ESV® Text Edition: 2007. The ESV® Bible is adapted from the Revised Standard Version of the Bible, copyright Division of Christian Education of the National Council of the Churches of Christ in the U.S.A. All rights reserved.

Scripture taken from *The Message* copyright © 1993, 1994, 1995, 1996, 2000, 2001, 2002. Used by permission of NavPress Publishing Group.

Scripture quotations taken from the *New American Standard Bible*® (NASB) copyright © 1960, 1962, 1963, 1968, 1971, 1972, 1973, 1975, 1977, 1995 by The Lockman Foundation. Used by permission. www.Lockman.org

Scripture quotations taken from the *New English Bible* copyright © Cambridge University Press and Oxford University Press 1961, 1970. All rights reserved.

Quotations marked NETS are taken from *A New English Translation of the Septuagint*, ©2007 by the International Organization for Septuagint and Cognate Studies, Inc. Used by permission of Oxford University Press. All rights reserved.

Scripture quotations marked NIV are taken from the *Holy Bible, New International Version*®, NIV®. Copyright © 1973, 1978, 1984, 2011 by Biblica, Inc.™ Used by permission of Zondervan. All rights reserved worldwide. www.zondervan.com. The "NIV" and "New International Version" are trademarks registered in the United States Patent and Trademark Office by Biblica, Inc.™

Scripture quotations marked NRSV are from the *New Revised Standard Version Bible*, copyright © 1989 National Council of the Churches of Christ in the United States of America. Used by permission. All rights reserved worldwide.

Scripture quotations marked RSV are from the Revised Standard Version Bible, copyright © 1946, 1952, and 1971 National Council of the Churches of Christ in the United States of America. Used by permission. All rights reserved worldwide.

"Suzanne" by Leonard Cohen. Copyright © 1967 by Leonard Cohen, used by permission of The Wylie Agency LLC.

Dedication

For Oliver O'Donovan
in gratitude

Table of Contents

Preface xiii
Abbreviations xv
Primary Sources xvii

I. INTRODUCTION

Interpreting Resurrection 2
Speaking of God 14
Life "In Christ" 23
Listening, Speaking, Waiting 29

II. LISTENING

CHAPTER ONE: Speaking for God? 33
Presuming to Speak 33
"By What Authority?" 37
Newbigin, Bosch, and the *Missio Dei*: An Initial Corrective 41
Performative Utterance: Doing Things with Words? 51

CHAPTER TWO: Reaching into Silence 58
The Words of Adam and the Word of God 58
Divine Commissives and Human Declaration 64
Perlocutionary Divine Speech 75
Speaking and Not Speaking: The Mystery of Silence 80
Only Drowning Men Can See Him 85
"Ears Thou Hast Dug for Me":
    The Difference Between Listening and Hearing 91
"I Fell Down at His Feet as One Dead" 93

III. SPEAKING

CHAPTER THREE: "He Being Dead Yet Speaketh" 99
Messengers of the Resurrection: "Who Is Sufficient for These Things?" 99
The Message of the Resurrection: "He Is Not Here" 111
Responding to Resurrection: The Necessity of Doubt 119

CHAPTER FOUR: Turning Back from Emmaus 127
Worst Sabbath Ever 128
Their Eyes Were Kept from Recognizing Him 131
Recognition 137
Two Ways of Preaching 148

CHAPTER FIVE: Third Space; Third Voice 156
Contesting Christian Space 156
Homi K. Bhabha and Third Space 161
Horizons Near and Far 169
"Whither Must I Fly?" 174
Third Voice and the Voice of Preaching 182
Postcolonial Homiletics:
    Preaching between Departure and Destination 188

IV. WAITING

CHAPTER SIX: God the Last Word 199
Saint Augustine's Purse: Making Space for God 200
Claiming and Being Claimed: A Disclaimer 207
Ever Holy Saturday 211
Preaching Resurrection 216
Resurrection Preaching as the Confession of Hope 229

Bibliography 233
Index of Modern Authors 247
Index of Early Literature 253

Preface

OCCASIONED BY AN EVER-EXPANDING appreciation for the profound complexity of discipleship, my preaching and major publications over the past two decades have focused principally on the cruciform shape of Christian identity. In particular, research leave during the academic year 2003–2004 gave rise to *We Preach Not Ourselves: Paul on Proclamation* (Brazos, 2008), an exploration of Paul's cruciform ministry as he explains it in 2 Corinthians 1–6. A subsequent research leave in 2011–2012 produced *Of Seeds and the People of God: Preaching as Parable, Crucifixion, and Testimony* (Cascade, 2015), which sought to articulate a cruciform homiletic in relation to the parables of Jesus and the vision of divine power that they express. The present study extends this trajectory toward its logical (and theological) conclusion, considering the homiletical implications of resurrection, which is the divine vindication and empowerment by which God both affirms the fragility of human existence and at the same time offers a reversal of suffering and defeat. It too is the fruit of a research leave, this one generously granted by the Senate of McMaster Divinity College over the Winter semesters of 2018 and 2019, respectively, for which I am deeply grateful.

The basic thesis of this study is that notwithstanding the unavoidable importance of sound exegesis, good grammar, logical structure, rhetorical winsomeness, and the like, spiritually transformative preaching depends above all on divine power, not human agency alone. Like the two previous volumes, this one is addressed both to working preachers and to academics within the homiletical guild who find themselves confounded by the occasional futility of their best preaching and the unexpected success of their worst. Those who would reduce Christian preaching to simple systems, formulas, or surefire strategies for success will find little of interest here. Rather, this study seeks to enter more deeply into the uncontrollable mystery that attends all efforts to speak in the name of Christ, above all on the subject of his (or our) resurrection. Such are the challenges of discipleship and the adversities of human experience that we have little difficulty identifying with Jesus' suffering and crucifixion; resurrection, by contrast, is another matter entirely. Here one can do little more than squint into the overwhelming light and invite others to peer in the same direction. Nonetheless, these three monographs seek to articulate a comprehensive vision of preaching that is modeled on the death and resurrection of Jesus as a single saving act, thereby addressing the theology, spirituality, and practice of Christian ministry.

Ongoing experience of the academic life only serves to deepen my conviction that scholarship is a communal endeavor (even for introverts who would prefer to sequester themselves in their faculty offices or study carrels!). Accordingly, I wish to thank my colleagues (both faculty and staff) at McMaster Divinity College for their consistent support and good humor. I am grateful to Phil Haskell for having undertaken the tedious task of proofreading, while Mike Krause's perceptive comments have sharpened my thinking and invited me to remedy a number of gaps and missteps in the logic of the argument. For the remaining flaws (at this point no doubt more obvious to others than to myself), I of course take full responsibility.

Eastertide, 2020

Abbreviations

ASV	American Standard Version
CD	Karl Barth. *Church Dogmatics*. Translated by G. T. Thomson et al. Edinburgh: T. & T. Clark, 1936–1977.
EHLL	*Encyclopedia of Hebrew Language and Linguistics*. 4 vols. Edited by Geoffrey Khan et al. Leiden: Brill, 2013
EncBudd	*Encyclopedia of Buddhism*. 2 vols. Edited by Robert E. Buswell Jr. New York: Macmillan Reference USA, 2004.
EncJud	*Encyclopaedia Judaica*. 22 vols. Edited by Michael Berenbaum and Fred Skolnik. 2nd ed. Detroit: MacMillan Reference USA, 2007.
ESV	English Standard Version
KJV	King James Version
L&N	Johannes P. Louw, Eugene A. Nida, et al. *Greek-English Lexicon of the New Testament: Based on Semantic Domains*. 2nd ed. 2 vols. New York: United Bible Societies, 1989.
LCL	Loeb Classical Library
LSJ	Henry George Liddell, Robert Scott, and Henry Stuart Jones. *A Greek-English Lexicon*. 9th ed. Oxford: Clarendon, 1996.
LW	*Luther's Works*. 55 vols. Edited by Jaroslav Pelikan and Helmut T. Lehman. Philadelphia: Muhlenberg/Fortress; St. Louis: Concordia, 1955–1986.
MSG	Eugene H. Peterson. *The Message: The Bible in Contemporary Language*. Colorado Springs: NavPress, 2002.

NASB	The New American Standard Bible
NEB	The New English Bible, with the Apocrypha
NETS	*A New English Translation of the Septuagint*. Edited by Albert Pietersma and Benjamin G. Wright. Oxford: Oxford University Press, 2007.
NIV	The Holy Bible: New International Version
NJB	New Jerusalem Bible
NRSV	New Revised Standard Version Bible.
NT	New Testament
PL	*Patrologia Latina Cursus Completus*
RSV	Revised Standard Version
Soncino	*The Babylonian Talmud, Translated into English with Notes, Glossary and Indices*. 35 vols. Edited by Isidore Epstein. London: Soncino, 1935–1952.
TDNT	*Theological Dictionary of the New Testament*. 10 vols. Edited by Gerhard Kittel and Gerhard Friedrich. Translated by Geoffrey W. Bromiley. Grand Rapids: Eerdmans, 1964–1976.
TDOT	*Theological Dictionary of the Old Testament*. 15 vols. Edited by G. Johannes Botterweck, Heinz-Josef Fabry, and Helmer Ringgren. Translated by David E. Green and Douglas W. Scott. Grand Rapids: Eerdmans, 1975–2015.
WA	*Luthers Werke: Kritische Gesamtausgabe [Schriften]*. 73 vols. Weimar: H. Böhlau, 1883–2009.
WA TR	*Luthers Werke: Kritische Gesamtausgabe: Tischreden*. 6 vols. Weimar: H. Böhlaus Nachfolger, 1912–1921.

Primary Sources
(accessed via Logos Bible Software 8.118.11.0.0017 © 2000–2020 Faithlife Corporation)

The Babylonian Talmud: A Translation and Commentary. 22 vols. Edited and translated by Jacob Neusner et al. Peabody, MA: Hendrickson, 2011.

The Babylonian Talmud, Translated into English with Notes, Glossary and Indices. 35 vols. Edited by Isodore Epstein. London: Soncino, 1935–1952.

The Greek New Testament: SBL Edition. Edited by Michael W. Holmes. Bellingham, WA: Lexham; Atlanta: Society of Biblical Literature, 2011–2013.

The Holy Bible: New Revised Standard Version. Nashville: Thomas Nelson, 1989. Unless otherwise indicated, Scripture citations are from the NRSV.

The Jerusalem Talmud: A Translation and Commentary. Edited and translated by Jacob Neusner et al. Peabody, MA: Hendrickson, 2008.

The Mishnah: A New Translation. Translated by Jacob Neusner. New Haven: Yale University Press, 1988.

The Tosefta: Translated from the Hebrew with a New Introduction. 2 vols. Translated by Jacob Neusner. Peabody, MA: Hendrickson, 2002.

I.

Introduction

I called through your door,
"The mystics are gathering
in the street. Come out!"

"Leave me alone.
I'm sick!"

"I don't care if you're dead!
Jesus is here, and he wants
to resurrect somebody!"

—Jalāl al-Dīn Rūmī (1207–1273)[1]

Attempting to offer a constructive account of the intersection between preaching and resurrection (whether this refers to preaching on the topic of resurrection, the resurrection of preaching as an activity in itself, or the resurrection of dead preachers) may seem at best implausible, at worst an exercise in futility. For while it is not difficult to encounter crucifixion without a resurrection, it is impossible to experience resurrection without the cross. That is what makes resurrection so difficult to

---

1. Barks, *The Essential Rumi*, 201–2. One of the most influential figures in Persian culture, Rūmī was a Sunni Muslim and Sufi mystic whose poetry frequently refers to Jesus.

preach about: from our perspective the one is plain, even without faith, whereas the other seems incomplete, even for those with great faith. Again, while human ingenuity has produced many unspeakable forms of torment without any help from God (crucifixion prominent among them), resurrection from death is impossible without divine assistance.

Resurrection is therefore, by definition, a dynamic over which preachers have no control. Much as we preach in the aftermath of Jesus' resurrection, there is no direct or causal trajectory that leads from the sermon to the resurrection of our hearers. To assert such a possibility would be to deny the essential character of resurrection itself as that which stands over against us and confounds, even sabotages, our normal categories of understanding and action. Nonetheless, the following study attempts to wrestle with the paradox of speaking (and thereby exercising human agency) about a premise that surpasses and subverts human agency both in principle and in practice.

Since resurrection entails fundamental questions about the nature of Christian faith, such an inquiry requires initial (if brief) clarification of two important questions. First, how is the resurrection of Jesus best understood, either in historical or theological terms, and, second, what is its relevance to Christian life and ministry, on the assumption that an essential purpose of preaching is the shaping of Christian discipleship? If, as Christian orthodoxy contends, Jesus' resurrection is indeed critical to faith, pilgrimage, ministry, and the gospel itself, what are we to make of it—and what does it make of us?

Interpreting Resurrection

Much effort has been expended on the task of articulating conceptual trajectories that can account for resurrection, so as to render the category in general or the resurrection of Jesus in particular intellectually plausible on the basis of some conceptual precedent or point of departure located within our normal understanding of the world we inhabit. So too, much effort has been expended on describing the impossibility of such a venture, contending that what the first disciples saw—or imagined they saw—can only be explained on the basis of simplemindedness and credulity, wish-fulfilment, group hallucination, metaphor, myth-making, or something of the sort. Accordingly, explanations of Jesus' resurrection fall generally into one of three categories: (1) psychological and existential; (2) literary, mythological, or theological; and (3) historical or quasi-historical.[2]

The first category locates the genesis of belief in Jesus' resurrection in the minds of his followers and nowhere else. Such recourse is required on the grounds that a literal, historical resurrection is incompatible with a scientific worldview: in the words of Rudolf Bultmann, language of resurrection reflects the obsolete "cosmology of a pre-scientific age."[3] Hence he speaks of "the incredibility of a mythical event like the resuscitation of a dead person" and "the impossibility of establishing the objective historicity of the resurrection no matter how many witnesses are cited." As he famously concludes, "An historical fact which involves a resurrection from the dead is utterly inconceivable!"[4] All that remains, on such a view, is the domain of subjective apprehension and privatized—existential—faith. Just so, John Spong speaks of Peter "having had in Galilee an experience of the inbreaking reality of God that he called resurrection, which included seeing Jesus of Nazareth as part of who God was and is."[5] Expanding on this approach, Gerd Lüdemann explains the faith of the earliest disciples in explicitly psychological terms:

> Peter received the first vision, which is to be interpreted psychologically as failed mourning and the overcoming of a severe guilt complex. He had "sinned" against Jesus by denying him. But under the impact of Jesus' preaching and death, through an appearance of the "Risen Christ," Peter once again referred to himself God's word of forgiveness which was already present in the activity of Jesus, this time in its profound clarity.
>
> This first vision became the initial spark which prompted the further series of visions mentioned by Paul in 1 Cor. 15. The subsequent appearance of Christ can be explained as mass

---

2. Although the literature on this topic is voluminous, the following offer representative surveys of the question (from a variety of perspectives): Allison Jr., *Resurrecting Jesus*, 199–213, listing the options as (1) orthodox belief; (2) misinterpretation; (3) hallucinations; (4) deliberate deception; (5) genuine visions; (6) belief in God's vindication; and (7) "Rapid disintegration of the body plus visions"; Braaten, "The Resurrection Debate Revisited" (to which the following review is directly indebted); Carnley, *Structure of Resurrection Belief*; Geyer, "The Resurrection of Jesus Christ"; and, above all, the magisterial and comprehensive review of Wright, *Resurrection and the Son of God*.

3. Bultmann, *Kerygma and Myth*, 3.

4. Bultmann, *Kerygma and Myth*, 39.

5. Spong, *Resurrection*, 277.

> psychoses (or mass hysteria). This phenomenon was first made possible by Peter's vision.[6]

Michael Goulder takes a similar approach, referring to resurrection testimonies as "collective delusion," on a par with UFO sightings or encounters with the Sasquatch.[7] For Lüdemann the conversion of Saul, who had initially persecuted the fledgling Christian community, is to be explained in much the same way as that of Peter before him:

1. In both, the vision of Jesus is inseparably related to the denial of Jesus or the persecution of his community.
2. In both a feeling of guilt is replaced by the certainty of grace.
3. Both figures may have put forward a doctrine of justification which was similar, indeed largely in agreement . . . Paul evidently agreed with Peter from the beginning that men and women are justified through faith in Christ and not through the law; indeed, this conviction led both to turn to Christ in their "Easter experience."[8]

In a manner that seems to contradict a plain reading of Paul's Letter to the Galatians (with its emphasis on the priority of divine action over human), the main premise of this explanation is that psychological and theological convictions are the primary cause of spiritual experience, rather than their immediate consequence. On this point, Rowan Williams is both blunt and categorical: "Jesus is not raised by our faith, but by God's prior act."[9]

Ironically, such interpretations fail to take into account what little we know about the "psychology" (although appeal to such concepts is anachronistic) of the earliest disciples. Lesslie Newbigin explains:

> In the effort to make Christianity acceptable to contemporary thought many theologians explain the scriptural accounts of the empty tomb and the appearance of the risen Jesus in purely psychological terms, as visions created in the minds of the disciples by their faith in Jesus. Thus the resurrection story is the result of a preexisting faith, in exact reversal of the biblical record, which

---

6. Lüdemann, *What Really Happened to Jesus*, 129–30, quoted in part by Braaten, "Resurrection Debate," 151.

7. Goulder, "Did Jesus of Nazareth Rise from the Dead?," in Barton and Stanton, *Resurrection*, 61–63.

8. Lüdemann, *What Really Happened to Jesus*, 130.

9. Williams, *Resurrection*, 5.

affirms that unbelief was turned into faith by what happened on Easter morning. Here is a classic example of the domestication of the gospel, of the attempt to defend it by co-option into the reigning plausibility structure.[10]

As Tom Long observes, such an approach "wants to view the mythological claims of Scripture as the outdated vestiges of an obsolete world view," but has "no issue with a God who operates inside the tiny tableau of our psyches."[11] On this point, he cites Paul Ricoeur's critique of Bultmann:

> "It is striking that Bultmann makes hardly any demands on [the] language of faith, whereas he was . . . suspicious about the language of myth." As Kevin J. Vanhoozer puts it, "Bultmann is critical of *mythos* . . . employed by the biblical authors for speaking of God's acts but uncritical of his own."[12]

To state the matter in somewhat more confrontational terms, it is hardly satisfactory to attribute to the credulity of a former age an explanation that does little more than satisfy the incredulity of one's own, especially so when the explanation itself is insufficiently self-critical in its expansive critique of others.

Further undermining any appeal to psychological dynamics is the prominence and persistence of skepticism among the disciples, both prior and subsequent to the various appearances of their resurrected Lord. Accordingly, preaching that proceeds from resurrection will need to account for doubt as much as it seeks to encourage trust in the one from whom resurrection proceeds. Anything less than this (any effort, that is, to deny the prevalence of disbelief, even for those who encountered the risen Christ face to face) is simply dishonest with regard both to the biblical witness and to the nature of faith itself. Conversely, if faith is no more than self-persuasion in the absence of anything external to itself, then

---

10. Newbigin, *The Gospel in a Pluralist Society*, 11. Here Barth's expression of annoyance seems apt: "Why is the Church so incredibly skilled in discovering in Divinity a thing capable of historical description or psychological analysis? . . .How distressingly correct and friendly the Church manages to make itself!" (Barth, *Epistle to the Romans*, 388).

11. Long, "Preaching Easter at Old First Gnostic," 22.

12. Long, "Preaching Easter at Old First Gnostic," 22; revised as Long, "Preaching the Gospel of Resurrection," in Campbell, *Preaching Gospel*, 78, both citing Ricoeur, "Preface to Bultmann," in *Essays on Biblical Interpretation*, 65, and Vanhoozer, *Remythologizing Theology*, 17.

preaching can be little more than psychological self-affirmation in the absence of anything other than its own words.

A second explanatory category is closely related to the first, but situates "resurrection" in the life of the community as a whole rather than that of any particular individual. On this view, to speak of resurrection is to say that the "cause" of Jesus continues in the life and ministry of the church: even though Jesus himself had been unjustly executed, the religious movement he began could not be so easily put down. "Easter has less to do with one person's escape from the grave," declares William Sloan Coffin, "than with the victory of seemingly powerless love over loveless power."[13] The earliest disciples continued to trust in God and await God's final intervention in history; just as Jesus had taught them to, they looked for God to bring an imminent end to the injustice and disarray of the present world order. Stories of his resurrection cast this hope in concrete form. Therefore the various Gospel accounts are to be read (so the explanation goes) not as factual historical narratives but as literary and theological responses to the immediate needs of the communities that first produced them.

So for Wes Allen, the conclusion of Mark's Gospel, which in the earliest manuscripts omits any resurrection appearances and (in the words of Elizabeth Goodman) concludes "using syntax only Yoda could love,"[14] represents "a parabolic ending to a parabolic narrative."[15] In his view, the primary historical event to which the resurrection corresponds is the destruction of the Jerusalem Temple, rather than anything in the biography of Jesus of Nazareth. Specifically, the destruction of the Temple signals the end of God's presence in our midst by that means and in that place; yet by "returning" to Galilee (at least metaphorically) as Jesus commands, Mark's readers will discover the presence of the Risen One as the basis for their new life:

> Read through the lens of Mark's attempt to deal with the theological challenge of the destruction of the temple, therefore, the story of the empty tomb without resurrection appearances offers to the readers the resurrection not as a past event but as a present and ever-future experience. As with the empty temple,

---

13. Coffin, "Easter and Forgiveness," 8.
14. Goodman, "Preaching the Easter Texts," 3.
15. Allen, "Mark 16:1–8," 8.

the empty tomb points to Jesus' presence with the [Markan] community.¹⁶

So too, for Peter Carnley, "The belief that Jesus was alive and that he had been raised . . . is not traced back to an experience or vision of the bodily Jesus of some kind, but to the continuing presence of the Spirit of Christ."¹⁷ What may not be true physically or historically is held to be true theologically, metaphorically, or in some other "spiritual" and existential sense. Hence preaching on Jesus' resurrection may appropriate particular narrative details in symbolic or allegorical fashion: the stone that seals the tomb, for instance, will represent doubt, the power of those who crucified him, or the weight of death. On such a view, Easter faith is anchored less in an experience of the resurrected Jesus than in the prospect of some more general divine intervention. As Samuel Wells explains:

> for Jesus, the stone . . . was the symbol that nothing can separate the Father from him or him from us. Every permanent, immovable, unshakeable obstacle you could possibly think of, between us and God, between death and life, between this life and the life to come—every single one of them is going to find itself going the same way as that stone: rolling, rolling, rolling.
> And what about your stone? What does the stone represent for you? Reflect for a moment on what is standing, heavy, unshakeable, immovable, between you and life, between you and love, between you and healing, between you and God.¹⁸

Intentionally or otherwise, such admonitions propose that the relevant New Testament accounts, along with New Testament faith as a whole, are reducible to symbolism and metaphor, without need for any grounding in historical reality other than the subjective perception of believers themselves. Fred Tappenden, for example, proposes that "resurrection" is a cognitive category that facilitates perception of new possibilities in the lives of disciples: "For Paul, metaphors of resurrection organize life in Christ. They function as performative scripts that Christ-devotees live by."¹⁹ Accordingly, says Mary Catherine Hilkert,

---

16. Allen, "Mark 16:1–8," 12.

17. Carnley, *Structure of Resurrection Belief*, 249–50, quoted in Buttrick, "Easter Preaching," 62.

18. Wells, "The Challenge and Opportunity of Easter Preaching," 29.

19. Tappenden, *Resurrection in Paul*, 231.

> What the preacher should be concerned about is evoking hope. Like the nature miracles, the resurrection narratives are rich tapestries of literary and theological symbolism. Regardless of their historicity, the narratives carry the power to engender hope and to empower action on behalf of justice, peace, the integrity of creation. As John Dominic Crossan once declared, "Emmaus never happened. Emmaus always happens."[20]

Notwithstanding its continued emphasis on psychology, symbolism, and/or existential conviction, this second explanatory category is considerably less solipsistic than might at first appear. In the words of David Buttrick,

> The awareness of the Spirit within early Christian communities is crucial to resurrection faith. Early Christians were absolutely sure that Christ was risen, because they were living in the Spirit, the same Spirit that was in Christ Jesus. Not only was Lord Jesus alive, he still broke bread with them, and still spoke to them through their preachers as well as via resident "Christian prophets" in their congregations.[21]

Here, as in Peter Carnley's account, pneumatology takes the place of historical verification or an historically-rooted Christology: situating Christian faith primarily in relation to corporate experiences of the Spirit (or spirit) of God allows for a measure of agnosticism with regard to the fate of Jesus' physical body. There is, nonetheless, an unintended irony in such explanations. The New Testament experience of the Spirit of God is one of powerful charismatic manifestations: of "signs and wonders and mighty works" (2 Cor 12:12; cf. Acts 6:8; Rom 15:19; Heb 2:4), dramatic healings (Acts 3:6–8), "miracles" (Gal 3:5), and awe-inspiring "deeds of power" (1 Cor 12:28) that attest to Jesus' cosmic authority and consequent sovereignty over present circumstances. Luke speaks of the risen Κύριος, "Lord" (that is, Jesus) as the one who personally grants "signs and wonders" through the ministry of the apostles (Acts 4:30; 14:3, etc.). So too the Apostle Paul unequivocally links the "power" of God's Spirit with Jesus' "resurrection from the dead" (Rom 1:4), which he understands to have entailed the transformation of the Messiah's physical body (1 Cor 15:35–44). In other words, the event of Jesus' resurrection, the presence

---

20. Hilkert, "Preachers of Grace, Witnesses to the Resurrection," 298–99, citing Crossan, "The Life of a Mediterranean Jewish Peasant," 1200.

21. Buttrick, "Easter Preaching," 63.

of God's Spirit, and manifestations of supernatural power are of a piece for the New Testament church.

Yet those who commend pneumatological interpretations of the resurrection tend, as a rule, to be allergic to "charismatic" or "Pentecostal" forms of experience. In other words, there is in such explanations an implicit distantiation between what seems intellectually respectable in our own day and the ostensibly more naive beliefs of a primitive church. Yet neither psychologizing nor "de-mythologizing" their testimony seems sufficiently respectful of the theological convictions and lived experiences of those to whom it is applied, and thus cannot escape the charge of intellectual conceit. At least as attested by the earliest Christians, evidence of divinely-authored resurrection is not to be located in some general sense of the church's faith and vitality despite all odds (as historical reductionism typically asserts), but in their encounter with terrifying, vivifying divine power of a sort not usually envisaged by liberal scholarship.

Still, acknowledging the genuinely historical character of the resurrection requires an equally honest acknowledgment of the historical difficulties to which doing so gives rise. As with any form of testimony, the first such difficulty is that of subjectivity and verification, a challenge nicely captured by the response of a fictional Abraham in Jesus' parable about a wealthy patron and a poor beggar named Lazarus (Luke 16:19–31). The rich man now in torment asks Abraham to resurrect a messenger who will warn the man's five brothers of the cost of moral responsibility:

> Abraham replied, "They have Moses and the prophets; they should listen to them." He said, "No, father Abraham; but if someone goes to them from the dead, they will repent." He said to him, "If they do not listen to Moses and the prophets, neither will they be convinced even if someone rises from the dead."
> (Luke 16:29–31)

At least in Luke's Gospel, this parable represents the capstone to a furious debate between Jesus and certain Pharisees about the scope and application of "the law and the prophets" (16:16). But Jesus and his opponents would have agreed on the paramount importance of Scripture, and would not have differed in principle on the prospect of resurrection. So what is the point of the parable? The point of contention is that of true openness to God, regarding which one's response either to "Moses and the prophets" or to resurrection is merely an indicator.

Still, saying this does not solve the problem: the Pharisees are more scrupulous than most in their religious observance, and according to Luke are among those of his generation who view Jesus as "a glutton and a drunkard, a friend of tax collectors and sinners" (Luke 7:29–34). Each, in other words, insists that they alone obey the will of God. To be clear: by setting this parable in the context of controversy, Luke understands that Jesus is likening the Pharisees to the rich man's wayward brothers, who neither observe Torah nor believe in resurrection, despite the Pharisees' own fervent claim to do both. Every religious position (whether as to doctrine or conduct) is always right in the eyes of its adherents, yet according to Jesus, true faithfulness is more a matter of inward disposition (that is, "spirituality") than of punctilious doctrinal orthodoxy or the most scrupulous obedience alone.

To press the matter further, it is not unreasonable to imagine that the wealthy man would have interpreted his own vast wealth as a sign of divine blessing, just as he would have seen the penury of poor Lazarus as righteous punishment from God. In addition to being thoroughly biblical (e.g., Ps 112:3), that such views were common is evident, first, from the disciples' assessment of the man born blind ("Rabbi, who sinned, this man or his parents?" [John 9:2]) and, second, from a saying attributed to Rabbi Meir of Tiberias, who flourished ca. 130–160 CE: "Poverty does not come from one's trade, nor does wealth come from one's trade. But all is in accord with a man's merit."[22] Prior to his untimely demise, the rich man has no reason to think otherwise. What he and his brothers are incapable of envisaging, therefore, is a world that operates on anything other than the evidence of their immediate senses. Jesus' inference is that the Pharisees suffer from a similar theological myopia: they already have such a confident purchase on the ways of God that even should a witness be raised from death, they are unlikely to be persuaded otherwise. In short, they are so fully engaged in the familiar dynamics of the present order and the way they understand God to work within it that they are unwilling or unable to see anything else beyond.

However indelicate such a response may seem, reductionist rationalizations (in all their many forms) must similarly be named for what

---

22. *M. Qidd.* 4:14; cf. *t. Sanh.* 11:8, which lists "beauty, power, wisdom, riches, long life, honor, glory, and children" as the blessings of righteousness (attributed to Meir's contemporary Simeon ben Yoḥai). Of course, acknowledging the prevalence of such views does not preclude other perspectives, even within the canon itself (notably Ps 73 and the book of Job as a whole).

they are: as attempts to sidestep the affront to common sense and human experience—Brian Blount calls it "reckless implausibility"—that the resurrection of Jesus clearly represents.[23] David Buttrick states the matter in straightforward fashion: "Repeated events are credible—what does happen is likely to have happened—and singular events are incredible. The resurrection was a singular event without precedent or repetition; it has always been unbelievable."[24] In this regard, John Dominic Crossan is surely correct when he asserts, rather famously, "I do not think that anyone, anywhere, at any time brings dead people back to life."[25] At least, he is correct to the extent that he speaks of the normal human course of things and, presumably, his own personal experience.

But any concept of "God"—more precisely, of divine agency—that can be reduced to the woefully limited scope of human conceiving alone is not worth preaching. When it comes to comprehending God and God's ways, our intellects cramp up at the effort and invariably fall short. If we are comfortable confessing, as we often do, that God's love exceeds all understanding, why should matters be otherwise when it comes to Jesus' resurrection? On this point, we would be well instructed by the medieval Sufi theologian Abū Ḥāmid Al-Ghazālī (1058–1111 CE):

> Praise be to God, alone in His majesty and His might, and unique in His sublimity and His everlastingness, who clips the wings of intellects well short of the glow of His glory, and who makes the way of knowing Him pass through the inability to know Him; who makes the tongues of the eloquent fall short of praising the beauty of His presence unless they use the means by which He praises Himself, and use His names and attributes which He has enumerated.[26]

Or as the Anglican Reformer Richard Hooker (1554–1600) asserts, alluding to Ecclesiastes 5:2 ("God is in heaven, and you upon earth; therefore let your words be few"):

---

23. Blount, *Invasion of the Dead*, xv.

24. Buttrick, "Preaching on the Resurrection," 279.

25. Crossan, *Jesus: A Revolutionary Biography*, 95. For Crossan, the resurrection accounts are symbolic embodiments of theological reflection: "Life out of death is how [Galilean peasants] would have understood the Kingdom of God, in which they began to take back control over their own bodies, their own hopes, and their own destinies" (95).

26. Al-Ghazālī, *Ninety-Nine Beautiful Names of God*, 1.

> Dangerous it were for the feeble brain of man to wade far into the doings of the Most High … our safest eloquence concerning him is our silence, when we confess without confession that his glory is inexplicable, his greatness above our capacity and reach. He is above, and we upon earth; therefore it behoveth our words to be wary and few.[27]

In her own exploration of Easter preaching, Barbara Brown Taylor captures the implications of the resurrection for Christian speech with characteristic eloquence and precision:

> I recently read a book review in which the author was praised for "leaving all the right things unsaid so that the silence resounds," and it occurred to me that we could use more silence in our sermons these days. By silence I do not mean the literal absence of speech, although that might not be a bad idea. I mean fewer, more carefully chosen words, with less presumption in them. I mean greater respect for the mystery of God which passes all understanding, and deeper humility about our own relative size in the universe.[28]

Or, finally, much as it may seem unfashionable to endorse the convictions of a children's author and essayist who confesses her own lack of formal theological training, Madeleine L'Engle (1918–2007) manages to explain what is at stake for faith and speech alike more eloquently than most:

> The only God who seems to me worth believing in is impossible for mortal man to understand, and therefore he teaches us through this impossible.
>
> But we rebel against the impossible. I sense a wish in some professional religion-mongers to make God possible, to make him comprehensible to the naked intellect, domesticate him so that he's easy to believe in. Every century the Church makes a fresh attempt to make Christianity acceptable. But an acceptable Christianity is not Christian; a comprehensible God is no more than an idol.[29]

It is not that we will have nothing at all to say concerning God—in this case, nothing to preach on the topic of resurrection—but rather that to say anything, we must do so on terms other than those we might plausibly

---

27. Hooker, *Of the Laws of Ecclesiastical Polity* I. ii. 2. (p. 6). Hooker published this first of an eventual eight volumes in 1594.

28. Taylor, "The Easter Sermon," 12.

29. L'Engle, *The Irrational Season*, 19.

INTRODUCTION 13

determine for ourselves. Why should we be surprised when contemplating resurrection draws us out well beyond our moral, conceptual, and existential comfort zones, for is that not its exact intent?

Accordingly, preaching of the Christian gospel (and of Jesus' resurrection in particular) must be distinguished from apologetics, at least with regard to the structure and direction of its logic. Whereas apologetics undertakes a task of correlation, working forward from the intellectual assumptions of some other foundational worldview (scientific rationalism or moralistic therapeutic deism,[30] for example) in order to demonstrate the plausibility of Jesus' resurrection on the basis of *those* presuppositions, the trajectory of proclamation moves in the opposite direction. It begins with the disciples' unaccountable encounters with a disturbingly substantial and articulate (apparently even hungry!) post-crucifixion Jesus, then goes in search of language that might suitably explain (but not explain away) such experience. As William Willimon observes, this is how Paul presents the resurrection to skeptical Corinthians. Just as Jesus' closest friends and followers found themselves unable to deny the evidence of their senses, so the fractious congregants know themselves to have been profoundly changed: not by Paul's preaching of the gospel *per se*, but by the power of the resurrection to which that preaching bears witness. "This," says Willimon, "is the logic of Easter":

> Sometimes the best sermons do not argue the congregation into something they have not yet known but rather point to and name that which the congregation undeniably knows. Having undeniably experienced resurrection, we now talk about it. Because your faith is not in vain, an Easter sermon is no lie, and Jesus is raised, therefore you are raised.[31]

On such a view, attempts to "rationalize" the resurrection in terms dictated by an Enlightenment worldview are understandable, but essentially misguided. In effect, they cede the field of enquiry and the rules of discourse to a perspective that, by definition, invalidates such a possibility even before debate can begin. It is helpful to acknowledge at the outset, therefore, that evidence for the resurrection of Jesus emerges in the

30. For this concept, see Smith and Denton, *Soul Searching*, with a summary definition at 162–63.

31. Willimon, *Proclamation and Theology*, 76; further, Beaudean, *Paul's Theology of Preaching*, 134–35. Paul employs a similarly abductive logic in 2 Cor 3:1–3 as a means of defending the validity of his own ministry, on which see Knowles, *We Preach Not Ourselves*, 112–18.

form of what scientists call "observational" rather than "experimental" data. Since the phenomenon of resurrection is not subject to control by a human observer, it can only be reported, not reproduced, quantified, or manipulated at will. In this case, moreover, the observational "data" calls into question many of our prior (essentially reductionistic) assumptions about how the world works: it calls for new explanatory proposals and a commensurate correction or abandonment of previous explanations that would deny its validity. As Willimon indicates:

> Resurrection is presented in the Gospels and the letters of Paul as an experienced fact, that is, though we may have trouble grasping this datum, it is a datum nonetheless, a fact that is external to the constructs of our imagination, an experience that is neither of our making nor at our disposal but which invades human reality, changing our destiny. The risen Christ meets us, and then we attempt to bring that meeting to speech. The modern notion that resurrection is a projection of human longing, an inward experience of the believer, knows no basis in Scripture. Resurrection is the supreme instance not of the fertile imaginings of our inner subjectivity but of the initiative and the active subjectivity of the God who comes to us.[32]

In short, as we have noted in part already, that Jesus' resurrection beggars imagination and blows apart our logic is our first hint that this may not be of our own making. It is a daring invitation for us to encounter—to be encountered by—a reality that is well beyond all expectation or control.

Speaking of God

Regardless of whether or not we find it intellectually expedient, the New Testament writers describe resurrection as an event both in the biography of Jesus and in the perception and experience of his followers. Notwithstanding troublesome contradictions between their respective accounts, all four evangelists report encounters in which Jesus not only appears in bodily form, but also speaks (Matt 28:9–10; Luke 24:17–25; John 20:15–17, etc.), breathes on the remaining disciples (John 20:22), eats food (Luke 24:42–43), and on one occasion goes so far as to prepare breakfast over a charcoal fire for weary fishermen (John 21:9). He is sufficiently corporeal that the two Marys can grasp his feet (Matt 28:9). Christian testimony,

---

32. Willimon, *Proclamation and Theology*, 77.

whether ancient or modern, unfolds as a consequence of such encounters. New Testament language for these appearances often includes an important detail, explanation of which will require a brief detour into certain details of Greek grammar and Hebrew theology.

Jewish devotional tradition is famously circumspect when it comes to speaking of God, as is evident already from the Ten Commandments: "You shall not misuse the name of the Lord your God" (Exod 20:7; Deut 5:11 NIV). But pious restraint extends well beyond reluctance to utter the actual name of the deity. Even in prayer, one might at most venture to ask, "May your name *be sanctified* . . . May your will *be done*" (Matt 6:10), rather than daring to insist that God get up and "do" something. Use of the passive voice provides a suitably indirect manner of speaking about (all the more so, for indirectly addressing) Almighty God.[33] So, for instance, the Mishnah records that Judah b. Tema, a little-known rabbi of the late second century, was accustomed to pray, "May it *be found pleasing before you*, O Lord our God, that you rebuild your city quickly in our day and set our portion in your Torah" (*m. ʾAbot* 5:20). Even Jesus, on intimate terms with the One he calls "Father," adopts this manner of speech.

Expressing requests indirectly is not only a matter of deference and due humility; it also acknowledges (as prayer implies in principle) that God is the One with power to fulfill such petitions. This is how things work in God's kingdom: "To all those who have," says Jesus, "more *will be given*, and they will have an abundance; but from those who have nothing, even what they have *will be taken away*" (Matt 25:29). Just so, Paul uses the passive voice to describe divine action in his famous description of the transformation that results from an encounter with Christ: "All of us, with unveiled faces, seeing the glory of the Lord as though reflected in a mirror, are *being transformed* into the same image from one degree of glory to another; for this comes from the Lord, the Spirit" (2 Cor 3:18). So too for the creedal confession that appears in 1 Timothy 3:16:

> Without any doubt, the mystery of our religion is great:
> He *was revealed* in flesh,

---

[33]. "The worshipper does not address God forcefully in language which could be considered too direct and presumptuous, as if he [sic] were telling God what to do. A prayer which uses the stylistic device 'May it be Thy will' expresses an appropriate amount of reverence and restraint, for the worshipper only asks that it be God's will to grant his request, and not that God do his bidding"; so Heinemann, "The Background of Jesus' Prayer," 83–84.

> *vindicated* in spirit,
> *seen* by angels,
> *proclaimed* among Gentiles,
> *believed* in throughout the world,
> *taken up* in glory.

Alongside the faith and proclamation of human agents and insight on the part of angels are revelation, vindication, and exaltation by the power of God alone.

This convention applies in particular when it comes to describing theophanies, or visible appearances of God. Thus we read in the Septuagint that "the angel of the Lord *appeared* [ὤφθη]" to Moses in a flaming bush (Exod 3:2; so also Acts 7:30, 35), just as God tells Moses, "I am YHWH. I *appeared* to Abraham, Isaac, and Jacob as El Shaddai..." (Exod 6:3; likewise Acts 7:2). Both in the Septuagint and in the New Testament, use of the passive voice generally and the aorist passive ὤφθη in particular implies that God is at work.[34] This explains why Luke, for example, chooses the same grammatical form when he says that an angel of the Lord "appeared" to Zechariah in the Temple (Luke 1:11); that tongues of fire "appeared" on the Day of Pentecost (Acts 2:3); or that a vision of a Macedonian man appealing for help "appeared" to Paul in a dream (Acts 16:9).[35]

Above all when used as a technical term for appearances of the risen Christ, the same aorist passive, ὤφθη, implies divine action: even where God is not directly named, divine agency is unmistakably in view.[36] So, for instance, when the two travelers return to Jerusalem from Emmaus, the eleven tell them, "The Lord has risen indeed, and ... *has appeared* to Simon!" (Luke 24:34); Ananias explains to the newly converted Saul, "Brother Saul, the Lord Jesus, who *appeared* to you on your way here, has sent me so that you may regain your sight and be filled with the Holy Spirit" (Acts 9:17); even as Paul, preaching at Pisidian Antioch, says of Jesus, "God raised him from the dead; and for many days he *appeared* to

---

34. Further: Michaelis, s.v. ὁράω, κτλ., *TDNT* 5:331–33.

35. With respect to this particular verb, use of the passive voice is not limited to directly visionary experience: Christ, says the writer to the Hebrews, "having been offered once to bear the sins of many, *will appear* a second time" (Heb 9:28); similarly, 1 John explains, "This life *was revealed*, and we have seen it and testify to it, and declare to you the eternal life that was with the Father and *was revealed* to us" (1 John 1:2). In each case, divine agency is implied.

36. Cf. ὁράω, κτλ., *TDNT* 5:358–59.

those who came up with him from Galilee to Jerusalem" (Acts 13:30–31). Perhaps the most concentrated collection of such language in the entire New Testament occurs in Paul's account of the basic Christian tradition about Jesus' death and resurrection:

> For I handed on to you as of first importance what I in turn had received: that Christ died for our sins in accordance with the Scriptures, and that he was buried, and that he *was raised* [ἐγήργεται] on the third day in accordance with the Scriptures, and that he *appeared* [ὤφθη] to Cephas, then to the twelve. Then he *appeared* to more than five hundred brothers and sisters at one time, most of whom are still alive, though some have died. Then he *appeared* to James, then to all the apostles. Last of all, as to one untimely born, he *appeared* also to me. (1 Cor 15:3–8)

From this discussion of theology and language, two corollaries ensue. The first is that New Testament writers recount experiences of the resurrected Jesus (with or without uncertainty on the part of some witnesses) in the same manner as they do sea voyages, riots, judicial arrest, financial transactions, public speaking, or any other biographical event. Apart from his somewhat alarming ability to pass through locked doors unimpeded (John 20:19, 26), the disciples' encounters with Jesus after his resurrection differ from encounters with him prior only in terms of reduced frequency and public visibility. As Peter explains in his sermon at the house of Cornelius, "God raised him on the third day and allowed him to appear, not to all the people but to us who were chosen by God as witnesses, and who ate and drank with him after he rose from the dead" (Acts 10:40–41). In this sense, the authors in question plainly understand such experiences to be "historical"—that is, rational, experiential, biographical—events. Whether subsequent readers wish to accept them as such is another matter entirely, but if the purpose of proper exegesis is the recovery of authorial intent (delusional or otherwise), this is the only inference available. In response to the account of Jesus consuming a morsel of broiled fish (Luke 24:42–43), Joseph Fitzmyer observes rather tartly that "only Luke among the evangelists indulges in this sort of realism about the existence of the risen Christ; and for this he is castigated, by twentieth-century readers!"[37] Fitzmyer is mistaken in his assertion that Luke alone is guilty of producing realistic narrative, although doubtless

---

37. Fitzmyer, *Gospel according to Luke X–XXIV*, 1577.

correct about the modernist response. But such critique says more about certain of Luke's readers than it does about the evangelist himself.

The second conclusion to be drawn is that the New Testament authors manifestly believe God to be active within human history and the personal experiences of those of whom they write (as well as in their own lives). This foundational conviction is embedded in the forms of language they employ. In principle, then, language concerning resurrection—whether that of the biblical text or of our own sermons—challenges us to consider the question of God. More precisely, our decisions around language—again, both our own and that of the text—hinge on what we are willing to accept and confess with regard to the identity of Jesus and the activity of the One he called "Father." The two sides of this question are commensurate: we will allow the text to say as much (or as little) as we allow ourselves to say, and vice versa. In other words, while we and our hearers each remain free to accept or to reject the testimony of the canonical text, in so doing we reveal the true nature of our own theological convictions concerning trust in and knowledge of God.

This is not to suggest that the New Testament writers conceive of resurrection as being in any way "normal." The careful wording of Peter's sermon at the house of Cornelius indicates otherwise: fellowship with the risen Jesus is limited to those whom God has previously chosen to be witnesses of the fact. They know as well as anyone that in the normal course of events, the crucified remain irreversibly dead (Hebrews 11:35 notwithstanding). Should proof be required, they need only recall that around 88 BCE, the Hasmonean king Alexander Janneus had eight hundred Pharisees crucified in Jerusalem, not one of whom subsequently returned to life.[38] Resurrection is a category that confounds the normal course of history. Rather than affirming our usual manner of thinking, it contradicts us; whether as a general possibility (for, say, the Christian faithful) or with reference to Jesus in particular, resurrection is explicable only on the basis of extraordinary divine intervention. As with any other episode in history, it may be announced in advance and described in normal human language, but as to the details of causality it remains humanly inexplicable. The silence of all four evangelists on this point concedes as much (only John Updike dares specify that "the molecules reknit, the amino acids rekindle").[39] For Francis Watson, such theological indirec-

---

38. Josephus, *War* 1:97–98; *Ant.* 13:380–83.
39. Updike, "Seven Stanzas at Easter," line 3.

tion accounts for Mark's famously abrupt conclusion: "In speaking of this event only in the form of a non-narration, the Marcan narrator indicates that the divine act of raising Jesus from the dead is not intelligible, imaginable, and therefore reproducible as other events are. Narrative testimony to it must therefore be indirect and fragmentary."[40]

Accordingly, Karl Barth prefers to consider the resurrection as an eschatological event, one in which the eternal touches human history at a point of singularity akin to the intersection of a tangent with a circle (although a better image might be that of an infinite plane intersecting a finite sphere, in three dimensions rather than two). In his commentary on Romans (the first edition of which appeared in 1918), Barth asserts that "the raising of Jesus from the dead is not an event in history elongated so as still to remain an event in the midst of other events. The resurrection is the non-historical relating of the whole historical life of Jesus to its origin in God."[41] The key here is the concept of intersection, the dynamics of which are akin to incarnation, which does not deny historicity (in the sense of permitting historical encounter) while at the same time remaining irreducible to the limitations of human history alone. As Barth will later insist, alluding to the words of Paul in 1 Corinthians 15:14-17, "If Jesus Christ is not risen—bodily, visibly, audibly, perceptibly, in the same concrete sense in which He died, as the texts themselves have it—if He is not also risen, then our preaching and our faith are vain and futile; we are still in our sins."[42]

In line with such logic, the following study begins with the assumption that there is no point of departure within the bounds of scientific or empirical rationalism from which we may arrive at belief in, or full

---

40. Francis Watson, "'He Is Not Here,'" in Barton and Stanton, *Resurrection*, 101. Watson continues, "The fragmentary nature of this particular narrative [i.e., Mark] is therefore not an accident, but is integral to its meaning; it is an expression of the narrator's reticence in the face of the mystery of the divine action" (101); again, referring to all four Gospels, "the narratives are agreed in their refusal to dispel the mystery by penetrating into its heart" (103).

41. Barth, *Epistle to the Romans*, 195; cf. 30. As Long ("Preaching the Gospel of Resurrection," 75) observes, "the resurrection cannot be described without viewing it in two frames of reference: the historical, immanent, and material, on the one hand, and the eschatological and transcendent, on the other. To lose the first renders the resurrection a spiritualized abstraction and to lose the second renders it absurd." So, similarly, Purves, *Resurrection of Ministry*, 94-96.

42. Barth, *CD* IV.1 351-52. Similarly, "If [the apostles] were true witnesses of His resurrection, they were witnesses of an event which was like that of the cross in its concrete objectivity" (352).

understanding of, Jesus' resurrection. On the contrary, resurrection stands over against us and shatters our expectations, because it originates from beyond the horizon of normal human history. It is *sui generis*, representing the irruption of divine ultimacy into our world.[43] From the perspective of apocalyptic theology, resurrection represents God's invasion of our world with the power of life.[44] More particularly, resurrection is the first instantiation of a new or renewed creation, something that the old creation is incapable of producing on its own:

> The problem is not that we must try to think the impossible but that we must try to think the ineffable . . . So here is the central paradox that confronts us when we try to think about the resurrected Jesus: he is the central perspective from which all of Christian faith is determined, yet we have no human categories of thought by which to bring him to expression.[45]

Desperate for some suitable analogy, the preacher may speak of a butterfly that emerges from its cocoon, of buds on fruit trees in springtime, or of a chastened Jonah emerging from the belly of the whale (Matt 12:40). In a pinch, we may even call upon the phoenix, the mythical bird that arises from the ashes of its own conflagration, as if new life might arise spontaneously from the defeat of death (so 1 *Clem.* 24:1—26:3).[46] Except that crematoria do not report this happening. Ever. Resurrection is a solely divine prerogative and, as such, a phenomenon that, to date, has taken place just once, in the crucified body and biography of Jesus.

As demonstrated by Jesus' own experience, it is accessible only by way of death. Materially, and notwithstanding occasional resuscitations (Lazarus, Jairus' daughter, the son of the widow of Nain), none of us will fully experience resurrection this side of the grave. Neither will we fully understand it. Conceptually, and notwithstanding the utility of human speech, to confess the limitations of such speech (along with

---

43. Cf. Watson, "'He Is Not Here,'" 104–5.

44. So Blount, *Invasion of the Dead*, 21, and passim: "The resurrection, then, *is* the apocalypse, the revelation of God's intent for the cosmos. The cross is apocalyptic because of the resurrection; the resurrection, by its very nature, stands as apocalyptic on its own" (62; emphasis original).

45. Purves, *Resurrection of Ministry*, 35. Purves makes the important point that discussion of resurrection is less concerned with an event, concept, or category *per se* than with the personhood and identity of Jesus.

46. Dating from the end of the first century, *First Clement* is one of the oldest non-canonical documents in the patristic corpus.

the conceptual categories that speech employs) testifies to the validity of resurrection rather than its opposite. At this point especially, encouraged by the likes of al-Ghazālī and Richard Hooker, we will do well to ponder Paul's assertion in 1 Cor 1:25 that the folly of God is wiser than human wisdom and the weakness of God is stronger than human strength. As John Updike insists,

> Let us not mock God with metaphor,
> analogy, sidestepping transcendence;
> making of the event a parable, a sign painted in the faded credulity of earlier ages:
> let us walk through the door.[47]

Such an approach requires one further word of explanation. In working through the testimony of the four evangelists, little attempt is made to reconcile or harmonize their variously overlapping and divergent accounts, even if this gives the appearance of what Robert Morgan terms "diplomatic evasion."[48] Although others more able may wish to undertake such a task, here the resurrection appearances are simply read for what they are—testimonies in human language to a reality for which words alone are insufficient. In effect, disagreements about this detail or that confound "the wisdom of the wise"; they serve to remind us that the events in question cannot and will not be reduced to simple categories. In other words, these narratives function much as does the risen Lord himself: as embodied, human testimony to a reality that is at the very limits of human understanding.

To reiterate: belief in the resurrection is not a destination at which we may arrive by virtue of negotiating an appropriate material, moral, or intellectual strategy. On the contrary, the resurrection of Jesus is explicitly *sui generis*, unprecedented in human history apart from prior divine interventions of which this is the climax and capstone. By definition, the resurrection is a divine act that wrests control of God's kingdom out of the hands of God's people. Because death—especially death at the hands of the ruthlessly efficient Romans—is the absolute terminus of human control (intellectual and otherwise), resurrection represents the inception of a new divine order. It is from this perspective that Barth insists,

---

47. Updike, "Seven Stanzas at Easter," lines 13–16.
48. Robert Morgan, "Flesh in Precious," in Barton and Stanton, *Resurrection*, 9.

"Under no circumstances and in no sense ought we to desire to be *creatores Creatoris*. Ours is not to give *birth* to God but to give *testimony* of him."[49]

In his own survey of different hermeneutical approaches to resurrection, Stephen Barton contrasts ideologically driven historical reconstructions and a-historical literary-critical readings, on the one hand, with the possibility of engaged reading in the context of Christian discipleship and community, on the other. He suggests that we replace our customary hermeneutic of suspicion with a hermeneutic of deliberate and deliberative trust:

> According to the latter, the Gospels would be approached differently. Instead of playing off one against the other, the interpreter might seek to discern how the Gospel accounts *complement* one another . . . What this involves is not, however, a return to rationalistic attempts to harmonize the various details of the Gospel accounts. Rather, it is a question of asking, in a way that is sympathetic to the tradition, what each Gospel testimony contributes to resurrection faith and Christian living.[50]

Proposing what he describes as a "resurrection hermeneutic—that is, an understanding and experience both of the life of the resurrection and of 'communities of resurrection' which help to foster a life-transforming (rather than a reductionist or even nihilist) approach to the text," Barton quotes philosopher Nicholas Lash with approval:

> I would wish to argue that the fundamental form of the Christian interpretation of Scripture is, in the concrete, the life, the activity and organization of the Christian community, and that Christian practice consists (by analogy with the practical interpretation of dramatic, legal and musical texts) in the performance or enactment of the biblical text: in its "active reinterpretation."[51]

As Lash further explains, "Christian practice, as interpretative action, consists in the *performance* of texts which are construed as 'rendering,'

---

49. Barth, *The Word of God and the Word of Man*, 131.

50. Stephen Barton, "The Hermeneutics of the Gospel Resurrection Narratives," in Barton and Stanton, *Resurrection*, 52–53.

51. Barton, "Hermeneutics," 54, citing Lash, "What Might Martyrdom Mean?," in *Theology on the Way to Emmaus*, 75–92; here, 90.

bearing witness to, one whose words and deeds, discourse and suffering, 'rendered' the truth of God in human history."[52]

This observation helps to clarify the theological character of Christian preaching. According to Lash, "It follows that, for the practice of Christianity, the performance of the biblical text, to be true, it must be not only 'true to life,' but 'true to *his* life'; and not only 'true to his life,' but 'true to God.'"[53] Lash argues, in effect, that the Christian life is not just a performance of the canonical (in this case, New Testament) text, but more precisely a performance of the identity and theological orientation of Jesus, who is the focus of that text. Accordingly, preaching resurrection is not simply a matter of apologetic intent, exegetical acumen, suitable language, or rhetorical skill; in addition to all these (sometimes despite or instead of them), it entails existential involvement in Jesus' own unique identity. It is a question of spirituality rather than of concepts and words alone. To see how this is so requires a brief description of Christian spirituality in general, followed by a succinct explanation of how proclamation of God's death-defying power offers a particularly clear and focused illustration of that more general orientation.

Life "In Christ"

To claim that Jesus' resurrection is unique, its power outside human control, might make it seem irrelevant for discipleship and as such beyond the scope of preaching. Paradoxically, the opposite is true, for its relevance is guaranteed by the theological implications of Jesus' incarnation. For Paul, whose correspondence predates the Gospel accounts, Christian discipleship is defined at its most basic as life "in Christ." "I have been crucified with Christ," he tells the Galatians; "it is no longer I who live, but . . . Christ who lives in me" (Gal 2:19–20). The same is true, he writes, for the believers at Colossae, with a slight alteration of the metaphor: "For you have died, and your life is hidden with Christ in God" (Col 3:3). The apostle's rhetorical challenge to these congregations—"If you have been raised with Christ, seek the things that are above, where Christ is" (Col 3:1)—implies a simple logic: what Christ himself experienced determines their own experience by virtue of being joined to him. More precisely,

---

52. Lash, "Performing the Scriptures," in *Theology on the Way to Emmaus*, 42 (emphasis original).

53. Lash, "Performing the Scriptures," 45 (emphasis original).

the theological mandate of unity with Christ constitutes an existential and moral obligation, as indicated by (*inter alia*) the NIV rendering: "*Since*, then, you have been raised with Christ . . ."[54] Their task is not to construct a meaningful personal identity for themselves, for death by conjoined crucifixion (as Paul explains in Gal 2:20) implies just the opposite. Rather, all that remains for them is active yielding to the new *post mortem* identity and life that Christ himself provides: "seek the things that are above, where Christ is."

A similar dynamic undergirds all four Gospel accounts. Just as Jesus calls God "Father" (Matt 11:25–26/Luke 10:21–22), so he invites his disciples to do the same (Matt 6:9/Luke 11:2). Much as the Spirit of God descends on Jesus at his baptism (Mark 1:10), empowering his ministry (Luke 4:14, 18–19), so at the conclusion of John's Gospel, the risen Jesus breathes on the disciples, saying "Receive the Holy Spirit" (John 20:22). Even before this, Jesus promises that the Spirit of his Father will be their defense when the disciples face persecution (Matt 10:20/Luke 12:12), as followers share the fate of their Lord (Matt 10:25/John 15:20). In practice, they participate in his ministry of proclaiming God's reign: preaching, casting out demons, and healing the sick (Mark 3:15; 6:12–13; 13:10). Indeed, for Matthew, the disciples' message, "The kingdom of heaven is at hand," is identical to that of both John the Baptist (3:2) and Jesus before them (Matt 3:2; 4:17; 10:7). More broadly, allusions to the exodus in the missionary instructions (Mark 6:8–11) imply radical reliance on divine provision as basic to discipleship, which is a signal feature of Jesus' own piety (John 4:32).[55] Nowhere is the identification of sender and sent more obvious than in Jesus' assurance, "Whoever receives you receives me" (Matt 10:40 ESV; cf. Luke 10:16; John 13:20). Thus to follow Christ is to share his fate; to be "in Christ" is to participate in the basic dynamics of his life, death, and vindication at the hand of God. As Dietrich Bonhoeffer observes,

> To be conformed to the image of Jesus Christ is not an ideal of realizing some kind of similarity with Christ which we are asked to attain. It is not we who change ourselves into the image of God. Rather it is the very image of God, the form of Christ, which seeks to take shape within us (Gal. 4:19). It is Christ's own form which seeks to manifest itself in us. Christ does not cease

---

54. Cf. L&N §89.4 and Rom 6:8.

55. For fuller discussion of these themes, see Knowles, "Mark, Matthew, and Mission," 69–72, 85–87.

> working in us until he has changed us into Christ's own image. Our goal is to be shaped into the entire form of the incarnate, the crucified, and the risen One.⁵⁶

Again, this is not simply a question of imitating Jesus (*imitatio Christi*) so much as it is one of participating with him in his life before God (*participatio Christi*), above all with respect to his absolute reliance on God in all things, even for life itself. Nowhere is this orientation more obvious than in the contrapuntal polarity of crucifixion and resurrection, which describes the basic contours of conversion as well as, at the Lord's Supper and in terms of eschatology, of Christian experience both present and future.

This proposal requires two important qualifications. The first concerns mystical participation in the full range of Jesus' human experience. Unless it is balanced with an equal orientation to crucifixion, identification with Christ's resurrection can be overstated, eliding into triumphalism, elitism, perfectionism, esoteric speculation, and/or a preterist perspective. From the Patristic era onwards, one manifestation of this tendency has been Gnosticism, according to which "Salvation [is] understood as a flight from human finitude, embodiment and dependence into a 'spiritual' realm of godlike existence."⁵⁷ Yet this is to misconstrue the character of resurrection itself. As Sri Lankan theologian Vinoth Ramachandra explains, the Patristic response to Gnosticism applies equally to all denials of creatureliness—our own and that of Jesus alike:

> Such visions of transcendence and human perfection were profoundly challenged by the Christian proclamation of a God who had not only created and sustained the material world but who had himself embraced finitude, vulnerability, dependence and even evil and death through the incarnation, crucifixion and resurrection of Jesus. This is what love entails—the capacity to be hurt by the other and to transform that hurt into creative action. The resurrection represented not the overcoming of the human but its fulfillment.⁵⁸

---

56. Bonhoeffer, *Cost of Discipleship*, 341, as quoted in Pasquarello, *We Speak Because We Have First Been Spoken*, 23. Compare the parallel passage in Bonhoeffer, *Ethics*, 93: "Formation occurs only by being drawn into the form of Jesus Christ, by being conformed to the unique form of the one who became human, was crucified, and is risen" (emphasis original).

57. Ramachandra, *Subverting Global Myths*, 212.

58. Ramachandra, *Subverting Global Myths*, 212–13.

Conversely, overemphasis on crucifixion can effectively deny the redemptive power of God in present experience, relegating Christian hope to an as yet inaccessible future. Paul, however, steadfastly insists that life "in Christ" entails participation in abasement and exaltation alike, as illustrated by his own experience of ongoing affliction and consolation—apparently in equal measures:

> We are afflicted in every way, but not crushed;
> perplexed, but not driven to despair;
> persecuted, but not forsaken;
> struck down, but not destroyed;
> always carrying in the body the death of Jesus, so that the life of Jesus may also be made visible in our bodies. (2 Cor 4:8–10)

Clearer still in this regard are the polar contrasts that buttress his account of grace in 2 Cor 6:8b–10:

> We are treated as impostors, and yet are true;
> as unknown, and yet are well known;
> as dying, and see—we are alive;
> as punished, and yet not killed;
> as sorrowful, yet always rejoicing;
> as poor, yet making many rich;
> as having nothing, and yet possessing everything.

The paradox in such experience—and this kind of preaching—is that it encompasses weakness and power, folly and wisdom, futility and authority alike, each hidden within the other so that they are all but indistinguishable.

Yet (as the second necessary qualification) such is the paradox and complexity of pilgrimage that even though we are captured by Jesus' death and life, there will always be a distance between ourselves and him. For the moment, the contours of our discipleship will be at most cross-*like* and resurrection-*like*—cruciform but not crucified, transformational but not yet fully transformed. Metaphor and analogy will come to an end only at the moment of our full identification with Jesus' biography as we share his experience of physical death, followed by—we trust!—physical resurrection at a suitable point thereafter.

Even so, our interim association with Jesus is both real and substantive, as Christian discipleship is drawn toward the arc of his biographical experience. However imperfect in practice, discipleship is an empowered performance of the life of Christ by virtue of being overtaken by and enfolded within that life. This "performance" or "enactment" (to borrow Lash's terms) will necessarily include resurrection, if only in preliminary or proleptic fashion, because resurrection is not simply an event in Jesus' life history. Rather, it is intrinsic to his identity: as he declares categorically in John 11:25, "I am the resurrection." Accordingly, a fully-orbed program of Christian preaching and teaching will engage the practical implications of Jesus' resurrected life, of "new creation," and of acclaiming Jesus as Κύριος, "Lord," over every dimension of our lives. It will discuss Jesus' resurrection as the basis for Christian hope and the doctrine of eschatology: for the life of the Christian community, its engagement with contemporary society, and its mission in the world.[59] More particularly, a comprehensive program of preaching will explore Jesus' cross and resurrection from the perspective of our relationships with each other and with God; with respect to its impact on personal and congregational formation; and for its contribution to social justice, liberation, and healing.[60]

Yet much as these are vitally important subjects in their own right, the primary focus of the present study is on the implications of Jesus' resurrection for the activity of preaching itself. It is not that we must somehow imitate Jesus' manner of proclamation (as if such a thing were possible), nor even that fidelity to tradition requires that we repeat the specific content of his teaching (much as that remains the case). Rather, to be incorporated into the resurrected life of Jesus of Nazareth implies that our preaching should be informed, structured, and empowered by that life, joining that life in its utter dependence upon God. To consider preaching as an activity conducted "in Christ" requires that we account for it not simply in terms of technical or methodological excellence, rhetorical virtuosity, or any other aspect that lies within the scope of human endeavor, but on directly theological grounds, and as a response to divine initiative. As Joni Sancken comments, in her own discussion of resurrection and Christian proclamation,

> The ability to bring new life out of death is God's work alone. We cannot do it. So while humans have God-granted potential,

---

59. These are among the concerns addressed by Seamands's insightful chapters on preaching resurrection in *Give Them Christ*, 99–138, as well as more fully (for Christian apocalypticism) by Blount, *Invasion of the Dead*, 24–28, etc.: "Apocalyptic preaching focuses out beyond the present crisis of living death with the expectation of certain hope" (68); "our task is to focus [congregations] on life: resurrected life and all that it socially, ecclesiastically, politically, economically, and spiritually means" (103).

60. So Sancken, *Stumbling Over the Cross*, 38–72.

the cross and resurrection ground human potential in God's work rather than our own work... In the events of Good Friday and Easter, all human efforts reach their end, meaning both our limit and our future. It is only through Christ's power that we are empowered to be the people God created us to be.[61]

Like every other aspect of Christian life and ministry, preaching on the subject of cross and resurrection is itself subject to the conditions of cross and resurrection. As James F. Kay explains, the fact that such preaching stands at the intersection between "old" and "new" creation has critical implications for the function of human language in proclamation of the gospel:

> The cross does not mean we forsake the language of human beings or of our culture for that of the angels. The word of the cross always retains a human form. Nevertheless, what the crucified Christ reveals is that no creaturely form has in itself the power to render the identity or the reality of the new creation... rhetoric (and poetics) cannot be unquestionably baptized for Christian use in some version of "pulpit eloquence" or "sacred rhetoric" or "communication theory." Rather, the word of the cross overturns reigning rhetorical strategies, "taking them captive" (2 Cor 10:5) in the service of its message.[62]

Hence preaching modeled on resurrection is an act of trusting speech that takes Christ and the text at their word with respect to God's willingness and ability to raise dead hearers to life (preachers foremost among them). Faithful preaching does not claim authority for itself or endeavor by virtue of its own persuasive power to coerce or inspire a suitable response (much less to bestow the gift of life), but leaves to God the prerogative for effecting the transformation of which it speaks. Even before inviting hearers to enter into this dynamic for themselves, the first "active reinterpretation" of the text must therefore be the preacher's own. It is an exercise in yielding, and of ceding authority, to God. As Michael Pasquarello wisely observes, "Speaking of God cannot be reduced to saying things

---

61. Sancken, *Stumbling Over the Cross*, 16.
62. Kay, "The Word of the Cross at the Turn of the Ages," 48 (quoted in part by Sancken, *Stumbling Over the Cross*, 59); "Ultimately, the truth of the cross, its logos, is conveyed or enacted not by the compelling power of Paul's word, but by the power of God at work in the cross and its word or message" (49).

about God; rather, speaking of God will draw us into a relationship with God, in union with Christ, so that prayer and preaching are inseparable."[63]

For this reason, as with J. I. Packer's contrast between pilgrims and balconeers,[64] preachers and their hearers will ultimately be less concerned with theories of resurrection than with its operational implications for Christian discipleship and ministry. Of course, there is a certain irony here. The worse the preaching, the more relevant the topic of resurrection becomes: the preacher longs for congregants to respond in some more lively manner, while members of the congregation blame inadequate preaching for their own lethargy and confusion. Both yearn for a deeper experience of the Christian life, and the sermon seems as good a culprit as any. Addressing homiletics in light of Jesus' resurrection will help to explain why preaching sometimes fails to provide what it promises (despite the preacher's best efforts), and why even a sermon that is shallow or theologically faulty, or offered by a morally suspect preacher, can sometimes succeed beyond all reasonable expectation. In addition, directing our attention to the ways and work of God will help to remedy our preoccupation with ourselves and with the allegedly lamentable state of contemporary preaching. As implied by Rūmī's poem from more than seven centuries ago, our sense of our own frailty and decay matters considerably less than Christ's ability to reverse it.

Listening, Speaking, Waiting

The sections that follow are entitled "Listening," "Speaking," and "Waiting." The first of these addresses the necessity of silence as a prelude to Christian speech. Just as the incarnate Jesus desists from speaking, initially as an infant and later with his death on the cross, so intrinsically human modes of speech (of which there are many) must yield to the Word that God proclaims. If they are to bear the eventual weight of resurrection, our words and voices must first be crucified and fall silent. More specifically, our claims of verbal agency (our attempt, as speech act theory would have it, to "do things with words") must give place to the Word of God and to words given us by God. The second section explores what kind of words these might be. Drawing on resources as diverse as Luther's understanding of the Christian gospel and Homi K. Bhabha's

---

63. Pasquarello, *We Speak Because We Have First Been Spoken*, 148.
64. Packer, *Knowing God*, 5–6.

concept of "Third Space," it will discuss the unique and difficult character of Christian proclamation as discourse poised somewhere in the liminal space between the human and the divine. Stated more simply, the first two sections of the study will describe preaching as characterized more by withdrawal and humility (emulating the death of God's Word on the cross) than by argumentation or imposition, and thus as constituting testimony rather than dialectic. In conclusion, the third section will discuss what takes place after the sermon has concluded, as preachers and congregants together wait upon God to validate the word that has been spoken. Each section will include commentary on particular New Testament texts that describe or reflect on Jesus' resurrection and the way in which it shapes Christian experience.

> *Hosanna* to the Prince of Light
> That cloath'd himself in Clay,
> Entr'd the Iron Gates of Death,
> And tore the Barrs away.
> —Isaac Watts (1674–1748)[65]

---

65. Watts, *Hymns and Spiritual Songs* 2:149 (#76: "The Resurrection and Ascension of Christ").

II.

Listening

1

Speaking for God?

> Words strain,
> Crack and sometimes break, under the burden,
> Under the tension, slip, slide, perish,
> Decay with imprecision, will not stay in place,
> Will not stay still. Shrieking voices
> Scolding, mocking, or merely chattering,
> Always assail them.
>
> —T. S. Eliot, "Burnt Norton" (1935)[1]

Presuming to Speak

AT LEAST WHEN WEDDED to the "can-do" attitude that typifies much Western preaching, Paul's identification of proclamation of the Christian gospel as itself the "Word of God" is more of a problem than a clear explanation of what goes on Sunday by Sunday in the average North American pulpit. "We also constantly give thanks to God for this," he writes in his first letter to Thessalonica (one of his earliest epistles), "that when you received the word of God that you heard from us, you accepted it not as a human word but as what it really is, God's word, which is also at work in you believers" (1 Thess 2:13). Not once but twice he describes his preaching as a λόγον θεοῦ, a word of or from God—not, he insists, a merely "human word [λόγον ἀνθρώπων]." His explanation to the Galatians is more nuanced, but of similar intent: "For I would have you know," he says, "that the gospel which was preached by me is not according to man

---

1. Eliot, *Collected Poems*, 194; §V lines 13–19.

[κατὰ ἄνθρωπον]" (Gal 1:11 NASB). Yet two clues suggest that more is going on here than seems evident in translation. First, he says, the same divine word is "at work [ἐνεργεῖται]" in his hearers. Although Paul does not pause to clarify the relationship between the word that he speaks and the word at work within them (which is problematic in itself), the term he uses typically describes the power of Christ's resurrection in the life of the believer (a topic to which we will return in due course). Second, Paul turns at once to correlate their experience of suffering and persecution with that of the Judaean churches, as well as of Christ himself, thereby recalling the description of his own suffering with which the chapter began (1 Thess 2:1-2, 14-16). In other words, his reference to resurrection power and the word of God, which attributes divine authority to human preaching, is bracketed by acknowledgment that the larger contours of Christian experience remain persistently cruciform.

Regardless, to conceive of one's Sunday sermon as the "word of God" is an intoxicating proposal. According to John Calvin (1509-1564), mortal preachers are the primary means by which God now communicates eternal truth: "For, among the many excellent gifts with which God has adorned the human race, it is a singular privilege that he deigns to consecrate to himself the mouths and tongues of men, in order that his voice may resound in them."[2] As he comments on 1 Pet 1:25 (invoking 1 Cor 4:15),

> It is God alone who regenerates us, but for that purpose He employs the ministry of men ... It is indeed certain that those who plant and those who water, are nothing; but whenever God is pleased to bless their labor, He makes their doctrine efficacious by the power of His Spirit, [and the voice which is in itself mortal, is made an instrument to communicate eternal life].[3]

---

2. Calvin, *Institutes of the Christian Religion* IV.i.5 (2:1018). This translation is from the 1559 Latin edition of the *Institutes*.

3. "Solus quidem est Deus qui nos regenerat, sed ad eam rem utitur hominum ministerio ... Certum quidem est eos qui plantant et rigant, nihil esse: sed quoties Dominus benedicere vult eorum labori, spiritus sui virtute facit ut efficax sit eorum doctrina: et vox quae per se mortua est, vitae aeternae sit organum" (*Ioannis Calvini opera* 55:231). ET Johnston, *Epistle of Paul the Apostle to the Hebrews*, 255. In his revision of the earlier ET, Johnston's use of capitalization appears to introduce a christological reference that is without warrant in the Latin text ("and the *Voice* which is in itself mortal, is an instrument of eternal life"). Accordingly, the final clause is here cited from Owen, *Commentaries on the Catholic Epistles*, 60.

Moreover, for Calvin the power and authority of preaching are God's chosen means of vicarious rule over the church:

> [God] alone should rule and reign in the church . . . and this authority should be exercised and administered by his Word alone. Nevertheless, because he does not dwell among us in visible presence . . . he uses the ministry of men to declare openly his will to us by mouth, as a sort of delegated work, not by transferring to them his right and honor, but only that through their mouths he may do his own work—just as a workman uses a tool to do his work . . . to be interpreters of his secret will and, in short, to represent his person.[4]

Calvin's views are on a par with those of Martin Luther (1483–1546), who comments (in June of 1542, thus expressing his mature theological perspective), "God the creator of heaven and earth speaks to you through his preachers . . . These are the words of God, not of Plato or Aristotle. It is God Himself who speaks."[5] This view becomes a core principle of the Reformation, articulated most clearly in the Second Helvetic Confession of 1566: *Praedicatio verbi Dei est verbum Dei* ("The preaching of the Word of God *is* the Word of God").[6] As Luther explains in his *Church Postil* of 1522,

> Since the advent of Christ the gospel, which used to be hidden in the Scriptures, has become an oral preaching. And thus it is the manner of the New Testament and of the gospel that it must be preached and performed by word of mouth and a living voice. Christ himself has not written anything, nor has he ordered anything to be written, but rather to be preached by word of mouth.[7]

The influence of such views upon the English Reformation is evident from the work of the radical Calvinist and Puritan preacher Paul Bayne (or Baynes, ca. 1573–1617), whose massive and influential commentary on Ephesians was published posthumously. Bayne sees in Eph 2:17 ("he came and proclaimed peace to you who were far off and peace to those

---

4. Calvin, *Institutes* IV.iii.1 (2:1053).

5. WA TR 4:531 §4812, cited in Wood, *Captive to the Word*, 93.

6. *Confessio Helvetica Posterior* I, 4, quoted in Greidanus, *The Modern Preacher and the Ancient Text*, 9.

7. WA 10.1.48, cited in Wood, *Captive to the Word*, 90; cf. *LW* 52:205–6.

who were near") evidence that Christ employs human instruments for the preaching of good news:

> We see that *Christ is present, and hath a part in preaching, even when men preach* . . . For this is the office of Christ our great Prophet, not only in his own Person, to open to us the will of his Father . . . but to be present, and teach inwardly in the heart with that Word which is outwardly sounded unto the ear by men, extraordinary or ordinary . . . This must teach us to look up to Christ as the chief Prophet among us, and the chief Preacher whosoever speaketh.[8]

In today's church, assertions of authority and sermonic efficacy are commonplace at both ends of the theological spectrum, although in different forms. The claim is frequently made that words (the words of the sermon in particular) are sufficient to accomplish the things of which they speak, whether by virtue of their inspirational and motivational value or on account of divine authorization. Taking his cue from Paul's instructions in 1 Tim 4:11 (NIV), "Command and teach these things," John MacArthur says of preachers, "We are commanders. We speak with authority." Not just with authority in general, he argues, but according to Titus 2:15, "'We speak with all authority.' That is to say the authority is unassailable and the authority is comprehensive."[9]

From an entirely different theological standpoint, Mary Donovan Turner appeals to Jesus' citation of Isaiah 58 and 61 as the basis for Christian preaching:

> "The Spirit of the Lord is upon me, because he has anointed me to bring good news [εὐαγγελίσασθαι] to the poor. He has sent me to proclaim [κηρύξαι] release to the captives and recovery of sight to the blind, to let the oppressed go free, to proclaim [κηρύξαι] the year of the Lord's favor." (Luke 4:18–19)

In her words, "The purpose of preaching is, as it was for the prophets and as it was for Jesus, to disrupt life so that a space can be created, a space in which that Holy Spirit can work, a space in which the community can rethink, revisit priorities, or receive."[10] However, where MacArthur surely claims too much for preaching, Turner—in one sense—surely claims too

---

8. Bayne, *An Entire Commentary*, 306–7.

9. MacArthur, "The Authority of the Preacher."

10. Mary Donovan Turner, "Disrupting a Ruptured World," in Childers, ed., *Purposes of Preaching*, 135.

little, proposing to replace a "theology of word" for preaching with a "theology of voice" in which the biblical canon "becomes not a slate of norms, but offers models of struggles and emerging visions that, through the leading of God's spirit, opens us up to potential transformations."[11] Concerned to empower the powerless and give voice to the voiceless, she asserts that

> The notion of a word from God that freezes revelation at a particular point in time and within a particular text promotes disempowerment. Persons no longer take responsibility for participating in meaning making . . . The speaking and listening God continues to be present, bringing new insight, challenging and interrupting a fraudulent finality of understanding . . . Preaching, then, is that which contextualizes the Word so that it can interrupt our living; God's spirit enables the preacher to bring it new and afresh to the community and to the world.[12]

To be fair, Turner's position is a good deal more nuanced than that of MacArthur and, from a certain perspective, simply acknowledges the interpretative latitude found in sermons and sermonic application of all theological stripes. Nonetheless, she too expresses great confidence in a preacher's ability to speak on behalf of God. Among numerous "purposes of preaching" that she acknowledges (from a longer list proposed by her students), she includes "to give God a voice"; "to illuminate truth"; "to make present the living Spirit"; and "to mend our alienation from God." Through the spoken word, she concludes, "we are empowered by God's spirit to find a bold voice in the midst of a broken, ruptured world, to speak a new and radical and revolutionary word."[13] Abstracted from their distinctive (and very different) sociopolitical and theological contexts, MacArthur and Turner sound like they are saying much the same thing.

"By What Authority?"

Notwithstanding forceful counterclaims in postmodern homiletic theory, there is no question that Jesus grants a measure of authority to some, at least, of those who speak on his behalf. He grants the Twelve "power and authority over all demons and to cure diseases," sending them out "to

---

11. Turner, "Disrupting a Ruptured World," 137.
12. Turner, "Disrupting a Ruptured World," 137.
13. Turner, "Disrupting a Ruptured World," 139–40.

proclaim the kingdom of God [κηρύσσειν τὴν βασιλείαν τοῦ θεοῦ] and to heal" (Luke 9:1–2). Subsequently commissioning a cohort of seventy itinerant preachers, Jesus declares, "Whoever hears you hears me" (Luke 10:16). Perhaps for this reason, it is not uncommon for the programmatic description of Jesus' ministry in Luke 4:18–19, with its catena of citations from Isaiah 58 and 61, to feature prominently in present-day ordination liturgies: "The Spirit of the Lord is upon me, because he has anointed me to bring good news to the poor [εὐαγγελίσασθαι πτωχοῖς]. He has sent me to proclaim release to the captives and recovery of sight to the blind, to let the oppressed go free, to proclaim [κηρύξαι] the year of the Lord's favor." Yet nothing in Luke 4 suggests that the words of Isaiah apply to anyone other than Jesus himself. Just because *Jesus* proclaims liberation to the captives and healing for the blind does not necessarily imply that preachers should be capable of accomplishing as much. Even were the parallel to be granted on other grounds, neither Isaiah, Jesus, or Luke explain *how*. Indeed, we will search in vain for ministries to which these words apply in the same sense as they did for the Messiah (although the Apostle Paul may offer a partial exception). My own experience is, in fact, lamentably un-messianic. I find it difficult to raise the dead, even metaphorically speaking. I manage on occasion to amuse, distract, or in some measure enlighten my hearers, but bestowing new life seems beyond the power of even my most fervent and "inspirational" language. Doing so in the manner of Jesus with Lazarus or the son of the nameless widow of Nain is neither realistic nor realizable. At the synagogue in Nazareth, Jesus does not even claim this much for himself. Maybe he was simply being modest; perhaps he just wanted to avoid trouble in his hometown synagogue, and so settled for deliberate understatement. But whatever the reason (although I am inclined to take the quotation at face value), Jesus claims remarkably little for himself: rather, he indicates that he is simply an instrument through whom the Spirit of the Lord, the *ruach YHWH*, will act to liberate others. Yes, Jesus will "bring good news to the poor"; he will proclaim "release to the captives" and "the year of the Lord's favor." But the plain sense of the text is that Jesus is anointed to announce rather than to achieve. At least for those who heard him that day, the most natural meaning of his words would have been as intended by the prophet Isaiah, that these are forms of liberation that only God, YHWH himself, can accomplish. Centuries of post-Chalcedonian devotion tend to obscure the bareness of Jesus' meaning.

Along the same lines, it helps to understand the intent of the Greek verb εὐαγγελίσασθαι, "to announce good news." In the ancient world, a εὐαγγέλιον does not achieve anything of itself. It is simply a triumphant announcement of what God, or the gods, have already accomplished; without this prior divine act, there is nothing to announce. It also helps to recognize that behind our somewhat optimistic reading of Luke 4 lies the idolatry of human agency typical of much Western (or at least, Eurocentric) thinking. Some years ago two fellow ministers (both of them personal friends whose anonymity I have chosen to preserve) had a disagreement about the best plan of action for a joint ministry initiative. One (a woman of European heritage) began at once to propose various courses of action, confident in their ability to achieve whatever objectives the two of them had been assigned. Her partner in ministry (a young man of African ancestry) bluntly interrupted her by declaring, "You are so *white* . . ." It is important to point out that it was the female pastor who related the story and that she was—after her initial shock—ultimately grateful for the rebuke. For, as she went on to explain, what her fellow pastor meant by his politically incorrect rebuttal was that she had begun the planning process by assuming the power of personal agency. She had assumed that with good intentions, readily available resources, and a measure of gumption, their ministry was bound to succeed. Her approach was entirely reasonable from the point of view of one whose culture had fostered her self-confidence. She planned for success because, in her experience, success was the normal consequence of a properly executed plan of action. Her colleague, by contrast, his thinking tempered by a cultural legacy of disempowerment and lack of access to resources, made no such assumptions. His instinct was to begin instead with prayer—not a superficial, "let's get this thing blessed" sort of prayer, but the desperate prayer of those who know their own weakness and poverty, above all when it comes to doing the work of God.

We are caught in a strange contradiction. We are often reluctant to preach about the cross because it seems so pessimistic and judgmental, when the congregants who patiently bear our sermons want nothing so much as a little encouragement. But we are equally reticent when it comes to preaching resurrection, whether because we find it difficult to explain or because it seems so far removed from the concerns of everyday life. So rather than waiting for God, it seems much simpler to take the tasks of encouragement, inspiration, and empowerment upon ourselves. After all, whatever else we may think, we believe ourselves responsible for the spiritual well-being of our congregants. Everything in our culture, our sense of identity as ministers of the gospel, and our homiletical formation encourages us in this direction.

Not to put too fine a point on it, most theologies of preaching are at least implicitly *messianic*, which is to say, they assert for the hearers a Messiah-like responsibility to enact the values and mission of Jesus in their local situation. More particularly, they imply for preachers the ability to motivate, inspire, and empower listeners, and in so doing to actualize the conditions of God's reign. Just so, having reviewed a representative sample of contemporary homiletical theories, Charles Campbell observes,

> In all of the works I have discussed there is a rather naive confidence in homiletical technique to bring about transforming, experiential events. Further, this confidence in technique is frequently accompanied by an equally naive confidence in individual experience and choice, just at a time when the very notion of the free, autonomous "self" is being questioned in the postmodern world.[14]

In context, Campbell is primarily concerned to acknowledge the corporate and cultural dimensions of preaching, yet his broader argument with regard to misplaced confidence remains valid. John Rottman perceptively observes that such overconfidence in the power of preaching has a direct parallel in exaggerated claims of clerical authority to enact sacramental efficacy.[15] The irony here is that however much preachers on the left of the theological spectrum disavow the authority of the pulpit and those on the right boldly embrace it (despite, in their case, notional deference to the authority of Scripture), the immediate, operational focus of both approaches is on human agency, whether that of preachers, congregants, or the two in tandem. What the preacher alone cannot accomplish, the hearers must. One clear indicator of this tendency is the consistent neglect of pneumatology: few textbooks on preaching offer more than a passing reference to the work of the Holy Spirit, when the Third Person of the Trinity is mentioned at all.

More specifically, much homiletical theory and much actual preaching operate on the assumption that the sermon is an operational action

---

14. Campbell, *Preaching Jesus*, 144. Similarly, with particular attention to the theoretical presuppositions of the New Homiletic, Gaarden, *Third Room of Preaching*, 45, 93–94, 104–7, etc.

15. Rottman, "Performative Language," 82n46.

comprised of causal links. We assume that the appropriate application of the proper homiletical technique will produce powerful preaching, just as powerful preaching will, in turn, produce spiritual fruit in its hearers when heard and applied in the proper manner. But any preacher who has spoken more than two Sundays in a row knows this to be manifestly untrue: last week's unexpected success is this week's homiletical flop, despite equivalent investments of time, effort, and sermonic ingenuity. The inconsistent results of a consistently applied method is one of the great mysteries of pulpit ministry.

What seems missing from much contemporary theory is the ability to account for both the intermittent authority and—so far as we can tell—the not-infrequent futility and fruitlessness of our preaching. If, as is often alleged, confession is good for the soul, perhaps this is a moment for quiet confession, if only among preachers and professional homileticians: since some are bold enough to admit grave doubts about the resurrection in any non-metaphorical sense, might we also have courage to concede that preaching doesn't always work the way we tell others that it should? In theory, preaching should indeed "disrupt life," "illuminate truth," "make present the living Spirit," "mend our alienation from God," and much else besides. But in practice, this is only sometimes the case, and often not. Whichever the case, we preachers are often the last to know. To be blunt, our failures either to slay the living or to rejuvenate the dead far outnumber our successes, and we often wait in vain at the church door for exiting congregants to say much more than a perfunctory "Thanks for the sermon, Pastor," in response to our magnificent preaching and the many hours of preparation that we have invested in it. As Will Willimon points out with characteristic wit and precision, the miracle is not that preaching sometimes works, but that it works at all.[16]

Newbigin, Bosch, and the *Missio Dei*: An Initial Corrective[17]

Whether directed to those who are members already or those as yet outside its fellowship, preaching is (according to some proponents) an

---

16. Willimon, "Preaching After Easter," 40–41: "While it is aggravating for those of us who talk about Jesus to have Jesus come and go as he pleases, preaching keeps generating faith in me because of the wonder that Jesus shows up at all" (40).

17. One of the benefits of supervising doctoral research is the extent to which supervisors learn from the work of their students, as has been my own experience with

expression of the church's larger mission to proclaim and thus implement the reign of God. On another view, preaching is simply one aspect of the church's larger project of joining God in God's own mission to an alienated humanity. The difference between these two proposals is subtle, yet significant, reflecting a fundamental shift in missiological thinking that derives in large part from the work of Lesslie Newbigin and David Bosch.[18] In essence, it calls into question the theological presumption of missional strategies that operate on behalf of, and thus in place of God. Whatever their theological commitments, methodologically-oriented approaches to mission rely largely on human initiative and ingenuity to establish the conditions of God's kingdom here on earth. If sometimes unintentionally, they are theologically deist or, at most, assume that God will bless the work of human hands so long as such work is carried out in faith and faithfulness to the divine command. On this view, Christ at his ascension entrusts his saving mission into the hands of his followers, whose heirs we have now become. Given the methodological latitude that such an approach allows, it is hardly surprising that Christian mission has frequently entailed cultural imperialism, a colonial mentality (regardless of the "target" population), and reliance on strategies derived from other fields of human endeavor with insufficient attention to their theological implications.

In response to what has proven to be, in practice, an anthropocentric and instrumentalist approach, Newbigin, Bosch, and the missional church movement that builds on their work all seek to reclaim the concept of the *missio Dei*, whereby "mission" is not a human activity that proceeds from the life of the church, but rather a primarily divine activity from which the life of the church itself proceeds.[19] Viewed from a Trinitarian perspective, Christ embodies the saving initiative of a missionary God and, as such, is the source of the church's very life and being. Stated succinctly, "It is not the church which 'undertakes' mission; it is the *missio Dei* that constitutes the church."[20] As Bosch observes in an

---

Marilyn Draper. The following discussion is indebted to the more complex analysis offered by her PhD dissertation, "Lived Doxology: A Spiritual Theology for the Church in Mission," and, in particular, her schema of mission conducted "For God"; "With God"; "In God"; and "To God" (i.e., as doxology).

18. In particular, Newbigin, *Open Secret*, and Bosch, *Transforming Mission*.

19. See further Guder, ed., *Missional Church*; Van Gelder and Zscheile, *The Missional Church in Perspective*; and Draper, "Lived Doxology," 90–163.

20. Bosch, *Transforming Mission*, 519.

earlier study, "mission in the New Testament is more than a matter of obeying a command. It is, rather, the result of an encounter with Christ . . . Mission is therefore, according to the New Testament, a predicate of Christology."[21] On this view, the church undertakes its ministry not by acting on behalf of God, but by yielding to and being shaped by Christ's own ongoing (and, as such, irreplaceable) mission to a creation in need of salvation. The church is therefore the consequence, not the cause of "mission": rather than consisting of activities extrinsic to the church's identity, mission, and ministry are expressions of that identity. Thus we engage in mission not as privileged intermediaries tasked with dispensing grace to those "outside," but as its perpetual recipients and beneficiaries, simply sharing with others that which we ourselves continue to receive. Far from relieving the church of responsibility for proclaiming the gospel of Christ, this redefinition contextualizes human agency in such a way as to account for human and divine action alike:

> Mission, then, in biblical terms, while it inescapably involves us in planning and action, is not *primarily* a matter of our activity or our initiative. Mission, from the point of view of our human endeavor, means the committed *participation* of God's people in the purposes of God for the redemption of the whole creation. The mission is God's. The marvel is that God invites us to join in.[22]

Seeking to safeguard the priority of divine action in the shared task of mission, Marilyn Draper clarifies the nature of the church's "participational union" with the Triune God by distinguishing carefully between *imitatio Christi* ("imitation of Christ") and *participatio Christi* ("participation in Christ").[23] Notwithstanding occasional references to life "*with* Christ" (Rom 6:5–8; Col 2:12, 20; 3:1, etc.), the basis for this distinction is the predominant New Testament metaphor for discipleship discussed above, which is that of life "*in* Christ."[24] The two metaphors overlap to some extent, yet mission and ministry conducted "with" Christ potentially envisages human actors as co-equals and co-redeemers who work

21. Bosch, *Witness to the World*, 81–82.
22. Wright, *Mission of God*, 67 (emphasis original).
23. Draper, "Lived Doxology," 182–223.
24. For two recent explorations of this theme, see Macaskill, *Union with Christ in the New Testament*, and Thate et al., *"In Christ" in Paul*. Adopting the schema proposed by Campbell in *Paul and Union with Christ*, 413 (and passim), Draper further distinguishes between "union," "participation," "identification," and "incorporation."

shoulder to shoulder with the Son of God. By contrast, the classic formulation of life "in" Christ preserves a Reformed theological emphasis on divine initiative—in particular the ontological and soteriological priority of Christ's own work. Not only, according to this definition, does Christian identity derive from identification and mystical union with Christ (with forensic and ethical implications), but incorporation into Christ provides the theological and operational basis for collective, universal participation in his ongoing ministry. Conceived of in this manner, mission and ministry are activities of the whole church in the power of the Holy Spirit, rather than of particular individuals authorized by the church to act on its behalf, as a second-order extension of its life. Nor is this distinction of merely theoretical interest, as it has important practical implications for clergy who battle the never-ending demands of congregational ministry:

> Apart from union with Christ, ministry is cast back on us to achieve. This is a recipe for failure, for we all fall short of the glory of God. The understanding and practice of pastoral work in this case is a burden too heavy to bear and follows a path that denies the gospel. We do not heal the sick, comfort the bereaved, accompany the lonely, forgive sins, raise up hope of eternal life, or bring people to God on the strength of our piety and pastoral skill. To think that these tasks are ours to perform is not only hubris, but also a recipe for exhaustion and depression in ministry.[25]

In terms of preaching specifically, nowhere is the curious inutility of human testimony better expressed (at least in narrative terms) than by the heavenly voice in Revelation that declares over those whose deaths are collateral damage in the battle between Michael and the infernal serpent, "They have conquered him by [διά] the blood of the Lamb, and by [διά] the word of their testimony, for they did not cling to life even in the face of death" (Rev 12:11). Although John's grammar seems initially to suggest that "the blood of the Lamb" and "the word of their testimony" are instruments of conquest in the hands of the martyrs, they prove to be so only by affirming that the power is not their own.[26] The

---

25. Purves, *Reconstructing Pastoral Theology*, 45. Its aptness is such that I previously cited this passage in *Of Seeds and the People of God*, 96, as does Draper, "Lived Doxology," 229.

26. *Pace* Blount, *Invasion of the Dead*, 24, who offers a somewhat more agential reading of this passage: "Through their testimony, they participated in God's conquest of the powers that haunt this age. Through their testimony to resurrection life, with

slaughter of the faithful is proof enough that words of attestation are only as powerful as the events to which they bear witness. Accordingly, the NASB better captures the theological intent of John's prepositions: "they overcame him *because of* the blood of the Lamb and *because of* the word of their testimony."²⁷ Just so, the testimony of the faithful (that of faithful preachers included) is more declarative than instrumental, testifying to the primacy of Jesus' mediation by joining him first in death, and thereby yielding to his agency rather than wielding power of its own.

In a manner that seems to reflect an operational understanding of Christian ministry, homiletical theory has for some time been occupied with questions of rhetorical method, or what Jacques Ellul calls "technique."²⁸ Notwithstanding the democratizing emphases of the New Homiletic, in particular its wholly appropriate repudiation of coercive authority and its insistence on more participatory modes of speech,²⁹ preachers and their hearers nonetheless remain in place as the primary agents of spiritual transformation. Homiletical theory, anthropologically conceived, is thus liable to the charge of *hubris*, as a catalogue of operational strategies that seek to act in the place of an apparently absent (whether historically past, irretrievably risen, or unaccountably metaphysical) God. Yet insofar as Christianity is an intrinsically covenantal faith, homiletical theory within the Christian tradition is more properly constrained by the radical asymmetry of the divine-human relationship.³⁰ On this point, no less capable an accuser than Karl Barth demands:

God, they have conquered death!"

27. In commenting on this passage, Aune (*Revelation 17-22*, 702) notes the close parallel in 1 Cor 15:57, "But thanks be to God, who gives us the victory through [διά] our Lord Jesus Christ."

28. In *The Technological Society*, Ellul comments, "The term *technique*, as I use it, does not mean machines, technology, or this or that procedure for obtaining an end. In our technological society, *technique* is the *totality of methods rationally arrived at and having absolute efficiency* (for a given state of development) in every field of human activity" (xxv, emphasis original). Or as Draper observes ("Lived Doxology" 70), Ellul is concerned with "the fundamental, universal, and essentially rational characteristic behind technology which seeks efficiency, manipulation, and control of pre-determined results." On "technique" in relation to preaching, see also Knowles, *Of Seeds and the People of God*, 188–91; for a similar critique of homiletical instrumentalism, in conversation with Thomist theology, see Pasquarello, *We Speak*, 113–17.

29. For a concise description, see Wilson, "New Homiletic."

30. Rottman, "Performative Language," 82–86.

> What are you doing, you man, with the word of *God* upon *your* lips? Upon what grounds do you assume the rôle of mediator between heaven and earth? Who has authorized you to take your place there and to generate religious feeling? And, to crown all, to do so with results, with success? Did one ever hear of such overweening presumption, such Titanism, or—to speak less classically but more clearly—such brazenness! One does not with impunity cross the boundaries of mortality! One does not with impunity usurp the prerogative of God![31]

Barth's conclusion is unequivocal: "The word of God on the lips of a man is an impossibility; it does not happen; no one will ever accomplish it or see it accomplished."[32]

This conviction provided the theological foundation for a highly popular seminar on preaching that Barth offered at the University of Bonn in 1932 and 1933.[33] Barth's opening salvo is well known and widely quoted: "Preaching," he insists, "must conform to revelation." While such an assertion seems unexceptional in itself, its implications are both categorical and profound: "First, this means negatively that in preaching, we are not to repeat or transmit the revelation of God by what we do. Precisely because the point of the event of preaching is God's own speaking (*Deus loquitur*), there can be no question of our doing the revealing in any way."[34]

Anticipating the concerns of Newbigin, Bosch, and the missional church movement as they apply to preaching, Barth directly challenges exaggerated claims of rhetorical efficacy:

> Preaching may not try to create the reality of God. Reference might be made to slogans which imply a progression from mere word to reality, from doctrine to life. Preaching, it is said, has the task of building up the kingdom of God, of converting, of leading to decision. It must confront us with the reality of God. It must be vital and communicate an experience. It must bring to light our situation and set us before God . . . All these things

---

31. Barth, *The Word of God and the Word of Man*, 125–26 (emphasis original).

32. Barth, *The Word of God and the Word of Man*, 124. Further: "Nothing else can satisfy the waiting people and nothing else can be the will of God than that he himself should be revealed in the event. But the word of God is and will and must be and remain the word of *God*" (125; emphasis original).

33. Thane, "Speech-Act Theory," 190–91; cf. 192 on the genesis of Barth's *Homiletik*.

34. Barth, *Homiletics*, 47; cf. 50; on this key criterion, see further Thane, "Speech-Act Theory," 193–94.

may well happen in a sermon, of course, but they are acts which God himself wills to perform and which can never, therefore, be a human task . . . Preachers are under a constraint, an *anankē* (1 Cor. 9:16) that strips them of all their own proposals and programs.[35]

If Barth is concerned with theological presumption, Luther concedes the simple limitations of human speech: "Where God does not provide the message, a sermon is useless . . . For wherever God does not suggest the words, there is no sermon at all, or it is a vain and pernicious sermon."[36] In characteristic fashion, Luther makes a clear distinction between human and divine action: "It is easy enough for someone to preach to me," he insists, "but only God can put it into my heart. He must speak it in my heart, or else nothing at all will come of it. If God remains silent, the final effect is as though nothing had been said."[37] Accordingly, he differentiates sharply between the physical limitations of human speech and the more profound efficacy of God's own Word:

> [God's] Word should be allowed to work alone, without our work or interference. Why? Because it is not in my power or hand to fashion the hearts of men . . . I can get no farther than their ears; their hearts I cannot reach. And since I cannot pour faith into their hearts, I cannot, nor should I, force anyone to have faith. That is God's work alone, who causes faith to live in the heart. Therefore we should give free course to the Word and not add our works to it. We have the *jus verbi* [right to speak] but not the *executio* [power to accomplish]. We should preach the Word, but the results must be left solely to God's good pleasure.[38]

Calvin, characteristically, laments the epistemological obstinacy of fallen creatures:

---

35. Barth, *Homiletics* 48-49.

36. *LW* 13:12 (WA 8:12-13), on Ps 68:11, cited in Ferry, "Martin Luther on Preaching," 273.

37. "Sermons of 1522," WA 10:3, 260; "Sermons of 1525," WA 17:2, 174; as cited in Althaus, *Theology of Martin Luther*, 39.

38. "The Second Sermon, March 10, 1522, Monday after Invocavit"; *LW* 51:76; WA 10:15. Here, Luther combines German and Latin terms: "wir haben wohl *ius verbi* aber nicht *executionem*." Cf. WA 29:381, where Luther observes that the preacher "corporaliter verbum praedicet docente deo interne [preaches the Word physically while God teaches internally]"; quoted in Büttgen, "Luther et l'objet de la predication," 569n16.

> God's word ought indeed to be enough to engender faith in us, if our blindness and stubbornness did not prevent it. But since our spirit is inclined to futility it can never hold to God's truth and since it is stupefied it cannot see His light. That is why the bare word profits nothing without the illumination of the Holy Spirit, from which it is clear that faith is above all human understanding . . .
> God's word is like the sun, for it shines on all to whom it is proclaimed, but it is without effectiveness among the blind. Now we are all naturally blind in this matter; that is why it cannot enter into our spirit unless God's Spirit, who is the inward Master, gives it access by His illumination.[39]

Taken on their own, such assertions leave little room for any human contribution to the work of God, however much Barth, Luther, and Calvin may all have given themselves to preaching. Yet it is here that the missional church conversation can help, because (in addition to posing difficult questions of methodology), its key insight is to reclaim the rôle of human agency, albeit re-envisioned in light of a more robust Trinitarianism and a more accurate reading of christological anthropology.

A key purpose of preaching is, surely, to make God known, notwithstanding the fact that God cannot be fully known, that preachers in particular do not always know God well, and even if they did, that they are persistently opaque and unreliable vehicles for divine revelation. A christocentric missiology recalls that self-disclosure is, in fact, the domain of the Father, Son, and Holy Spirit, acting in concert. As an expression of God's own mission, preaching may yield to and thus participate in divine self-revelation, while yet not presuming to act as its necessary substitute. In this sense, the purpose of preaching is to announce the salvation declared in Christ by its own proclamation of the gospel message. More precisely, its purpose is the linguistic *contextualization* of the gospel, articulating the universally relevant claims and promises of God in terms that apply to the hearers of a given moment. Yet all such efforts are themselves qualified and contextualized by the unsubstitutable character of the incarnation itself, which preachers are hardly in a position to imitate (much less supersede), as well as by the power of the Holy Spirit, which rhetoric alone cannot presume to match. Even though preachers at every point on the theological spectrum affirm that sermons aim to

---

39. Calvin, *Institutes of the Christian Religion: 1541 French Edition*, 188–90. Here, Calvin's French corresponds closely to the revised 1559 Latin version of *Institutes* 3:2.33–34.

transform and empower their hearers, they themselves possess no such power, insofar as transformation—as Barth and Luther both insist—is the sole domain of the Spirit of God. Stated differently, for preachers to empower others, they and their words need first to be empowered, since Christian discipleship is not, at root, a process of self-improvement on the basis of pooled resources (as liberals and conservatives alike not infrequently imagine), but rather a slow and difficult discipline whereby we learn to rely instead on divine grace.

By the same token, the principle of *participatio Christi* indicates that preachers do not partake of or participate in the life and ministry of Christ any more or less than do their congregants. Far from reinstating the preacher as the sole authority for spiritual truth in the life of a congregation (as those on the theological right would insist), such an emphasis situates them as fellow recipients and co-hearers of the gospel with their congregations, as much subject to the demands of the word of God as those to whom they proclaim it. But neither does it allow preachers to abdicate responsibility for declaring a definitive, authoritative gospel that is focused on the life, death, and resurrection of Jesus of Nazareth (as those on the theological left seem at times to imply). Neither preachers nor congregations are free to make of Christian faith what they will (with or without claims of divine endorsement). To the contrary, both are constrained, first, by the historical character of Jesus' incarnation, together with the gospel message that proceeds from it and, second, by the suprahistorical character of Christ's lordship, demonstrated above all by his resurrection from death.

As is evident from his post-resurrection appearances and throughout the book of Acts, Christ does indeed entrust his mission into the hands of a fledgling church (whose faults and failings have not lessened in the centuries since). Hence the need for direct reliance on the Spirit of God to save us from our tendency to assume responsibility for ministry, claiming even its most intermittent and imperfect successes as our own. Although Mark reports that Jesus' parable of the rebellious tenants (Mark 12:1–12 and parallels) was originally directed against certain religious leaders of his own day, and the church has frequently turned this interpretation against Judaism as a whole, both approaches overlook its more obvious application to the presumed inheritors of the vineyard. On one level, the parable concerns social conditions, viticulture, and the contractual obligations that bind tenant farmers to absentee landowners. But Jesus does not intend either to advocate or to condemn peasant revolt *per se*, since his focus is not primarily political, sociological, or mercantile (much as his ministry has critical implications for each). On either side of an escalating and deadly dispute, master and mastered battle for control, one invoking the force of law and the others implementing rough justice of their own. Yet all of them are equally mistaken, for in Jewish tradition the fruit of the earth comes ultimately from God, in which case it is to God that they owe primary allegiance. The whole point of Jesus' agricultural parables, after all, is that neither the most resentful stewardship (as here) nor the most neglectful (as in the parable of the lazy farmer, Mark 4:26–29) alters the fact that God alone is the giver of life, as much for homileticians and ministry professionals as for tenured vineyards and ancient fig trees.

If, therefore, as Jesus warns, "the kingdom of God" is to be taken from the faithless "and given to a people who will produce its fruit" (Matt 21:43 NIV), surely the new stewards are no less responsible than the original ones for giving credit where theological credit is due. If, as Christians have always claimed, Jesus is here identifying his own followers as the rightful inheritors of a squandered legacy, surely these later disciples will be no less subject to judgement should they fail to acknowledge the true source of all fruitfulness. In fact, neither the old stewards nor the new can take responsibility for "producing" the fruit of the vineyard: since they are not the ones who make the vines flourish, they have no reason to claim the produce as their own. This is the error of the wealthy farmer whose fields produce a bountiful crop (Luke 12:16–24): he fails to recognize that everything he gathers into his barns is the gift of divine abundance and generosity. In much the same way, simply attending to recent developments in the literature of mission should be enough to qualify our confidence in the power of language and recall us to a more vivid reliance on divine agency in the preaching moment as the source of spiritual "fruit."

Critiquing exaggerated claims of rhetorical efficacy leaves us with important questions: since we are, despite everything, still called to preach, what is the proper rôle of language in the kingdom of God and what are its proper limits? Answering these concerns invites a consideration of performative utterance and its application to the ministry of proclamation.

Performative Utterance: Doing Things with Words?

Speech act theory, and the concept of "performative utterance" in particular, offers a helpful test case for assessing both the power and the limitations of human language, especially as applies to proclaiming the word and reign of God. Although the concepts in question are rather technical, their implications for how we preach are altogether concrete and practical.

How do we know whether the words of a sermon (for example) will have any effect on the hearer? Are they not, after all, simply words like any others? To questions such as these, J. L. Austin's aptly named study, *How to Do Things with Words*, suggests a compellingly simple answer.[40] Austin (who was a philosopher of language) distinguishes between words themselves and the effects that they produce. More precisely, first, he names meaningful speech as a "locutionary act," by which he means the act of saying something that the hearer can reasonably understand. Second, he describes the intended effect of that speech as an "illocutionary act": the speaker employs words in order to bring about a certain result: "I apologize"; "I accept your apology"; "I nominate you as chair"; "I resign," etc. These are not aimless or empty words, but words by which the speaker intends to make a particular difference within a particular situation or circumstance (by means of apologizing, nominating, resigning, etc.). Third (although the distinction is subtle) the effect itself is designated a "perlocutionary act." In other words, a "perlocutionary" act is an act performed by saying something (the consequence of locutionary and illocutionary acts), such as persuading, inspiring, encouraging, or otherwise directing a listener.[41] To speak in these terms is to assert that words not only proclaim reality (for instance, by describing something that the listener cannot directly see); more precisely, proclamation actually establishes the reality to which the words refer: "Saying something

---

40. Austin, *How to Do Things with Words*. In contrast to its employment as an approach to biblical interpretation (reviewed by Botha, "Speech Act Theory and Biblical Interpretation") or to establish a theological account of Scripture as divine locution (cf. Berry, "Speech-Act Theory"), application of speech act theory to homiletics has to date been limited.

41. For Austin's summary of these categories, cf. *How to Do Things with Words*, 109, 116–18, 121 ("Thus we distinguished the locutionary act . . . which has a *meaning*; the illocutionary act which has a certain *force* in saying something; [and] the perlocutionary act which is *the achieving of* certain *effects* by saying something" [emphasis original]).

will often, or even normally, produce certain consequential effects upon the feelings, thoughts, or actions of the audience, or of the speaker, or of other persons: and it may be done with the design, intention, or purpose of producing them . . ."[42] On this view, language does more than convey propositional content; it communicates the disposition of the speaker, above all with regard to the proper ordering of their environment.[43] Indeed, language serves as a means by which the speaker seeks to establish that intended order. Not that speech act theory seeks to reconstruct an author's psychological state at the point of composition (an especially problematic endeavor across barriers of culture and history). Rather, as Kevin Vanhoozer explains, "understanding the intention of the language user is not a matter of recovering psychic phenomena but of reconstructing a public performance in terms that make its nature as an intended action clear."[44]

In addition to distinguishing between, for instance, "explicit" and "implicit" forms, Austin divides illocutionary speech acts into more precise categories, with these categories further refined by John Searle into the following five:[45]

1. Representatives (alternatively, "assertives") which "commit the speaker (in varying degrees) to . . . the truth of the expressed proposition . . . the psychological state expressed is Belief [that something is the case]."

2. Directives, "which are attempts (of varying degrees . . .) by the speaker to get the hearer to do something . . . Verbs denoting members of this class are ask, order, command, request, beg, plead, pray, entreat, and also invite, permit, and advise."

---

42. Austin, *How to Do Things with Words*, 101. Following his own description of these categories, Graham (*J. L. Austin*, 59) notes that "the theory of illocution plays a central part in [Austin's] own philosophy, and it is almost impossible to exaggerate its influence in contemporary philosophy."

43. So Berry, "Speech-Act Theory," 83–85.

44. Vanhoozer, *Is There a Meaning in This Text?*, 252; cf. 230.

45. Definitions are cited from Searle, "A Classification of Illocutionary Acts," 10–14, which appears in nearly identical form as "A Taxonomy of Illocutionary Acts"; cf. the list of verbs for each category in Searle and Vanderveken, *Foundations of Illocutionary Logic*, 179–216, and Austin, *How to Do Things with Words*, 151–63.

3. "Commissives... are those illocutionary acts whose point is to commit the speaker (again in varying degrees) to some future course of action."

4. Expressives, which "express the psychological state specified . . . about a state of affairs specified in the propositional content. The paradigms of Expressive verbs are 'thank,' 'congratulate,' 'apologize,' 'condole,' 'deplore,' and 'welcome.'"

5. Declarations, which "bring about some alteration in the status or condition of the referred to object . . . solely in virtue of the fact that the declaration has been successfully performed." These are instances in which "saying makes it so," for which Searle offers the examples "I resign"; "You're fired"; and "I excommunicate you."

Despite the fact that its operations are varied and complex, into which of these categories might preaching fit, broadly speaking?[46] Which of them best account for the effect that preachers intend their sermons to have?[47] In terms of the first category ("assertives") preachers are certainly committed to the truth of their words, although we would want to acknowledge that "belief" as an expression of spirituality implies relational trust as much as confidence in the propositional accuracy of the assertions themselves. Likewise (second) a sermon might incorporate "directives"—as, for instance, when the preacher admonishes the congregants to increase their tithes in order to meet his salary. Again (third) the faithful pastor commits herself to the congregation when she speaks of her intent to shepherd them through whatever challenges lie ahead, just as she may (fourth) express her gratitude (or her apologies!) for her ministry and congratulate them for their achievements. Searle himself proposes that religious forms of speech are often "declarations" (his fifth category) which depend for their efficacy on some form of external authorization: "Thus, in order to bless, excommunicate, christen, [or] pronounce guilty . . . it is not sufficient for any old speaker to say to any old

---

46. As Austin (*How to Do Things with Words*, 38) wittily observes, "We must at all costs avoid over-simplification, which one might be tempted to call the occupational disease of philosophers if it were not their occupation."

47. Searle notes that, on the one hand, "there are a rather limited number of basic things we do with language: we tell people how things are, we try to get them to do things, we commit ourselves to doing things, we express our feelings and attitudes and we bring about changes through our utterances." Yet he acknowledges that "often, we do more than one of these at once in the same utterance" (Searle, *Expression and Meaning*, 29).

hearer 'I bless,' 'I excommunicate,' etc."[48] In such cases, the speech act in question only proves effective by virtue of certain attendant conventions that validate the utterance:

> There must exist an extra-linguistic institution and the speaker and hearer must occupy special places within this institution. It is only given such institutions as the Church, the law, private property, the state and a special position of the speaker and hearer within these institution that one can excommunicate, appoint, give and bequeath one's possessions or declare war.[49]

In the absence of proper authorization, therefore, a "declarative" fails. For instance, "If I say 'I declare you man and wife' when I have not had vested in me the right to conduct the marriage ceremony then I have not succeeded in marrying you."[50] Or we may think of the famous instance in which, on March 30, 1981, American Secretary of State General Alexander Haig responded to the attempted assassination of Ronald Reagan by insisting, "I am in control here," when, constitutionally, that was not in fact the case. Because it lacked external validation, his attempt at self-assertion failed (as, for the same reason, must all claims of self-authorization). Indeed, the more closely we examine them, the more apparent it becomes that declaratives prove truly "performative" only in a limited set of circumstances, and even then only under a narrow set of conditions.[51] These limitations lead Graham to conclude that performatives of this sort "can only be effective against the appropriate *social* background. The act of speech is one necessary component, but the attitude of those surrounding that act is another."[52] Still, there are exceptions to this rule also,

---

48. Searle, "A Classification of Illocutionary Acts," 6.

49. Searle, "A Classification of Illocutionary Acts," 14; cf. Austin's extended discussion of "appropriate circumstances" (*How to Do Things with Words*, 12–38, etc.).

50. Graham, *J. L. Austin*, 55; further, "We could put this briefly by saying that there must be an accepted conventional procedure involving the uttering of the words in question, that this must be properly and correctly invoked by the parties to the exchange, and that they must all perform correctly and completely according to the principles of the procedure they are invoking." For an entertaining account (originally a BBC Radio address) of ways in which performative utterance may in fact fail to perform, see Austin, "Performative Utterances [1956]," in *Philosophical Papers*, 237–41.

51. Graham (*J. L. Austin*, 58–67) notes Austin's own dissatisfaction with this category (e.g., Austin, "Performative Utterances," 246–51), yet deems such dissatisfaction premature.

52. Graham, *J. L. Austin*, 84.

among them what Searle calls "supernatural" declarations, as "When God says, 'Let there be light.'"[53]

Even for denominations with a minimal sense of clerical authority, this last category makes a good deal of sense, at least when it refers to human speech. Pulpit committees select, and churches ordain, preachers able to provide a compelling account of the gospel message, thereby naming the reality that the congregants seek to embrace. At least notionally, churches of Reformation heritage defer to the authority of the preached word, while more sacramentally-oriented churches assert the right to bestow authority on their clergy. But whether by way of recognition or impartation, every church takes responsibility for selecting leaders whom it authorizes to speak both to and for its members, all in the service of the Christian gospel.

Just so, Keith Graham assesses performative utterance (generally speaking) in terms of "the capacity which human beings have to *map* the structure of the world." By this he means that

> in some way people can reproduce, in their thought, speech and perception, a representation of some part of reality. When beings possess this capacity it is one further step in sophistication to be able to map not only the actual world but also possible worlds. It can then be argued that in order to act, in the fully human sense, we must be able to form a conception of the world as it is and also as it might be, and be able to bring about the change from the first to the second.[54]

Put simply (although the matter is far from simple), performative utterances are part of the larger project by which we not only envisage but also endeavor to bring about such change: "in one way or another the performative brings about the truth of its own content."[55] Yet even though "people can change the world, create new states of affairs, by *conceiving* it differently,"[56] we are still left with the problems of authority and consensus with which our discussion began. Accordingly, much subsequent debate has focused on the question of how, in what measure, or why, performatives may be thought to enact the conditions that they name.[57]

---

53. Searle, "A Classification of Illocutionary Acts," 15n3.
54. Graham, *J. L. Austin*, 53.
55. Graham, *J. L. Austin*, 75.
56. Graham, *J. L. Austin*, 84.
57. See, e.g., Gunther Grewendorf, "How Performatives Don't Work," in

That is to say, in our context, that preachers may utter any number of assertions or declarations, but why should a congregation take their word for things?

For all its initial promise, applying the concept of performative utterance to proclamation of the Christian gospel runs up against two significant objections, one rhetorical (or sociological), and the other theological. As to the first category, the general tenor of the New Homiletic has been to renounce authoritative (therefore necessarily authoritarian) declarations from the pulpit, deferring to the authority of the listener to determine the meaning of God's word for each. Logically, then, just as preachers cannot impose meaning on their hearers, so no one hearer can impose their personal interpretation on any other. Without ruling out the possibility of consensus,[58] such an approach quickly bogs down in the quagmire of infinite deferral: if every congregant is truly free to arrive, unconstrained, at their own conclusions, there can be no limit in principle to the number of interpretations available. Although, from a certain perspective, allowing for unlimited possibilities of meaning is an essential feature of the freedom required for individual moral accountability, the gospel risks becoming, in practice, whatever we choose to make of it.

Against such a possibility (and this is the second objection), the most basic Christian confession, at least according to Paul, is Κύριος Ἰησοῦς—"Jesus is Lord" (1 Cor 12:3). Whatever other implications it may entail, confessing Jesus to be "Lord" means that he is not ours to command, least of all in the arena of preaching. With respect to the larger principle, christological confession is not a gesture by which we elect Jesus to office, but rather an act of capitulation to his antecedent sovereignty. This is important to acknowledge in a culture that values personal choice and assumes the normalcy of democratically elected leadership. More specifically, with respect to preaching, the sermon does not represent a kind of "performative utterance" on the simple grounds that Jesus is not obligated to "perform" when called upon to do so. Because she is merely a servant of Christ, the preacher cannot command either the written or the living word of God; rather, she is first and foremost a fellow listener with those to whom she preaches. Situating the preacher closer to God than her congregants, as one who speaks in place of God, is thus

---

Grewendorf and Meggle, eds., *Speech Acts, Mind, and Social Reality*, 25–39, esp. 26–30.

58. Stanley Fish offers this solution in his well-known essay, "Is There a Text in this Class?"; in *Is There a Text in this Class?*, 305–21.

to be rejected on theological even more than sociological grounds. She may invite submission while yet not commanding it, thereby modelling the posture that she advocates even in the manner of her address. If we are to arrive at a more suitable category for the sermon, preaching must always be a kind of humble listening even as it is more obviously a form of speaking.[59]

Clearly, therefore, confessing that "Jesus is Lord" represents the very opposite of performative utterance.[60] In this case, the "extra-linguistic institution" to which Christian speech attests is that of divine sovereignty itself, together with the epistemological prerogative that it implies. Because such confession merely acknowledges a reality to which, by definition, the speaker yields control, all that it changes is the cognitive or volitional disposition of the one who speaks in this manner. Paradoxically, preaching is therefore "performative" only with respect to the speaker: conforming to the first of Searle's five categories ("Representatives" or "Assertives"), a sermon can do little more, humanly speaking, than express the beliefs and convictions of one who utters it.

Whether, therefore, speech act theory can be more substantively reconciled with traditional categories of Christian proclamation (and *vice versa*) remains for the moment an open question.

> "What is truth?" said jesting Pilate, and would not stay for an answer.
> —JOHN LANGSHAW AUSTIN (1911–1960)[61]

---

59. "Preaching excellence will be the fruit of listening to God's prior Word . . . before we ourselves presume to speak. And because the depth and riches of God's Word are too great to absorb in a lifetime, we will have cause to listen for eternity" (Pasquarello, *We Speak*, 4).

60. Along the same lines, Poythress ("Canon and Speech Act," 348) warns against the possible assumption in speech act theory "that a speaker has essentially god-like powers over language, and god-like powers over his [*sic*] own meanings."

61. Austin, "Truth," in *Philosophical Papers*, 117.

2

Reaching into Silence

> Jesus was a sailor
> When he walked upon the water
> And he spent a long time watching
> From a lonely wooden tower
> And when he knew for certain
> Only drowning men could see him
> He said all men will be sailors then
> Until the sea shall free them,
> But he himself was broken
> Long before the sky would open,
> Forsaken, almost human
> He sank beneath your wisdom like a stone.
>
> —Leonard Cohen, "Suzanne"[1]

The Words of Adam and the Word of God

THE NET RESULT OF the discussion thus far seems to be that while the words of a sermon (dialogical or otherwise) can enable congregants to imagine the conditions of God's kingdom, they can do little more than this to bring it about in practice. On this point, and despite the initial proviso in his comments, David Buttrick is nonetheless deeply confident in the power of language, the language of preachers in particular:

---

1. This poem first appeared in Cohen, *Parasites of Heaven*, 70, and subsequently as the lyrics of "Suzanne" on his debut album "Songs of Leonard Cohen" (CBS 63421), released by Columbia Records on December 27, 1967.

> Words do not create the world—only God creates with a Word—but language does constitute the world-in-consciousness, the significant social world in which we live. People and places, things, symbols, social roles and moral values, lands never visited, persons never met, cosmologies, psychological "models"—all these are named into consciousness and become a "world" in which people live together ... With words, we *name* the world.[2]

Echoing Keith Graham on the question of our capacity to map the structure of the world, Buttrick proposes that every infant is like Adam in the garden, naming and thereby ordering their environment: "Like diapered Adam, every baby learns to name the world."[3] This, for Buttrick, is the elemental human disposition that gives rise to preaching, as preachers name the ways of God within the conceptual world that we inhabit: "Preaching can rename the world 'God's world' with metaphorical power, and can change identity by incorporating all our stories into 'God's story.' Preaching constructs in consciousness a 'faith-world' related to God."[4] Indeed, says Buttrick, the work of the preacher is in essence that of Adam, to whom God brings "every animal of the field and every bird of the air ... to see what he would call them" (Gen 2:19). As Buttrick goes on to explain,

> Preachers use words. So preaching can reshape the world in consciousness and transform identity: Preaching can build a faith-world in human consciousness. If preaching speaks boldly then, perhaps, like astonished Adam, once more we may walk God's mysterious world, name it good, and see ourselves with tender wonderment as characters in God's great story of salvation.
> Story and naming are the stuff of *Christian* preaching.[5]

According to Buttrick (whose contribution to contemporary homiletics is incalculable), "Preaching can build a faith-world in human consciousness." It is possible to interpret this assertion as a gesture of methodological humility, one that limits the "construction" of new worlds to the internal realm of consciousness (or imagination) alone. On this view, preaching does no more than cast a vision of what could be, leaving the task of realization, implementation, or fulfillment to God and

---

2. Buttrick, *Homiletic*, 9.
3. Buttrick, *Homiletic*, 6.
4. Buttrick, *Homiletic*, 11.
5. Buttrick, *Homiletic*, 20.

the hearers. Still, conceiving of it in this manner fails to address questions of "failure" and "success"—why some sermons take root, rise up in consciousness, and bear rich fruit, while others wither on the homiletical vine, failing to produce any measurable response among their hearers.

Yet just when we might seem to have reached an impasse, Buttrick's appeal to Adam, on the one hand, combined with aspects of performative utterance, on the other, offers the possibility of a way forward. Examining the first of these requires more detailed recourse to the account of Adam naming animals in the second chapter of Genesis:

> Then the LORD God said, "It is not good that the man should be alone; I will make him a helper as his partner." So out of the ground the LORD God formed every animal of the field and every bird of the air, and brought them to the man to see what he would call them; and whatever the man called every living creature, that was its name. The man gave names to all cattle, and to the birds of the air, and to every animal of the field; but for the man there was not found a helper as his partner. So the LORD God caused a deep sleep to fall upon the man, and he slept; then he took one of his ribs and closed up its place with flesh. And the rib that the LORD God had taken from the man he made into a woman and brought her to the man. Then the man said, "This at last is bone of my bones and flesh of my flesh; this one shall be called Woman, for out of Man this one was taken." (Gen 2:18–23)

Adam names the animals as part of the larger search for a solution to his solitude. As the wordplay in 2:23 confirms (happily operating in Hebrew [*ish/ishshah*] as well as English ["man/woman"]), language is the means by which Adam articulates his relationship to the different creatures that God brings to him. At least in this account, corresponding language signals corresponding identity, just as lack of linguistic correspondence indicates an unequal or incommensurate relationship. However venerable the tradition according to which his bestowal of names serves primarily to indicate Adam's wisdom and capacity for intellectual ordering,[6] the point of the original story is that he fails by this means to discover a suitable mate: "for the man there was *not* found a helper as his partner." Far from producing the communion and intimacy for which he yearns, none of the creatures to which Adam assigns a place in his mental geography proves to be a fitting companion.

---

6. Further, Jacobs, "Naming of the Animals."

These details are important for the conclusion that Buttrick seeks to draw from the story. Whereas in the first chapter of Genesis God "names" creation into existence, here God fashions living creatures "out of the ground" (2:19), just as Adam himself is formed "from the dust of the ground" (2:7). In this chapter, and in contrast to the creation account, "naming" is a human rather than divine task. Thus on mortal lips it is clearly a derivative, second-order activity: Adam can only name what God first presents before him. To borrow Buttrick's terms, Adam's ability to articulate a "world-in-consciousness" is wholly dependent on the prior and more substantive creativity of God. Nowhere is this distinction more evident than in the formation of "Eve," who is neither named into being nor fashioned "from the earth," but carved out of Adam by the hand of God. Against Buttrick's claim that human words create meaning and community in their ability to evoke the things of God, Adam cannot do even this much. He can only acknowledge the limit of his own efforts—lexical or otherwise—compared to the full sufficiency of what God provides: "This *at last*," he exults, "is bone of my bones and flesh of my flesh; this one shall be called Woman, for out of Man this one was taken" (2:23). He recognizes that the community and companionship for which he longs indeed derives from him, but only because God has brought them forth. In effect, Adam proves incapable of realizing the potential that lies within himself; hence this climactic "naming" amounts to an admission of the limited force of human language.

In much the same way, all properly Christian speech, together with its effects and consequences in the life of the church, are founded on prior divine action and prior divine speech. As Joe Jones observes, "The confession that the church speaks because God has first spoken and revealed Godself is fundamental to Christian witness and self-understanding."[7] The preacher may well evoke possibilities and recount the promises of God, but the limits of Adam's speech are the limits of all human speaking: the most the preacher can do is to catalogue the consequences of a generous divine creativity, whether these are already manifest or as yet only promised. Christian speech is by nature both deferential and referential, directing attention beyond its own words to the veracity and fidelity of the One whose self-declaration we echo and whose enduring commitment to grant life provides the basis for our own salvation. This being the case, the authenticity, integrity, and authority of Christian speech (such

---

7. Jones, *A Grammar of Christian Faith*, 79 (originally in italics).

as they are) are ultimately rooted not in the efficacy of our language or the winsomeness of the preacher, but in the character of God. To say this does not mean simply that God can be trusted to keep promises or to act in a manner that is consistent, but that the God of Adam, Abraham, Moses, and Jesus is fundamentally trustworthy, such that divine fidelity, expressed in divine speech, is what evokes the human response of faith.[8] Christian community, which modestly and imperfectly echoes the word of God in every facet of its existence, therefore forms neither in recognition of nor in answer to its own needs, but in response to the self-declared reality of God. As Luther says of the church's liturgy, "Our dear Lord himself speaks with us through his holy Word and in response we speak with him through prayer and praise."[9] Rowan Williams explains that "speaking of God is speaking to God and opening our speech to God's speech, and it is a speaking of those who have spoken to God and who have thus begun to form the human community, the unrestricted fellowship of humbleness that is the only kind of universal meaning without the tyranny of a total perspective."[10] To answer divine speech with worship (whether in the form of hymnody, baptismal liturgy, eucharistic prayers, creedal confession, lamentation, or preaching) is to assume a new, theologically modest identity as those whose words turn them away from themselves and toward the One whose Word they heed.

This dynamic of "second-order" naming (testimony that defers to a prior divine word) is fully visible in the book of Psalms, where worshippers joyfully expound the fidelity of Israel's God:

> I will sing of your steadfast love, O LORD, forever;
>   with my mouth I will proclaim your faithfulness to all generations.
> I declare that your steadfast love is established forever;
>   your faithfulness is as firm as the heavens. (Ps 89:1–2)

Throughout the psalms, as I noted in a previous study, "The saving works of Yahweh . . . provide the source and content of testimony among the faithful":[11]

> I have not hidden your saving help within my heart,
>   I have spoken of your faithfulness and your salvation;

---

8. On the linguistic basis for this claim, see Knowles, *Unfolding Mystery*, 149–66.

9. Cited in Hughes, *Worship as Meaning*, 161 and n45; hence, as Hughes observes, "the language of worship consists primarily in the vocative case" (282).

10. Williams, *On Christian Theology*, 8.

11. Knowles, *Unfolding Mystery*, 158.

> I have not concealed your steadfast love and your faithfulness
> from the great congregation. (Ps 40:10)

In the New Testament, it is Jesus of Nazareth who represents—and bears witness to—the fidelity of a faithful God. Playing on the same Hebrew vocabulary that underlies the psalmists' celebration of a trustworthy God, the book of Revelation refers to Christ as "the Amen, the faithful and true witness" (Rev 3:14; cf. 1:5). Christ as divine witness thus creates the possibility of Christian witness: hence the author of Revelation describes himself as having "testified to the word of God and to the testimony of Jesus Christ, even to all that he saw" (Rev 1:2). In similar fashion, the Letter to the Hebrews begins not by asserting its own authority, but by attending instead to prior divine speech: "Long ago God spoke to our ancestors in many and various ways by the prophets, but in these last days he has spoken to us by a Son, whom he appointed heir of all things, through whom he also created the worlds" (Heb 1:1–2). In his Letter to the Romans, Paul explains that "faith comes from what is heard, and what is heard comes through the word of Christ [διὰ ῥήματος Χριστοῦ]" (Rom 10:17), whether we take the final clause as a qualitative genitive ("the word concerning Christ") or a genitive of source ("the word that is from Christ").[12] The Gospel of John is even clearer on this point, with its declaration, unmistakably indicating Jesus of Nazareth, that "he whom God has sent speaks the words of God [τὰ ῥήματα τοῦ θεοῦ]" (John 3:34).

Thus, conflating the two creation stories of Genesis 1–2, the "words" of Adam can only catalogue, classify, and name the creatures to which God's word first gives life. In similar fashion, the poets and prophets of Hebrew tradition bear witness to what they have heard and seen, on which basis their own testimony is eventually incorporated into the canon. For their part, New Testament writers echo a definitive word of God articulated in the person of Israel's Messiah. Each of the texts in question models the deferral characteristic of testimony in principle and—in the New Testament—of Christian speech in particular. The same holds true for Christian preaching more specifically: just as the words and works of Jesus articulate the will of the One who sends him, preachers offer words that are defined by Jesus' own testimony to the ways of God. Since naming Jesus "Lord" is itself a gesture of capitulation rather than authorization,

---

12. Lukaszewski et al., *Lexham Syntactic Greek New Testament, SBL Edition*, in loc. On the text critical issue in this verse (the alternative reading is ῥήματος θεοῦ), see Longenecker, *Epistle to the Romans*, 832.

to do so acknowledges in principle that Jesus' definitive articulation of the divine character determines the content and character of Christian testimony. Whether for New Testament authors or for preachers who appeal to the authority of these texts, Christ himself thus provides the warrant for testimony offered "in his name." Far from forbidding authoritative speech with regard to God, God's prior "word" makes such speech possible.

Divine Commissives and Human Declaration

Our review of human "naming" (and the example of Adam in particular) necessitates a reconsideration of performative utterance. Recalling the first three main categories of speech act theory, much as a sermon will (1) likely offer assertives (it will "argue," "inform," "confess," and "testify"), possibly also (2) various directives (so as to "urge," "command," "forbid," "warn," "entreat," etc.), its chief *theological* purpose (at least within Christian tradition) will be to acknowledge (3) the commissive speech of God, articulated both in the biblical text generally and more particularly in the person of Jesus. "Commissive" speech acts are those by which the speaker commits to performing the words that they utter. The guarantee of their authenticity or efficacy is thus twofold: first, the character of the speaker and, second, the speaker's ability to bring the intent of their words into being. Austin proposes that verbal commitment to an act, disposition, or outcome on the part of the speaker—in the form of first person speech—is in many instances a basic characteristic of all performative utterance, distinguishing it from simple description or statement.[13] Appropriately, Searle notes in this category the verbs "commit," "promise," "vow," "pledge," "offer," "assure," and "covenant,"[14] all of which appear in Scripture as characteristic of God's disposition toward a recalcitrant humanity. Even Searle's example of a supernatural "declarative," cited above, is equally commissive in the sense that it proves valid and effectual simply by virtue of the One who speaks: "Then God said, 'Let there be light'; and there was light" (Gen 1:3).[15] Isaiah's prophetic

---

13. Austin, "Performative Utterances," 242–43; however, Warnock ("Some Types of Performative Utterance," in *Essays on J. L. Austin*, 73–74, and passim) notes that this condition is not absolute, since extra-linguistic convention (which is not absolute either) takes precedence in establishing operativity or "performance."

14. Searle and Vanderveken, *Foundations of Illocutionary Logic*, 192–98.

15. So Evans, *Logic of Self-Involvement*, esp. 151–65, on creation and covenant as

oracle is thus representative of all divine speech, as God pronounces himself the guarantor of his own words: "I have spoken, and I will bring it to pass; I have planned, and I will do it" (Isa 46:11; cf. 55:10–11). In canonical prophetic speech, as Walter Brueggemann observes, the words of the prophets "are cast as God's own speech, the authority for which is not found in any visible circumstance but in the trustworthiness of the God who speaks."[16] Indeed, divine commitment is directly encoded within the grammar of Hebrew verb tenses: employing the so-called "Prophetic Perfect," speech uttered on behalf of God expresses future actions as though they were already complete, since God is incapable of failing to follow through on a promise once it has been made.[17]

When it comes to the promises of the Christian gospel (which he summarizes in terms of 1 Cor 15:1–5, with its appeal to the death and resurrection of Jesus), James F. Kay invokes the identity and involvement of Christ, on whose behalf the preacher speaks:

> When we hear the kerygma with "commissive force," as a promise directed to us, such force necessarily entails the Promissor's self-involvement and simultaneously calls for our correlative response of faith in the promise. Since a promise always entails its promisor, when the kerygma is heard as a promise *of* Christ, then it is heard in faith as a promise *from* Christ himself (Rom 10:17; 2 Cor 5:20, 13:3). Thus, the *Christus praesens* is logically entailed by the promissory character of his word.[18]

At the same time, Kay insists that such promises cannot be received in isolation, but require narrative texts to flesh out, as it were, the character of Christ as one in whom hearers may place their trust.[19] Since, that is,

---

commissive divine speech acts (with exercitive and verdictive force) that call forth corresponding commissives from the people of God.

16. Brueggemann, *Cadences of Home*, 22, quoted in Jacobsen, "Promise as an Event of the Gospel in Context: Toward an Unfinished Homiletical Theology of Grace and Justice," in Jacobsen, ed., *Toward a Homiletical Theology of Promise*, 115.

17. See further Muraoka, "Prophetic Perfect," *EHLL* 3:279b–80a.

18. James F. Kay, "Promissory Kerygmatics," in Jacobsen, ed., *Toward a Homiletical Theology of Promise*, 98–99; cf. 90. Kay cites Bultmann with approval: "Christ is correctly preached not where something is said *about* him, but only where he himself becomes the proclaimer" (97–98).

19. "On the one hand, speech-act theory helps us to move conceptually and plausibly beyond Jesus Christ as a mere inference or reference in proclamation to Jesus Christ as a commissive Referent or acting Subject of an utterance heard in faith as a promise from God. Divine agency in kerygmatic proclamation is thus personal and

hearers are not invited to trust in words *about* Christ or even the words *of* Christ in isolation, but rather to trust Christ himself, something more must be said about him. In a certain sense, this second assertion risks undermining the first, at least if it is taken to suggest that the "presence" of Christ as promisor is insufficient in its own right. Hence the implications (and operations) of *Christus praesens* will require further clarification at a later juncture. Nonetheless, preaching that reiterates divine fidelity may fairly be described as a form of "promissory narration," to the extent that it narrates the faithful action of a God who commits in the person of Jesus Christ to keeping promises (so 2 Cor 1:20: "All the promises of God find their Yes in him" [ESV]), even if certain of those promises remain as yet imperfectly fulfilled.[20]

To reiterate, the first consideration that underlies our claim to base Christian preaching on the commissive speech of God, both broadly and narrowly understood, is direct acknowledgment of the divine character. If we are to speak, we must first listen, and if we are to listen well, we must know the character of the One whose word we seek to hear. As much, then, as trustworthiness—commitment to faithful action—facilitates commissive speech on the part of God, so trust—conscious submission to divine fidelity—provides the foundation for faithful testimony on the part of those who hear.

As a second consideration that clarifies the potentially performative character of Christian preaching, divine commissive speech matches trustworthiness with executive force, or power.[21] Without getting bogged down in the semantic minutiae that evidently delight philosophers of language, it is helpful at this point to observe Austin's distinction between "meaning" and "force," since it is essential to the difference between locutionary, illocutionary, and perlocutionary speech acts.[22]

---

existential rather than impersonal or mechanistically causal . . . Nevertheless, *while a promise entails a self-involving promisor, it cannot reveal the content of the promisor's character or commitments. For this reason, we not only need promissory kerygmatics, but we need kerygmatic narratives to identify who Jesus was as Lord and Christ . . .*" (Kay, "Promissory Kerygmatics," 101 [emphasis original]).

20. As David Jacobsen aptly notes, "a homiletical theology of promise . . . must be named in the midst of struggle, in both the overflow of promise and the undertow of its failure" ("Homiletical Theology, the Vocative Word *Extra Nos* and the Task of a Revisionist Eschatology," in Jacobsen, ed., *Homiletical Theology in Action*, 125).

21. So Evans, *Logic of Self-Involvement*, 163–64.

22. So Austin, *How to Do Things with Words*, 100; cf. L. W. Ferguson, "Locutionary and Illocutionary Acts," in Warnock, ed., *Essays on J. L. Austin*, 167–71.

Whether in the mouth of God or the inarticulate first-time preacher, "meaning" is a matter of making oneself understood, at least in a general sense, whereas "force" refers to specific intent. When, for instance, the pastor says, "God bless you," it is clear that he is referring to the deity and to benediction. But whether the congregant to whom he is speaking has simply sneezed, or he is praying for the miraculous healing of her sinus cold, involves a difference of rhetorical "force" and intent. Expanding on this distinction, there is a further difference between what the speaker intends by the words in question and whether or not that effect actually takes hold (which is where factors beyond the words themselves come into play). Anyone can pray, for example, in a manner that is both clear and comprehensible as to the intent of the prayer itself. But the nature of prayer is such that its ultimate, material "force"—its concrete effect on the situation for which one has offered this petition—depends entirely on the manner in which God chooses to respond. Even if, with James 5:16, we affirm that "the prayer of the righteous is powerful and effective," it is not so because the prayer itself has exercitive force, but because God acts in such a way as to implement its intended outcome.

So when God speaks, the efficacy of that communication (whatever form it may take) lies first in the nature of divine fidelity and second in the fact of God's power to enforce its purpose. Indeed, for God "speaking" and "acting" are held to be one and the same: "God said . . . and it was so" (Gen 1:9, 11, 24). So when God proclaims, "Let there be light," there is light of sufficient quality and quantity that God at once pronounces it "good" (Gen 1:3-4). The same is true for Jesus of Nazareth and the "authority" (or "power," since the term ἐξουσία encompasses both; Mark 1:22, 27, etc.) with which he speaks. Matthew observes that "he cast out the spirits *with a word*" (Matt 8:16), and all four Gospels record any number of commands that take immediate effect:

"Follow me." (Mark 1:17; 2:14; John 1:43)
"Be silent, and come out of him." (Mark 1:25; cf. 5:8; 9:25)
"Be made clean!" (Mark 1:41)
"Peace! Be still." (Mark 4:39)
"Go; let it be done for you according to your faith." (Matt 8:13)
"Young man, I say to you, rise!" (Luke 7:14)
"Peace be with you." (John 20:19, 21, 26)

Certain utterances are deemed so potent as to require transliteration of the original Aramaic:

He took her by the hand and said to her, "*Talitha cum*," which means, "Little girl, get up!" (Mark 5:41)

Then looking up to heaven, he sighed and said to him, "*Ephphatha*," that is, "Be opened." (Mark 7:34)

The immediate efficacy of Jesus' words is central to one of his earliest healings, and to our understanding the offense that such utterances occasion:

> When Jesus saw their faith, he said to the paralytic, "Son, your sins are forgiven." Now some of the scribes were sitting there, questioning in their hearts, "Why does this fellow speak in this way? It is blasphemy! Who can forgive sins but God alone?" At once Jesus perceived in his spirit that they were discussing these questions among themselves; and he said to them, "Why do you raise such questions in your hearts? Which is easier, to say to the paralytic, 'Your sins are forgiven,' or to say, 'Stand up and take your mat and walk'? But so that you may know that the Son of Man has authority on earth to forgive sins"—he said to the paralytic—"I say to you, stand up, take your mat and go to your home." And he stood up, and immediately took the mat and went out before all of them . . . (Mark 2:5–12)

The controversy at hand concerns the nature of religious language: in the view of certain onlookers, Jesus makes a declarative utterance ("Your sins are forgiven") that he lacks power or authority (ἐξουσία) to enact. Since, in their view, such declarations are the prerogative of God alone, his words are presumptuous—indeed, blasphemous—rather than performative. Jesus responds by uttering a second declaration, this one more demonstrably effective: "I say to you, stand up, take your mat and go home." He demonstrates, in effect, that especially when it comes to the word and work of God, performatives must be judged on the basis of performance itself. In terms of speech act theory, perlocution validates locution and illocution alike.

By contrast, and for all their many words, preachers prove unable to achieve similar results. At the simplest level, the fact that human speakers make verbal commitments is no guarantee of the ability to fulfill them. Marriage vows, for instance, may be uttered with perfect sincerity—"to have and to hold from this day forward . . . till death do us part"—yet the divorce rate in most Western societies illustrates the difference between "meaning," "intent," and "efficacy," even for the most heartfelt of commissive utterances. When it comes to the sermon in its congregational context, human speech may nonetheless have force on at least two grounds. First, institutional authorization grants the preacher authority to speak in church, to the church, in some instances on behalf of the church, whether as concerns baptism, marriage, or proclaiming the message of the gospel week by week. Stated more finely, the denomination or local judicatory makes a commissive utterance over the preacher's declaratives, thereby creating the conditions for authoritative speech, at least within the bounds of a particular administrative or confessional polity. Yet the truth of the Christian gospel does not ultimately depend on the validity of ordination, nor is a congregation likely to be swayed by clerical authority alone. Thus a second and countervailing condition for homiletic "force" must be that of assent on the part of the hearers. Of course, the veracity and "force" of preaching cannot be limited to the antecedent preferences or convictions of those who hear it (for in that case a sermon could do no more than reiterate what they already believe). Moreover, since neither ecclesiastical authority nor congregational assent are sufficient to heal the sick and raise the dead (Matt 16:19 notwithstanding), further authorization is required if human speech is to be correlated with the Word of God.

In fact, neither condition adequately accounts for the kind of transformative agency of which the gospel speaks, and to which faithful preaching bears witness. To the degree that the words of the preacher may be correlated with promissory or commissive *divine* speech, their veracity and force must to the same degree remain independent of their acceptance by the congregation or the *imprimatur* of judicatory authority. As David Lose concludes, in his own discussion of speech act theory, "in a 'preached' confession of faith, although the preacher/confessor desires the affirmation of her hearers, the integrity and validity of the confession stands independent of its reception and reciprocation. This, I believe, ensures the integrity of preaching as an assertive, but noncoercive activity..."[23]

Assent is, nonetheless, essential to Christian faith and discipleship. While it does not *establish* the veracity of the preacher's message, recognition on the part of its hearers nonetheless serves to acknowledge its force. Evans explains in the language of performative utterance:

> The idea of Jesus as the "Word" of God is of special logical interest in that His life, passion, resurrection and ascension could

---

23. Lose, *Confessing Jesus Christ*, 106–7.

> be interpreted as actions which have a "performative force" and "causal power" like words. It is as if God in the deeds of Jesus, *said*, "I hereby adopt you as sons and decree that you are brothers"; and *said*, "Become like this man Jesus." In each case the performative and causal efficacy of the "utterance" depends on the response of [the hearer]; it depends on whether [hearers] acknowledge the new institutional relation and word of command, and whether [they] allow themselves to be influenced by the divine power.[24]

The preacher then echoes and re-presents these claims in words of their own. What prevents such speech from being even implicitly coercive is that hearers offer their assent not to the preacher but to the One from whom such claims proceed.

Assent is likewise critical to the preacher's own rôle. Failure to be engaged by the reality of which we speak—failure, for instance, to acknowledge the substantive divine power manifest in Jesus' resurrection—leaves us liable to Jean Baudrillard's penetrating critique of "simulacra" and the "hyperreal." Baudrillard observes that contemporary Western culture has entered an "era of simulation" that replaces all reference to that which is "real" with its "artificial resurrection in . . . systems of signs . . . substituting the signs of the real for the real."[25] Our wholesale preoccupation with the multilayered artifice of television and "virtual reality"—attending, as a substitute for more banal personal experience, to patterns of electroluminescence in semiconductive material that delineate fictive projects and projections—is a good example. Nor is his choice of theological language accidental, since Baudrillard has a particular concern for "religion and the simulacrum of divinity":

> What if God himself can be simulated, that is to say can be reduced to the signs that constitute faith? Then the whole system becomes weightless, it is no longer itself anything but a gigantic simulacrum—not unreal, but a simulacrum, that is to say never exchanged for the real, but exchanged for itself, in an uninterrupted circuit without reference or circumference.[26]

To preach about the character and power of God without yielding to their actual force places the preacher in danger of "substituting the signs of

---

24. Evans, *Logic of Self-Involvement*, 167 (emphasis original).
25. Baudrillard, *Simulacra and Simulation*, 2.
26. Baudrillard, *Simulacra and Simulation*, 4–6.

the real for the real." Just as prayer can become routinized into mindless recitation of familiar phrases and liturgy can descend into a mechanical performance of ritual, so preaching can become self-actuated and self-perpetuating, with no substantive invocation of divine agency or expectation that God will enliven either the sermon or its hearers. If, then, the objective prerequisites for human trust are divine fidelity and power, a key subjective prerequisite is epistemic humility on the part of preacher and congregants alike, since humility is the precursor to assent. To engage the claims of Scripture as a preacher is to be engaged by those claims, submitting not simply to the text but to the God of whom the text speaks. But is submission alone sufficient?

In conversation with Jürgen Moltmann and James F. Kay, Paul Scott Wilson proposes that as a species of performative utterance, "preaching is more than reciting God's speech acts in the past, it is God reiterating those same promises in the present. The experience of agency is the experience of the Agent ('Whoever listens to you listens to me' Luke 10:16)."[27] Along the same lines, Sam Chan argues that

> to preach the gospel as the word of God is to re-locute and re-illocute the divine speech act, the gospel, which itself was once locuted and illocuted by the prophets, Jesus, and the apostles, and which now continues to be locuted and illocuted in the canonical Scripture . . . preaching ought to have the same locutionary force, illocutionary force, and intended perlocutionary effect . . . as that of the Bible passage being expounded.[28]

Likewise appealing to speech act theory, Duck Hyun Kim states the matter in even more provocative fashion: "the preacher's task is to re-enact the performance of the living voice of God in community"; "the presence of God can be performed in the sermon to create a new social reality."[29] That is, "Preaching is *basically a procedure of re-performing God's dynamic illocutions in Scripture* under [the] guidance of the Holy Spirit."[30] More

---

27. Wilson, "A Homiletical Theology of Promise: More Than One Genre?," in Jacobsen, ed., *Toward a Homiletical Theology of Promise*, 84. With respect to the eschatological promises of God, Wilson argues that "Christian language about the future performs the future in the now," not least because symbolic language (including resurrection language) "participates in the reality it represents" (84).

28. Chan, *Preaching as the Word of God*, 223.

29. Kim, "Homiletical Appropriation," 7, 125.

30. Kim, "Homiletical Appropriation," 11 (emphasis original).

specifically, he identifies "biblical illocutionary forces" that anticipate a "perlocutionary homiletical response."[31] That is,

> Scripture has its own illocutionary action whereby a revealed written text is part of a past event but its energy and theological purpose are continuously being echoed through the unique sequence of *biblical illocutionary forces*. In the light of this hermeneutical possibility, the preaching imitates [the] biblical author's illocutionary action and its own theological intention.[32]

Faithful preaching goes beyond the repetition of propositional statements or reproducing narrative form to create an "alternative reality in the modern world."[33] On this view, "Scripture uses the preacher; the preacher does not use the Scripture."[34]

But the argument of the present chapter is that the correlation of human and divine agency is nowhere near as simple as these statements seem to imply: continuity between divine and human speech acts cannot be assumed in any simple or straightforward fashion. Nor is it sufficient to claim (as Kim initially does) that "the language of the text has the inherent power to perform an act," or that "if interpreters have themselves been interpreted by the performative dimension of the text, the preacher then can execute its performative force,"[35] because the key dynamic in preaching has less to do with qualities inherent in the biblical text itself than with the divine reality to which the text bears witness. Neither exegesis nor eloquence are sufficient to raise the dead, nor can even a high view of biblical inspiration elide Paul's critical distinction in 2 Cor 3:3 between "letter" and "Spirit" (which applies as much to his own letters as to the words of Torah). Whatever our theological orientation, we must be inherently cautious of assuming too facile an equivalence between Jesus as the "Word of God," Scripture as the "Word of God," and the words of the preacher.

In a subsequent article, Kim further specifies that to speak of "the inherent power in the biblical text" or "the performative nature of

---

31. Kim, "Reframing the Hermeneutical Question," 39.
32. Kim, "Reframing the Hermeneutical Question," 41 (emphasis original).
33. Kim, "Reframing the Hermeneutical Question," 42.
34. Kim, "Reframing the Hermeneutical Question," 43.
35. Kim, "Homiletical Appropriation," 16, 69.

Scripture" is simply another way of describing the work of the Holy Spirit.[36] Accordingly, he restates his argument in more nuanced terms:

> Scripture has its own illocutionary force whereby a revealed written text is part of a past event but its energy and theological purpose are continuously being echoed through the unique sequence of the illocutionary force and the role of the Holy Spirit which [creates an] alternative reality in the modern world . . . In other words, it is the power of the Holy Spirit that uses the preacher and not the preacher manipulating the Scripture.[37]

This reformulation accords greater prominence to divine action, in effect recalibrating the force that speech act theory assigns to language in principle and suggesting a promising way forward for reformulating this model in the service of Christian homiletics. Even so, the overly optimistic correlation of divine and human action suggested here is contradicted in practice by a more intermittent or incomplete experience of the Spirit on the part of many preachers.

Only by acknowledging the profound limitations of human speech (and piety generally) do we come to recognize our need for divine authorization. Stated in more drastic fashion, only a conscious renunciation of constructive agency and the efficacy of language opens the way for divine agency to operate in its place. Just so John the Baptist, for instance, bears faithful witness to Jesus by renouncing any thought that he himself might be the Messiah (John 1:19–23). The twelve disciples prove incapable even of the ministry that Jesus himself has authorized them to perform (Mark 9:18; cf. 3:15; 6:12–13). Peter weeps bitterly because he has used his words to deny his Lord (Matt 26:75). Paul of Tarsus serves an apostolic ministry by acknowledging that he is "the least of the apostles, unfit to be called an apostle" (1 Cor 15:9). Most remarkable of all, Jesus himself confesses, "I can do nothing on my own" (John 5:30). In each case, the agent in question expressly repudiates agency as a condition of (potential) agency itself, of being empowered by a power not one's own.

Stated differently, Peter and his companions perfectly illustrate the problem of promissory speech on the lips of a disciple: "He said vehemently, 'Even though I must die with you, I will not deny you.' And all of them said the same" (Mark 14:31). "A promise," says Moltmann, "is a

36. Kim, "An Alternative Pneumatological Epistemology," 165; "The particular types of illocutionary points and their force in Scripture are based on the illumination of the Holy Spirit."

37. Kim, "An Alternative Pneumatological Epistemology," 170, 175–76.

declaration which announces the coming of a reality that does not yet exist."[38] In the case of the Twelve, however (Judas foremost among them), the actual value of the apostles' promissory speech is expressed in their abject inability to live by their own words. In their case, it is not just that the promised reality does not *yet* exist; it will *never* exist, because they lack the strength of character that such promises require. If this is the case for those who have walked with Christ and seen him face to face, on what possible grounds might later disciples (preachers among them) find within themselves the means to fund promissory speech of their own, however well intentioned?

If they could neither die with him nor bring themselves to wait with him while he died, it is not too much to expect that they might at least have cared for him after death. But the apostles cannot do even this much, in consequence of which it falls to a pair of timid crypto-disciples to take up the mutilated corpse (John 19:38-40). As John makes clear, neither Joseph of Arimathea (to whom, says Matthew, the tomb belongs) nor Nicodemus the Pharisee have previously had sufficient courage to be seen with Jesus by day. Yet now, as the light of day fails, they at last come out of hiding to minister in death to the one whom they could not follow in life.

For preachers, the most eloquent feature of this narrative is the silence and absence of those who knew Jesus best, a silence and absence that should make us question the moral and theological adequacy of either our obedience or our words. Yet it is these very failures who form the foundation of the New Testament church. Paradoxically, failure is the precondition and qualification for this future rôle, as Jesus himself predicts: "Simon, Simon, listen! Satan has demanded to sift all of you like wheat, but I have prayed for you [*singular*] that your own faith may not fail; and you, when once you have turned back, strengthen your brothers" (Luke 22:31-32). Of course, we would prefer not to derive a general principle from Peter's example, for our idealization of "apostolic" ministry focuses instead on authority, purity of doctrine, and fidelity to Christ. It is a daunting prospect to imagine that our betrayal of Jesus, even our abandonment of him, is what prepares us for the task of strengthening fellow disciples.

In terms of speech act theory, our main contention is that whether considered as declarative or directive, as assertion (in which, we recall,

---

38. Moltmann, *Theology of Hope*, 103.

"the psychological state expressed is Belief") or testimony to the ways of God, the efficacy of a sermon has relatively little to do with the power of human language *per se*. Nor does it concern a preacher's repudiation or embrace of "authority" vis-à-vis the congregation or denomination (as theorists on the left and right each contend). Nor even, in a more subtle degree, does preaching seek to persuade hearers to rely on God in the manner that canonical texts commend. Against all such alternatives, divine commissive speech—God's own self offering, attested in Scripture and the person of Jesus—constitutes the definitive authorization of human declaratives. What enables a preacher to participate verbally in the *missio Dei* is not mastery of method, but knowledge of the divine character and (as an initial step) direct and willing submission to God's saving power. Rhetorical form is not unimportant, of course, but "faithfulness" in speaking must concern theological substance and content before it concerns eloquence, social consensus, or institutional authority. More precisely, human words must defer to the Word of God (with its testimony to the absolute prerogative of divine agency) if they are to prove even indirectly transformative. To summarize the matter neatly in the categories that Austin and Searle delineate, substantive conformity to *divine* commissives is what renders the preacher's "assertives" into functional "declaratives," which is to say, into utterances that prove to be, in practice, "performative." Next to be considered are the concrete conditions under which this may be so.

Perlocutionary Divine Speech

In his own discussion of speech act theory as it applies to the authority of the biblical text, Nicholas Wolterstorff introduces the concept of double agency or "double agency discourse," whereby one individual is effectively authorized by and thus empowered to speak on behalf of another.[39] More precisely, Wolterstorff distinguishes between three forms of double agency. One so authorized may prepare forms of communication that await signature or some other *imprimatur* by the person whose more immediate authority they represent. Draft statements may be dictated in advance, or they may be composed independent of such direction by one who "knows the mind" of their superior. Such cases differ, notes

---

39. Wolterstorff, *Divine Discourse*, 38–42.

Wolterstorff, with regard to the "*degree and mode of superintendence*," as well in terms of how "*authorization*" is administered or bestowed.[40]

A second form of double agency is "deputized discourse," whereby the delegate is authorized to speak more freely, after the manner of an ambassador or other legal emissary. As one with "power of attorney," as it were, the deputy speaks within certain prescribed guidelines, yet without having been given exact words to repeat.[41] Here Wolterstorff notes the rôle of biblical prophets, as those who are authorized to speak on behalf of God, yet always in language of their own. Accordingly, canonical texts typically combine first person discourse in the prophet's own voice with passages *in vocem Dei*, whether or not the latter are explicitly signaled by means of oracular formulae. In this situation the question of verification (which is to say, evidence of authorization) comes to the fore, as hearers are required to differentiate between true and false prophecy—speech that faithfully conveys or falsely substitutes for the Word of God.

Third, there is what Wolterstorff calls "Appropriated Discourse," whereby a speaker simply adopts another person's prior utterance as their own.[42] Here there is no question of delegation or deputizing: it is a matter, rather, of embracing the speech of another (even without their express permission) and applying it in some related or quite different context. Citing another scholar in academic discourse is an exact illustration of this principle.

These categories (addressed in reverse order) offer a helpful framework for thinking about the sermon. Wolterstorff suggests that Scripture might, in its totality, represent an instance of "appropriated discourse," by which God chooses to embrace, even communicate via, the whole of the canon in all its human diversity.[43] The Song of Songs, the results of the first census in the wilderness, or the architecture of Ezekiel's ideal Temple come to mind as texts that are fully canonical while not presenting themselves as direct divine address. Not impossibly, God might appropriate

---

40. Wolterstorff, *Divine Discourse*, 41 (emphasis original).

41. Wolterstorff, *Divine Discourse*, 42–50.

42. Wolterstorff, *Divine Discourse*, 51–54.

43. However, he concedes the problematic nature of this claim: "It's not very plausible to understand it as God just taking some text, however produced, and doing something so as to being it about that these words serve as the medium of divine discourse. For what the writers *said* matters, that is, it matters what illocutionary actions they performed: what they were referring to, where they were speaking literally and where metaphorically, what cosmological picture served as background to their discourse, and so forth" (Wolterstorff, *Divine Discourse*, 53 [emphasis original]).

the sermon in a similar manner, not least when the sermon first endeavors to appropriate Scripture as the basis for its own discourse. Yet saying this does not clarify the conditions under which divine appropriation might take place, or explain the basis on which certain sermons might be adopted in such a manner and others disqualified.

As to Wolterstorff's second category, the New Homiletic (in keeping with the anti-authoritarian instincts of contemporary culture) expressly repudiates "deputized discourse" in the pulpit. With the possible exception of certain Pentecostal or Charismatic contexts, preachers are not usually identified with prophets (at least in the mold of biblical prophets such as Huldah, Jeremiah, or the four daughters of Philip). Much less are preachers to be confused with or mistaken for Jesus of Nazareth. They may well be authorized to speak (at least indirectly) in the name of Christ, whether by their local judicatory or in relation to a sense of personal divine vocation (preferably both). Yet in this case, linguistic and theological distance will be more obvious than any alleged proximity.

As an argument in favor of "deputized discourse," Paul concludes his apologia for a ministry of reconciliation by declaring, "So we are ambassadors for Christ, since God is making his appeal through us" (2 Cor 5:20). Interpreting this passage hinges in large measure on understanding the intent of his third person reference: to whom does this "we" refer? In context, given the breakdown in his relationship with the Corinthian congregation and his plea for them to acknowledge his leadership, it seems most likely that Paul is describing the nature of his own apostolic ministry, rather than characterizing all Christian ministry as ambassadorial in principle.[44] In comparing himself to Christ, his inference is that the congregants have treated him much the same way as Christ himself was treated—with contempt and rejection (so 6:3–10). Thus while the rôle of an apostle indeed entails considerable authority (so 2 Cor 10:8; 13:10), the similarity between himself and Christ is predominantly cruciform, as the Corinthians themselves would likely attest. No more than this may be inferred either for Paul or for the task of preaching generally. In any event, no more than an ambassador is coequal with a nation or a lawyer equivalent to their more powerful client should even the most conservative congregant imagine their preacher or pastor to be Jesus' (much less God's) personal plenipotentiary. The Corinthians themselves can hardly be accused of having done so with Paul.

---

44. See further Knowles, *We Preach Not Ourselves*, 237–41.

The most a preacher may do is to compose the sermon as a locutionary act, a discourse that yields to the sole authority of the One for whom it speaks, offering itself for authorization while not claiming that authority for itself. In this sense, the sermon will always be cruciform, an act of self-abandonment to God in recognition of the preacher's own frailty and finitude (which is to say, the preacher's own distance from God). More finely: to the extent that the preacher is guided by Paul's admonition in Philippians 2:5 that we embrace the "mind" or outlook of Christ, aspiring to imitate Christ will require that we renounce rather than appropriate divine authority for our sermons. Paradoxically, pretension to "equality with God" (Phil 2:6) is what bedevils pulpit ministry, yet true resemblance to Christ implies just the opposite.

This is the kind of humility, submission, and assent that the initial form of Wolterstorff's "double agency discourse" envisages. In the language of speech act theory, the deputy first performs a locutionary act, producing a form of discourse that is coherent and meaningful in its own right. Yet along the lines of Austin and Searle's appeal to "extra-linguistic" authorization, such action may be characterized as *illocutionary* only once the One in whom true authority lies affirms the validity of the utterance. Only at that point, having been adopted and affirmed by the One on whose behalf it was first drafted, does it become *perlocutionary* speech; that is, speech that produces concrete results by virtue of the authority of the God in whose name it is uttered. For the locutionary act of the sermon to be characterized as illocutionary—for it to be *heard* as authoritative or divinely sanctioned—and all the more so for it to produce its intended, perlocutionary effect is wholly dependent on the immediate agency of Christ who is present among those assembled in his name, and on the power of the Holy Spirit. Just so, Kevin Vanhoozer parses the matter in directly Trinitarian terms:

> If the Father is the locutor, the Son is his preeminent illocution, Christ is God's definitive Word, the substantive content of his message. And the Holy Spirit—the condition and power of receiving the sender's message—is God the perlocutor, the reason that his words do not return to him empty (Isa. 55:11).[45]

In its testimony to Christ, the sermon conforms to the conditions of resurrection as much as crucifixion, as a sacrifice taken up at the moment of its own death into the transformative power of the life of God.

---

45. Vanhoozer, *Is There a Meaning in This Text?*, 457.

While preachers may speak freely of God's gift of life, actual bestowal of that gift remains an unconstrained and unconstrainable divine prerogative. Hence Luther's incisive observation that "wir haben wohl *ius verbi* aber nicht *executionem* [We have the right to speak but not the power to accomplish]."[46] The preacher anticipates Christ's authority for the sermon even while the authority remains Christ's own. In practice, this is a difficult balance to maintain. Although Paul seems to have entertained few doubts on the apostolic authority that had been granted him (2 Cor 3:1–6; 10:5–6, etc.), the difficulty for most preachers is being able to discern whether or to what extent their own locutionary acts become the illocutionary and perlocutionary acts of God. But that, too (as Luther would also remind us) is an unavoidable aspect of the cruciform life.

A similar dilemma confronts the congregant: under what circumstances may the words of *this* sermon and *this* preacher assume immediacy and transformative power in *my* hearing at *this* present moment? At what point—and how—do these manifestly human words become the "Word of God"? As Wolterstorff explains, the answer that Karl Barth provides involves a series of important distinctions regarding the nature of testimony in relation to divine self-communication. First, Barth distinguishes between "God's *original* speech and God's *derivative* speech," which is the difference between the directly revelatory discourse of Jesus himself as the embodied Word of God and the church's subsequent proclamation of Christ.[47] More precisely, second, Barth distinguishes between Jesus as God's direct self-articulation, the church's attestation or proclamation of that Word, "and, third, that of God's effectively *communicating* to some person the content of God's revelatory speech on the occasion of that person's being confronted with a proclaimer of that revelatory speech."[48]

In a manner that recalls his own concept of "deputized discourse," Wolterstorff summarizes Barth as saying that "the present-day preacher must be understood as standing in a line of succession with the ancient prophets and apostles; all proclaim Jesus Christ." However, the critical distinction (in Wolterstorff's view) is "between the *primary* and the *secondary*: the proclamation of the contemporary preacher is dependent on, and governed by, that of the ancient prophets and apostles as known to

---

46. "The Second Sermon, March 10, 1522, Monday after Invocavit"; *LW* 51:76; WA 10:15, as quoted previously.
47. Wolterstorff, *Divine Discourse*, 64.
48. Wolterstorff, *Divine Discourse*, 64.

us in Scripture."[49] Stated differently, this is the difference between active and passive forms of testimony: whereas prophets and apostles bear direct and personal witness to definitive divine revelation in the person of Christ, preachers are constrained by that prior testimony in offering testimony of their own.

For this reason, it seems preferable to conceive of the sermon as a form of "appropriated discourse," one which embraces the words of Scripture in its own attestation of Jesus as the embodied Word of God, and on this basis becomes liable to appropriation by God. Again, however, an assurance of such appropriation rests not in the orthodoxy, authenticity, or integrity of the sermon *per se* (all of which are always incomplete) but in the unconstrainable authority of God who raises the dead to life (dead sermons and dead preachers among them). As Wolterstorff summarizes the matter, "God speaks in Jesus Christ, and only there; then on multiple occasions, God activates, ratifies, and fulfills in us what God says in Jesus Christ."[50] Between the first of these premises and the second, both of which preserve the integrity of divine initiative, lie the rôles and responsibilities of preacher and hearers alike.

Speaking and Not Speaking: The Mystery of Silence

Although not claiming this position for himself, Fred Craddock notes that to approach preaching from the perspective of Jesus' incarnation implies that "as the Word came in the flesh, so the Word comes in the form of human speech."[51] His summary captures an era of homiletical developments within Roman Catholic tradition, but it seems no less fair a description of mainstream Protestantism that seeks to model its own preaching on Jesus' compassion, piety, servanthood, and commitment to social justice. In terms of requiring the mediation of subsequent human voices, Luther too was convinced that the church's commitment to verbal proclamation was a matter of obedience and conformity to Jesus' own practice. But aspiring to speak in the manner of Jesus' human address runs up against a strange paradox: that of a divine Word that arrives and departs without words.

---

49. Wolterstorff, *Divine Discourse*, 66–72 (here, 66).
50. Wolterstorff, *Divine Discourse*, 73.
51. Craddock, *As One Without Authority*, 39.

T. S. Eliot's "Gerontion," first published in 1920, meditates on the birth of the Messiah:

> Signs are taken for wonders. "We would see a sign!"
> The word within a word, unable to speak a word,
> Swaddled with darkness. In the juvescence of the year
> Came Christ the tiger.[52]

Echoing the Matthaean scribes and Pharisees in their own search for signs (Matt 12:38 KJV), Eliot reflects on the relationship between words, signs, and wonders. In so doing, he misquotes a sermon that Archbishop Lancelot Andrewes preached on Christmas Day, 1618, which refers to the "*Verbum infans*, the Word without a word; the eternal Word not able to speak a word."[53] Eliot takes up the same motif (and corrects the allusion) ten years later in the poem "Ash Wednesday":

> If the lost word is lost, if the spent word is spent
> If the unheard, unspoken
> Word is unspoken, unheard;
> Still is the unspoken word, the Word unheard,
> The Word without a word, the Word within
> The world and for the world;
> And the light shone in darkness and
> Against the Word the unstilled world still whirled
> About the centre of the silent Word.[54]

Both of Eliot's meditations on the silent speech of God, like that of the learned archbishop before him, depend in turn on a tradition that reaches back to Irenaeus, Tertullian, Gregory of Nazianzus, and especially Augustine of Hippo.[55] Augustine's preaching frequently reflects on the *Verbum infans*, the eternal Word of God who comes to us unspeaking, an incarnate "infant" (since the Latin adjective *infans* means "without speech").[56] Eliot evidently relishes this paradox: since "Ash Wednesday" in particular (written following his own conversion) is about the struggle

---

52. Eliot, *Collected Poems*, 39; lines 17–19.

53. Andrewes, *Seventeen Sermons*, 200–201 [Sermon XII]; similarly, p. 91 [Sermon VII]; on the misquotation, see Rudrum, "T. S. Eliot."

54. Eliot, *Collected Poems*, 102; Stanza V lines 1–9.

55. On this theological tradition, see Meconi, "Silence Proceeding," 64–65, and the references cited there.

56. E.g., Sermon 184 §3; 190 §3 ("Quis est iste infans? Infans enim dicitur, quod non possit fari, id est loqui. Ergo et infans, et Verbum est" [PL 38 col. 1008]); Augustine, *Sermons for Christmas and Epiphany*, 104 and n18 (p. 206).

to articulate and maintain Christian faith, the silence of a wordless Word captures the difficulty both of hearing and of speaking God's word in an otherwise dark and broken world.

We may think of this as Jesus' first silence, whereby (*pace* David Buttrick) he wordlessly embodies complete inability to name his own world, much less the things of God. But this is only the first of several silences, each of them momentous. Although at the moment of his arrest he protests that he has always spoken openly (Mark 14:49), Jesus at trial refuses to answer his accusers. When the high priest presses him to respond, Mark records that (at least initially), "he was silent and did not answer" (Mark 14:61). The evangelists' own silence on the matter suggests that Jesus responds in the same manner when the guards strike him and command that he prophesy (Mark 14:65). But all these preliminary silences will soon be eclipsed by the absolute stillness of death, whereby the "Author of Life" (Acts 3:15), the one who possesses "the words of eternal life" (John 6:68), is finally rendered both wordless and lifeless. Notwithstanding the fact that Jesus embodies God's definitive self-communication to humanity, his death represents the failure of that communication, whether in terms of Jesus' own failure to persuade his pious opponents or failure on the part of his opponents to hear the divine Word that he brings. To acclaim him as the living "Word of God" requires us to confess—without blasphemy—that the Word of God falls silent in death, taking with him all attempts at speaking about (or for) God.

In this manner, Jesus' incarnate ministry—and the words that he speaks—are bracketed by absence of speech: just as the wordless cries of infancy are a necessary prelude to the teaching that will follow, so the brutal silencing that is his crucifixion awaits resurrection and the restoration of his voice after a space of three days. If our preaching is to take its cue from Jesus' incarnation—if, that is, the conditions of Jesus' ministry set any kind of precedent for the exercise of our own—we will have to reckon with silence as much as with speech, with letting God have the first and last word as the setting and context for our own abundance of words. More particularly, claiming that Jesus is the absolute Word who speaks through our own words imposes on us the conditions that govern his speech. Even were it not implied by virtue of his biography, silence is required on the grounds of our own. Preachers and their hearers fall silent, first, before the cross, because he has died when it should have been us: we and our sins have put the Author of Life to death. We fall silent, second, before his resurrection, knowing (if we have an ounce of humility or self-awareness) that we were not the ones who raised him to life again. Much less is his presence in our midst the result of our vaunted eloquence. Third, we join in the silence of heaven, if only for half an hour (so Rev 8:1), as the period during which beleaguered saints wait for God to answer their pleas with a word of his own.[57] And especially should those answers fail to materialize in the manner we desire (as the martyrs of John's Apocalypse so eloquently testify: Rev 6:10), we will certainly fall silent, fourth, at the moment of death. Addressing God with a prayer that he composed in anticipation of his own demise, Karl Rahner (1904–1984) reflects on the fate that awaits all preachers, pastors, and theologians alike:

> Then you will say the last word, the only word that abides and that one never forgets. Then, when all is silent in death and I have learned and suffered my last. Then will begin the great silence in which you alone resound, you who are word from eternity to eternity. Then all human words will be dumb... No human word, no image and no concept will ever stand between me and you; you yourself will be the one joyful word of love and life that fills all the spheres of my soul.[58]

If even the Messiah must fall silent in incarnation and death as the means of expressing his absolute self-abandonment to God, we who claim to be "in Christ" can hardly expect otherwise.

None of this, however, is the silence of the apophatic tradition, which chooses to be mute before the unfathomable greatness of God. Nor is it the silence of despair, as though God were stubbornly distant or hard of hearing. Rather, our silence is occasioned by the prohibition and assurance of Jesus' last word: "It is finished" (John 19:30). In our turning to him, it is the silence of waiting, reliance, and expectation: waiting, in the conviction that (despite the church's endless commentary on his accomplishment) there is nothing more to be said or done; reliance, which confesses the full sufficiency of another in our place; and expectation, in the assurance that the ministry of Christ will not fail to have its full effect, even in the face of death. Still, such silence proves elusive—especially for

---

57. On this motif and its background in Jewish tradition, see Bauckham, *Climax of Prophecy*, 70–83: "At the climax of history, heaven is silent so that the prayers of the saints can be heard, and the final judgment occurs in response to them" (71).

58. Quoted in Vorgrimler, *Understanding Karl Rahner*, 139. As another meditation on the silence from which preaching proceeds, compare Buechner, *Telling the Truth*, 23–24.

pastors and preachers—both because of the ambient noise of our environment and because we ourselves would much prefer to remain in control, establishing a relationship with God on our own terms. Admonishing a recalcitrant nation, the prophet Isaiah captures this dynamic exactly:

> For thus said the Lord God, the Holy One of Israel: In returning and rest you shall be saved; in *quietness* and in trust shall be your strength. But you refused . . . Therefore the Lord waits to be gracious to you; therefore he will rise up to show mercy to you. For the Lord is a God of justice; blessed are all those who wait for him. (Isa 30:15, 18)

Despite the invitation to quiet trust, God's people sometimes prefer to rely on their own devices. Paradoxically, God is the one who must first wait for us to wait, until we exhaust all other options and at last run out of things to say.

Having begun in rather abstract fashion by discussing linguistic theory in relation to homiletics, our consideration of theological silence concludes on a more practical note. Our argument has been that rather than attempting to remedy the challenge of hearing God speak with speech of our own, we must first join Christ when he too is without words. One such moment is that of his death, whereby the incarnate Word of God casts himself on God in order (at a minimum) to exemplify surrender and dependence. Just as the words of the living Word will prove performative only when they are given back to the source of all life, so too, on this model, must human words that bear witness to Christ unreservedly yield—that is, fall silent and die—in order for God to restore them to life and make them instruments of divine purpose. Jesus' previous silence, whereby he first accedes to the conditions of incarnation, is equally instructive. He enters fully into the circumstances of human existence not to berate, cajole, or condemn those who are far from God, but before all else to share in their humanity, their hope, and their desolation. Rather than speaking, the incarnate Word first listens. At the very least, preachers too must stop talking long enough to hear the voices in our culture that cry out for life, and for God. Far from imagining ourselves immune from the ills of the world on the basis of our faith and God's gift of new life, our first responsibility will be to "rejoice with those who rejoice" and to "mourn with those who mourn" (Rom 12:15 NIV).[59] Like that of the

---

59. Cf. Heb 13:3 (although with specific reference to the unjust suffering of fellow believers).

wordless Word, our silence will provide opportunity for identifying with the human condition in all its diversity, if only by virtue of listening to voices other than our own. What follows is a brief exploration of this process, as an exercise in the kind of listening that precedes faithful speech.

Only Drowning Men Can See Him

The beauty of "Suzanne," by Leonard Cohen (quoted at the head of this chapter), captures something of the paradox and incomprehensibility of the cross. Whether in the guise of prostitutes, tax-gatherers, or the *am ha'aretz* (the unlettered "people of the land" who were vilified for their lax observance of Torah),[60] only those who are "drowning" have eyes for Jesus and ears for his words. This should be the destiny of all who encounter Jesus, says Cohen, "But he himself was broken/Long before the sky would open/Forsaken, almost human/He sank beneath your wisdom like a stone." In other words, the logic of grace is sensible only to those who are already dead, or who know their death to be imminent. But whether in physical, emotional, spiritual, or some other existential terms, this is usually the last thing we are willing to admit. We are simply too committed to self-preservation, and too clever to put our confidence in something as improbable and intellectually unfashionable as the resurrection of a crucified Galilean rabbi.

Christians, it must be said, are on the whole a fairly sunny bunch. Whether by natural disposition or obedience to Scripture, we bear all things, believe all things, hope all things, and endure all things (so 1 Cor 13:7). Or at least we try to. But when Paul writes in these terms to the church of ancient Corinth, he is neither describing a general human capacity for love nor requiring that his readers exhibit such conduct. After all, Paul himself had been complicit in the death of Stephen, the first Christian martyr, on the grounds that love of God and uncompromising fidelity to God's commandments demanded nothing less. Although we tend to overlook the fact, 1 Corinthians 13 does not indicate a natural human capacity for fidelity and self-sacrifice (although the frequent citation of this passage in matrimonial liturgy seems to imply as much). Rather, the "charity" to which he refers is the ultimate gift of God's Spirit, above

60. Cf. *m. 'Abot* 2:5: "[Gamaliel III (3rd C)] would say, 'A coarse person will never fear sin, nor will an *Am haares* ever be pious, nor will a shy person learn, nor will an intolerant person teach, nor will anyone too busy in business get wise'" (Neusner, *Mishnah*, 676).

and beyond speaking in tongues, hospitality, prophecy, administration, miracles of healing, or any other divine charism.

Likewise when it comes to our capacity for faith and piety, Paul is far from optimistic. Recounting his treatment at the hands of saints and enemies alike, Paul confesses "We have become the scum of the earth, the garbage of the world" (1 Cor 4:13 NIV). Although his language is self-deprecating, its real target is those whose religious conduct it reflects. More shocking still, the same apostle who can speak proudly of being "a member of the people of Israel, of the tribe of Benjamin, a Hebrew born of Hebrews," can go on to say, "I have suffered the loss of all things, and count them as *refuse*" (Phil 3:5, 8).[61] His godly (and God-given) heritage, he says, is no more than σκύβαλα, a pungent term borrowed from the sewer or the barnyard. So we will find little encouragement in his writings for belief either in human potential and progress generally or piety in particular; as Paul sees it, whatever good we may aspire to will require a strong infusion of the Spirit of God.

Paul's apparent pessimism is echoed in reflections by any number of non-religious writers on the bleakness, brevity, and general futility of human existence. Perhaps the most famous such lament comes from Shakespeare's Macbeth, whose familiar soliloquy is a meditation on the death of his wife:

> Tomorrow, and tomorrow, and tomorrow
> Creeps in this petty pace from day to day
> To the last syllable of recorded time,
> And all our yesterdays have lighted fools
> The way to dusty death. Out, out, brief candle!
> Life's but a walking shadow, a poor player
> That struts and frets his hour upon the stage
> And then is heard no more. It is a tale
> Told by an idiot, full of sound and fury,
> Signifying nothing.[62]

Since life ends in death, life itself seems futile.

In his 1933 short story, "A Clean Well-Lighted Place," Ernest Hemingway depicts an elderly waiter who has endured the horrors of the First World War. Facing insomnia at the end of a long night, the old man, not unlike Macbeth, reflects on the desolation and emptiness of life:

---

61. Author's adaptation of Phil 3:8 ASV.
62. *Macbeth*, Act V, Scene 5, lines 19–28.

> What did he fear? It was not fear or dread. It was a nothing that he knew too well. It was all a nothing and a man was nothing too. It was only that and light was all it needed and a certain cleanness and order. Some lived in it and never felt it but he knew it all was nada y pues y nada y pues nada [nothing, and well, nothing, and nothing, and well, nothing]. Our nada who art in nada, nada be thy name thy kingdom nada thy will be nada in nada as it is in nada. Give us this nada our daily nada and nada us our nada as we nada our nadas and nada us not into nada but deliver us from nada; pues nada. Hail nothing full of nothing, nothing is with thee.[63]

The old man's protest is directly theological, subverting devotional language that has, at least in his case, failed to comfort or provide any meaning in the face of all he has suffered.

It would be comforting to think of such passages as little more than literary posturing (although Hemingway rather famously killed himself with his favorite shotgun). That others, both more and less perceptive, have come to similar conclusions, suggests otherwise. In *Life After God*, a semi-autobiographical collection of short stories, Douglas Coupland takes his own sense of desolation a step further:

> Now—here is my secret:
> I tell it to you with the openness of heart that I doubt I shall ever achieve again, so I pray that you are in a quiet room as you hear these words. My secret is that I need God—that I am sick and can no longer make it alone. I need God to help me give, because I no longer seem to be capable of giving; to help me be kind, as I no longer seem capable of kindness; to help me love, as I seem beyond being able to love.[64]

If despair is the death of hope, Coupland suggests that it is also, at least for some, a precursor to faith in God.

Although Christians may dismiss such views as the opinions of the ungodly and the godless, we must still account for similar convictions on the part of a certain preacher who claims King David as his father:

> The words of the Preacher, the son of David, king in Jerusalem. Vanity of vanities, says the Preacher, vanity of vanities! All is vanity. What do people gain from all the toil at which they toil under the sun? A generation goes, and a generation comes, but

---

63. Hemingway, "A Clean Well-Lighted Place," 150.
64. Coupland, *Life After God*, 259.

> the earth remains forever . . . All things are wearisome; more than one can express; the eye is not satisfied with seeing, or the ear filled with hearing. What has been is what will be, and what has been done is what will be done; there is nothing new under the sun . . . So I hated life, because what is done under the sun was grievous to me; for all is vanity and a chasing after wind. (Qoh 1:1-4, 8-9; 2:17)

This is neither boredom, nor pessimism, nor emergent depression, but rather a theological conviction regarding the folly and limitations of human endeavor. The key term *hebel* ("vanity"; LXX ματαιότης) refers to that which has no substance or reality; elsewhere it designates false idols.[65] Without the wisdom by which we learn to walk in fear of a holy God, says the Preacher (so Qoh 12:13-14), existence itself proves both empty and vain.

Returning to the New Testament, Paul concurs wholeheartedly with the Preacher's grim assessment of our human situation. In Romans 8, he contrasts the "vanity" or "futility" of the present age with the glory of that which is to come, employing the same term as in the Greek version of Ecclesiastes:

> I consider that the sufferings of this present time are not worth comparing with the glory about to be revealed to us. For the creation waits with eager longing for the revealing of the children of God; for the creation was subjected to futility [ματαιότης], not of its own will but by the will of the one who subjected it, in hope that the creation itself will be set free from its bondage to decay and will obtain the freedom of the glory of the children of God. We know that the whole creation has been groaning in labor pains until now; and not only the creation, but we ourselves, who have the first fruits of the Spirit, groan inwardly while we wait for adoption, the redemption of our bodies. (Rom 8:18-23)

A key question in this passage is determining who has subjected creation to "futility" or "purposelessness," whether Adam, Satan, God, or some other agent.[66] Despite the unusual grammar, Paul's claim that creation has been subjected to futility "in hope" suggests that he intends to weigh the prospect of future redemption against present evidence of judgement,

---

65. See further Seybold, s.v. הֶבֶל *hebhel*;* הָבַל *hābhal*, *TDOT* 3:313-20.

66. *Pace*, e.g., Wolters (*Creation Regained*, 56), the logic of the passage as a whole assigns responsibility to God; see discussion in Cranfield, *Epistle to the Romans*, 1:413-14; Fitzmyer, *Roman*, 507-9; Longenecker, *Epistle to the Romans*, 722-23.

both of which come from the hand of God. In any event, Paul clearly holds that even for followers of Jesus, our present existence is characterized by "sufferings" (v. 18), "futility" (v. 20), "bondage to decay" (v. 21), "groaning" (vv. 22–23), and hope that remains as yet "unseen" (v. 24).

Notwithstanding this odd agreement between the melancholy of (for example) Shakespeare's Macbeth, Hemingway's waiter, or Douglas Coupland, on the one hand, and the theological cynicism of Ecclesiastes and the Apostle Paul, on the other, such views are by no means universal in Western society, among scholars of religion, or in the Western church at large. Might it be, indeed, that our optimism and faith in human potential are what keep us from acknowledging our need of, much less experiencing, the transformative power of Jesus' resurrection? We may feel the need for a bracing spiritual tonic, a word of encouragement, or some assurance that God has matters in hand. But new life is not for people who are managing well enough on their own, or who require nothing more radical than a little cosmic prodding to keep them headed in the right direction. Nor is it suited to the kind of compartmentalization that appears in some visions of Christian discipleship (and preaching), whereby the sovereignty of Jesus concerns a privatized realm of "spirituality," but not therefore personal finances, human sexuality, voter registration, social relations, combat operations, or international affairs.

We reduce the resurrection to mere metaphor because we are optimists, buoyed by a stable social order and the benefits of Western political and economic dominance. The cause of Jesus continues, we say, and we are happy to contribute to its ongoing success. We interpret the confusion and factual contradictions in Gospel accounts of Jesus' post-crucifixion return as evidence of philosophical naïveté and literary fabrication largely because we can afford to be skeptical and a sense of intellectual superiority confirms us in our views. But the dead have no such luxury. If the resurrection accounts are not true in any hard, concrete, practical sense of the word, then those who have died will remain lifeless and inert. This assessment applies equally to those who find themselves "dead" in less tangible but no less real and personal terms, whether on account of sin, personal suffering, or intellectual nihilism. The "death" that resurrection requires of us is not only conceptual or theological (whereby we concede the limitations of human intellect), nor simply emotional and existential (the kind of weary nihilism espoused by Qoheleth and his heirs), but moral and material as well.

Even among those who acknowledge that resurrection is a matter of divine intervention, there remains a kind of optimism that we can somehow render ourselves worthy of resurrection by virtue of a faithful life. Nor are we the first to think so:

> R. Pinhas b. Yair says, "Heedfulness leads to cleanliness, cleanliness leads to cleanness, cleanness leads to abstinence, abstinence leads to holiness, holiness leads to modesty, modesty leads to the fear of sin, the fear of sin leads to piety, piety leads to the Holy Spirit, the Holy Spirit leads to the resurrection of the dead, and the resurrection of the dead comes through Elijah, blessed be his memory, Amen." (*m. Soṭah* 9:15)[67]

If these sentiments are anything to go by, theological conservatives seem as likely to place conditions on resurrection (if perhaps more subtly) as those of a broader metaphysical outlook.

When it comes to sermons, resurrection, and divine power (in all their various combinations), perhaps the issue is simply that we are reluctant to yield control of our preaching to an unmanageable God. Will Willimon suspects as much: "In my experience," he observes, "the last people to believe that preaching actually works are preachers—perhaps this is a defense mechanism against the reality of Easter. It is so tough to relinquish your life to a discipline over which you have so little control."[68] Far from proving immune to theological hardness of heart, preachers are sometimes poster children for what Tom Troeger calls "the human genius for resisting grace."[69] Eager for our sermons to have an impact, we cling to life, not realizing that doing so is likely to have quite the opposite effect. For to be engaged in the struggle to maintain our own hold on life is to preclude the possibility of yielding our lives into the hands of the one whom Jacques Ellul calls "le Tout Autre," the "Wholly Other" who is not subject to human command or control.[70] Therefore, as David Buttrick observes, "If we want to preach resurrection, we may have to restore the deadness of death."[71] Barbara Brown Taylor goes even further:

---

67. Pinhas (or Phineas) ben Jair lived in the latter half of the second century CE. For a later version of the same tradition, see *b. 'Avod. Zar.* 20b.

68. Willimon, "Preaching after Easter," 40.

69. Troeger, "Keeping in Touch with God," in Childers, ed., *Purposes of Preaching*, 116.

70. Ellul, "Témoignage et Société Technicienne," 446–48.

71. Buttrick, "Preaching on the Resurrection," 281.

> One thing that occurs to me is that we have a hard time celebrating Easter properly because we are wholly unwilling to die first. If anything, we are tempted to celebrate Easter as a festive denial of death—the day on which everyone is supposed to be happy, lovely, and well-fed. Faith in God means we do not have to worry about death. Jesus has taken care of it. Jesus *will* take care of it. All we have to do is believe.[72]

So Richard Lischer likewise concludes, "If Christian preaching—in its content and its craft—is to have the character of death and resurrection, something in it must die."[73]

Trite and obvious as it may sound, only the truly dead are truly in need of resurrection. The dead do not require lengthy speeches on the subject of resurrection (whether for or against, metaphorically or otherwise), but the power of resurrection itself. Since preachers and their sermons do not, of themselves, possess or command such power, they too will require divine intervention to bring them to life, apart from which they will remain buried in the "vanity" and futility of a creation as yet in bondage to decay.[74] Whether for preachers or their preaching, the resurrection of Jesus is neither an encouragement to moral living (as if exhortation alone could restore innocence) nor a simple human reboot (as if restarting the machinery of the old creation could return us to glory), but something radical and new, something that Paul calls a "new creation" altogether (2 Cor 5:17).

"Ears Thou Hast Dug for Me": The Difference Between Listening and Hearing

One of the more terrifying challenges with which Jesus confronts his listeners is "Whoever has ears to hear, let them hear" (Mark 4:9, 23; cf. Luke 14:35). Whether the ensuing discussion of his intent, with its allusion to Isaiah 6:9–10, can be taken to mean that God acts directly to prevent such hearing (Mark 4:10–12 and parallels) is another matter entirely. But what the discussion does make clear is that if "listening" is a physical activity, "hearing" is a question of more inward, spiritual perception. So, subsequently, when the disciples themselves mistake metaphor for literal

---

72. Taylor, "The Easter Sermon," 10.
73. Lischer, "'Resurrexit,'" 373.
74. Similarly Blount, *Invasion of the Dead*, 51.

description, Jesus responds, "Are your hearts hardened? Do you have eyes, and fail to see? Do you have ears, and fail to hear?" (Mark 8:17–18). The same distinction is central to the account in John's Gospel of the healing of the blind man: "Some of the Pharisees . . . said to him, 'Are we also blind?' Jesus said to them, 'If you were blind, you have no guilt; but now that you say, We see, your guilt remains'" (John 9:40–41 RSV).

The challenge is terrifying because it opens the possibility that we ourselves have merely listened to his words, but not truly heard them. It is this concern that leads Luther, Calvin, and Barth (among others) to make a clear distinction between outward listening and inward, theologically freighted perception. To all appearances, preaching seems to be a matter of crafting faithful forms of address, and preoccupation with the various nuances of speech act theory can only have deepened this impression. That a sermon cannot penetrate much further than the ears should by now be amply clear. But even prior to asking how our speech will be heard is the more difficult issue of the preacher's own ability to hear.

Hence the importance of silence, for silence is often required for the voice of God to reach us. Contemporary culture, of course, conspires to fill all our waking moments with sound, and advances in technology furnish ever more ingenious means of doing so. But attaining outward silence is, nonetheless, possible, with modest effort. Inward silence is much more elusive, and even when that is achieved a still more problematic issue awaits: that of accurately discerning the voice of God. Any exploration of meditation, contemplation, or spiritual self-examination is well beyond the scope of the present study, however vital such exercises are in the Christian life. Nonetheless, quiet and humble attentiveness to the words and Word of God will be essential preludes to the task of preaching: that we can only speak of what we have antecedently heard, seen, and know to be true seems basic to the life of the spirit (cf. 1 John 1:1).

Here in particular the conditions of grace must apply as much to preachers as to those who sit under their preaching. Eugene Peterson points out that most translations mask the plain sense of Psalm 40:6 (verse 7 in Hebrew) by paraphrasing its vivid metaphor of God digging out the psalmist's ears: "Sacrifice and offering you do not desire, but you have given me an open ear" (NRSV); "Sacrifice and offering you did not desire—but my ears you have opened" (NIV); "If thou hadst desired sacrifice and offering thou wouldst have given me ears to hear" (NEB). Peterson's own explanation strays far in the direction of hyperbole, but his point is well taken:

> What good is a speaking God without listening human ears? So
> God gets a pick and shovel and digs through the cranial granite,
> opening a passage that will give access to the interior depths,
> into the mind and heart . . . Our ears are so clogged that we
> cannot hear God speak. God, like Isaac who dug again the wells
> that the Philistines had filled, redigs the ears trashed with audio
> junk.[75]

Human obtuseness being what it is, our simply falling silent will not be sufficient, any more than death is an end in itself. The silence and death to which Christ calls us as preachers are not expressions of despair or helplessness, but represent a hopeful giving over of ourselves and our homiletical prerogatives in expectation of hearing the voice of God. They are thus (paradoxically) an active death and an expectant, listening silence, requiring that we turn away from ourselves to both the human and the divine Other, confident that God in Christ has already had, and will again have, the last word. Beyond this general theological principle, the final book of the Christian canon offers a single, compelling illustration of what such a hopeful falling silent might look like in practice.

"I Fell Down at His Feet as One Dead"

The book of Revelation begins in dramatic fashion, as the Apostle John hears "a loud voice like a trumpet," then turns to behold a terrifying and majestic figure whose face is "like the sun shining in full strength" (Rev 1:16). What concerns us here is not the particular details of his vision, but John's response to seeing the glory of the risen Christ: "When I saw him, I fell at his feet *as though dead*" (Rev 1:17). Collapsing face-first in holy dread is a familiar theological convention: Abram falls on his face when "God Almighty"(the conventional rendering of "El Shaddai") appears to him at the age of ninety-nine (Gen 17:1–3); Moses and Aaron do likewise on the threshold of the Tent of Meeting (Num 20:6); in the Chronicler's account, David and the elders of Israel prostrate themselves at the sight of the angel of judgement (1 Chr 21:16); Ezekiel falls before the vision of the heavenly chariot (Ezek 1:28; 43:3), as does Daniel in the presence of the angel Gabriel (Dan 8:17–18).[76] In Matthew's version of the

---

75. Peterson, *Working the Angles*, 101–2.

76. Cf. also Lev 9:24; Josh 5:14; Judg 13:20; 1 Kgs 18:39; Dan 2:46; 10:9; Matt 17:6; Rev 4:10; 7:11, etc.; on the motif generally, see Aune, *Revelation 1–5*, 99–100.

Transfiguration, Peter, James, and John not only see Jesus suffused with light; they also hear the voice of God declare, "This is my beloved Son." "When they heard this," writes the evangelist, "they fell on their faces, and were filled with awe" (Matt 17:5–6). Three times, Luke tells the story of Saul's dramatic encounter with Christ on the road to Damascus (Acts 9:3–9; 22:6–11; 26:12–18); in all three accounts, Luke retains the detail of Saul falling awestruck to the ground. Yet the opening scene of Revelation is distinctive in stipulating that John falls down before Jesus "as though *dead*."[77] Notwithstanding literary convention, it is a curious response to the very embodiment of resurrection power, and as such a contradiction in terms. Yet John's metaphorical "death" is no more than a prelude to the reaffirmation of life: "He placed his right hand on me, saying, 'Do not be afraid; I am the first and the last, the living one. I was dead, and see, I am alive forever and ever; and I have the keys of Death and of Hades. Now write what you have seen . . .'" (Rev 1:17–19). The living and glorified Christ, once dead, is now alive forever; John, who is alive on Patmos, falls down "as though dead." Still, despite him falling silent, to all appearances lifeless in the presence of glory, the Risen One now commissions John to bear witness concerning all that he has seen (and heard).

Two additional details invite brief comment. First, in the anthropology of Jewish and Hellenistic societies (as of many other ancient cultures), the right hand is the hand of authority and power, and positionally, therefore, the place of favor, whereas the left hand is in every sense its opposite (so Matt 6:3; 25:33, 41).[78] In context, we are told not once but three times that Christ holds "seven stars" (evidently symbolizing the seven congregations) in his right hand (Rev 1:16, 20; 2:1), just as the One on the throne grasps the scroll of history in his right hand (5:1, 7). At the risk of oversimplifying a vibrant, multivalent metaphor, these images insist that (notwithstanding persecution and suffering) Christ still sustains the life of the church. In 1:17, however, the imagery is more personal, for here the right hand of power and blessing rests on the prostrate apostle.

Accompanying this gesture (second) is the Lord's declaration, "I have the keys of Death and Hades" (1:18). These do not represent, in the first instance, power to impose death, but rather its opposite, in keeping

---

77. Aune (*Revelation 1–5*, 100) notes this feature elsewhere only in Matt 28:4 (the guards at Jesus' tomb), 4 Ezra 10:30 (Ezra and Uriel), and *T. Ab.* 9:1 (Abraham and Michael). In contrast to the Apocalypse of John, however, all three episodes describe responses to angelophany rather than theophany.

78. Cf. LSJ s.v. ἀριστερός A.3–4; εὐώνυμος A.III.

with the theological convention that "keys" in the hand of God indicate divine authority to grant life.[79] More precisely, possession of keys implies the authority to open what would otherwise remain closed, as in the later dictum attributed to Rabbi Johanan bar Nappaha (PA2; 3rd C): "Three keys are in the hand of the Holy One, blessed be he, that are not handed over to the hand of an agent, and these are they: the key to rain, the key to childbirth, and the key to the resurrection of the dead" (*b. Ta'an.* 2a; cf. *b. Sanh.* 113a). In context, the Talmud goes on to explain that God opens the heavens to bring forth rain, opens the womb to bring forth offspring, and opens the grave to bring forth its dead. So in the book of Revelation, it would seem, holding "the keys of Death and Hades" implies authority to release those who have been imprisoned by mortality and condemnation. The contrast between one who falls down "as though dead" and the other who holds the keys to release us from death could not be more pronounced.

If this scene is anything to go by, it seems that just as death is the necessary precondition for resurrection, so being reduced to awestruck silence is an essential prelude to faithful speech. The encounter between a metaphorically "dead" John and the resurrected, life-giving Christ provides a fitting and final illustration for the argument of the present chapter: to claim a capacity for articulating, evoking, or establishing the reign of God is to demonstrate our incapacity, for to attempt as much is both theological presumption and verbal idolatry. Yet to confess utter inability in this regard—to join the incarnate Jesus in silence and death—is to wait upon the possibility being commissioned and enabled by the Risen Lord, "the first and the last, the living one" who gives life to dying preachers and their inadequate words.

In Gal 2:19–20, Paul famously declares, "I have been crucified with Christ; it is no longer I who live, but it is Christ who lives in me. And the life I now live in the flesh I live by faith in the Son of God, who loved me and gave himself for me." In writing to the church, he declares the Christian gospel by proclaiming his own death in exchange for Christ's living presence within him; he therefore preaches as one both dead and simultaneously alive in Christ. In much the same vein is Martin Luther's widely quoted assertion that "living, nay, rather dying and being damned make a theologian, not understanding, reading, or speculation."[80] If Paul

---

79. See further Aune, *Revelation 1–5*, 103–4; Knowles, *Of Seeds and the People of God*, 92.

80. "Vivendi, immo moriendo et damnando fit theologus, non intelligendo, legendo

and Luther are to be believed, cadavers are powerful preachers and the damned make excellent theologians. Or at least, they have the potential to be so, once delivered into the hands of the Messiah. First, however, we require resurrection, in the absence of which neither the damned nor the dead will have much to say for themselves.

The following chapter outlines the first steps in this odd transformation, reviewing accounts from all four gospels of how the earliest witnesses respond to and are transformed by their own encounters with the resurrected Christ.

> Thus it is when *death* silently directs its gaze towards a man—that which causes all to fall into its own nothingness and precisely in doing this, provided only that it is willingly accepted (thus and only thus), does not strike man dead but itself transforms him, liberates him, endows him with that freedom which no longer appeals to or finds support in anything beyond itself, and yet at the same time is unconditional.
>
> —KARL RAHNER, SJ (1904–1984)[81]

---

aut speculando," from a 1520 lecture on Ps 5:11: WA TR 1:146.12; WA 5:63.28–29. The translation is that of Rupp, *Righteousness of God*, 102n2.

81. Quoted in Vorgrimler, *Understanding Karl Rahner*, 12 (emphasis original).

III.

Speaking

3

"He Being Dead Yet Speaketh"[1]

> Old men ought to be explorers
> Here or there does not matter
> We must be still and still moving
> Into another intensity
> For a further union, a deeper communion
> Through the dark cold and empty desolation,
> The wave cry, the wind cry, the vast waters
> Of the petrel and the porpoise. In my end is my beginning.
>
> —T. S. Eliot, "East Coker" (1940)[2]

> And then we encounter the power of the Resurrection: Christ *was raised from the dead through the glory of the Father*; impossibility becomes possibility.
>
> —Karl Barth (1886–1968)[3]

Messengers of the Resurrection: "Who Is Sufficient for These Things?"

With this remark from the second chapter of his second letter to Corinth, Paul concedes that he is wholly inadequate for the impossible task of bearing witness to the fragrance of life and stench of death that are

---

1. Hebrews 11:4 KJV.
2. Eliot, *Collected Poems*, 203–4; §V lines 17–19.
3. Barth, *Epistle to the Romans*, 195 (emphasis original, citing Rom 6:4).

conveyed by the gospel of Christ: "For we are the aroma of Christ to God among those who are being saved and among those who are perishing; to the one a fragrance from death to death, to the other a fragrance from life to life" (2 Cor 2:15–16). We might expect that his uncertainty arises first from the shamefulness of crucifixion itself (against which Paul must explain in Romans 1:16 why he is not, in fact, ashamed). Historically, this is certainly the case: among sensible Romans, for instance, crucifixion was not a subject for polite conversation, and to assert that one's divine Messenger had allowed himself to be executed in so ungodly a fashion would have been patently absurd, a contradiction in terms.[4] If this is the first embarrassment, the second is much like it: the chief witnesses to this awkward event appear singularly unqualified for their task.

Discussion of the Gospel resurrection accounts typically notes that women could not serve as witnesses for the purpose of legal deliberation.[5] Yet neither the evidence cited in favor of this view nor its applicability to the present situation are clear cut. As an indicator of later Jewish practice, the Mishnah describes instances of women's testimony with regard, for example, to their marital situation (*m. Yebam.* 15:1–16:2; *m. Ketub.* 2:5–6; 9:8). Even in so serious a matter as murder, the word of a woman is deemed valid (*m. Soṭah* 9:8). Yet it is equally clear that their testimony falls into the same category as that of a single witness (when two are normally required, according to Num 35:30; Deut 17:6; 19:15; *m. Mak.* 1:7–9) or a slave (*m. Yebam.* 16:7). Just so, certain biblical injunctions on the topic (in this case, Lev 5:1) are interpreted as referring to men and not to women (*m. Šebu.* 4:1). Likewise in discussion of who can and cannot offer valid testimony to the appearance of the new moon (of critical importance for the timing of seasons and festivals), women set the standard for ineligibility: "The following are ineligible: gamblers, usurers, pigeon-flyers, those who traffic in produce of the sabbatical year, and slaves. It is a general rule that for any testimony for which a woman is disqualified these also are disqualified" (*m. Roš Haš.* 1:8 [Soncino]).

Confirmation of the status of women as witnesses at the time of Jesus comes from the contemporary Jewish historian Flavius Josephus (ca. 37–100 CE), who tailors his twenty volumes of Jewish history to the interests of a learned, Greco-Roman audience. The first half of the *Jewish Antiquities* offers a summary of Hebrew Scripture, including the

---

4. See Hengel, *Crucifixion in the Ancient World*, 6–7 and passim.

5. On women as witnesses in Jewish tradition, see further Cohn and Sinai, "Witness," *EncJud* 21:115–25.

provisions of Mosaic law. In its original form, Deut 19:15 stipulates that "only on the evidence of two or three witnesses shall a charge be sustained." Josephus expands on the biblical text (likely adding details from personal observation) by specifying that potential witnesses are either qualified or disqualified on the basis of moral character:

> Let no witness be credited on his own, but three, or two at least, whose testimony is supported by their good lives. The testimony of women is not admitted, due to the *levity and audacity* of their sex. Neither let servants be allowed as witnesses, due to their baseness of soul, for they may not speak truth, either from hope of gain, or fear of punishment.[6]

Women, according to Josephus, are known for their preoccupation with trivia, as well as for their rashness and insolence (the sense of his phrase διὰ κουφότητα καὶ θράσος), on which grounds their word is not to be trusted. To be sure, the author is playing to the sentiments of his audience (predominantly male and Roman), yet the fact that he attributes this view to Moses and the sacred text lends it considerable weight, in which case it cannot be dismissed outright.

At a point of intersection between local custom and imperial power are the Roman provincial law courts, in which the Roman legal system exercises its dominion over the lesser details of life under military occupation. Near contemporary (in this case, early second century) evidence for the actual conditions under which Jewish plaintiffs and defendants might each plead their cause emerges from the so-called "Cave of Letters" in Nahal Hever. Confirming the uncertain middle ground that women occupy in both Jewish and Roman domains, Tal Ilan notes that

> in papyri from the Judaean Desert, which derive from the Roman provincial law courts, Babatha, the owner of one archive, always appears in court accompanied by a guardian. Thus we may suspect that women were not considered by these courts as

---

6. Josephus, *Ant.* 4:219, in the online translation by Patrick Rogers (emphasis added): http://www.biblical.ie/page.php?fl=josephus/Antiquities/AJE04#08. On this passage, see further Pearce, *Words of Moses*, 185–96 (esp. 191–94); "Josephus is . . . our earliest witness to the idea that Mosaic law prohibits the use of testimony by women or slaves—a position not otherwise attested until the writings of the Tannaim who themselves indicate that such a prohibition was not an absolute or universally agreed rule" (237).

fully fledged legal entities ... Yet they did appear before them and did make legal claims.[7]

Strictly speaking, the situation in Gospel accounts of Jesus' resurrection is not that of a law court, but rather involves religious belief or doctrine and its implications for discipleship. Here, too, women are largely without voice in the world of their day, if later rabbinic legislation (however idealized and prescriptive) can be taken to indicate their situation: "An unmarried man may not teach scribes. Nor may a woman teach scribes" (*m. Qidd.* 4:13). Although the context of this ruling suggests a more particular concern for sexual impropriety, no distinction is made between married and unmarried women (in contrast to the stipulation immediately prior): it evidently applies to women at large. Whether the subject matter in view here is literacy and penmanship specifically or the broader religious *content* of scribal tradition, such a prohibition is typical of rabbinic literature, which "views women's rôle in society as restricted and stereotypical: men operate in public, women in private only."[8] Indeed, even pious women (i.e., those envisaged by rabbinic dicta) are excluded from religious education: according to the influential Rabbi Eliezer ben Hyrcanus (T2; 90–130 CE), "Whoever teaches his daughter Torah teaches her obscenity."[9] Nor, along the same lines, are women permitted to read Scripture in the synagogue (*t. Meg.* 3:11); according to *Mishnah Qiddushin*, they are even exempt from rules concerning proper celebration of the Sabbath and annual festivals.[10]

Judith Lieu considers the attitude of Josephus (and, presumably, many in his audience) concerning the folly and insolence of women by itself "a disqualification that would ensure the derogation of the empty tomb tradition and its dependency on women."[11] If that is so with respect

---

7. Ilan, "Gender Issues and Daily Life," 51. On the historical background and contents of the archive, see Isaac, "The Babatha Archive."

8. Ilan, "Gender Issues and Daily Life," 48–49.

9. *M. Soṭah* 3:4 (Soncino); "This word may also mean 'lasciviousness' or 'silliness'" (so Feldman and Reinhold, *Jewish Life and Thought*, 201n71, citing a wide range of texts concerning attitudes toward women [197–203]). Cf. *y. Soṭah* 3:4, where Eliezer is reported to have said, "Let the teachings of the Torah be burned, but let them not be handed over to women." Further discussion of *m. Soṭah* 3:4 in Ilan, "Gender Issues and Daily Life," 59.

10. So *m. Qidd.* 1:7, although Ilan ("Gender Issues and Daily Life," 62–63) cites numerous other rulings and examples that illustrate female participation in the worship of contemporary Judaism.

11. Judith Lieu, "The Women's Resurrection Testimony," in Barton and Stanton,

to legal testimony, it applies even more fully to the teaching of religious doctrine: women are singularly unqualified to testify or instruct men in matters of faith and proper conduct.

Given the prevalence of such views, the male disciples' response to the testimony of the women should hardly surprise us. Luke's comment in this regard is particularly noteworthy: "Now it was Mary Magdalene, Joanna, Mary the mother of James, and the other women with them who told this to the apostles. But these words seemed to them *an idle tale*, and they did not believe them" (Luke 24:10–11). The word that Luke uses here (λῆρος) denotes "utter nonsense" (L&N §33.380), particularly with regard to foolish speech of any sort.[12] By way of illustration, another passage from Josephus offers a striking parallel to the women's testimony and its reception by worldly-wise disciples. Josephus recounts his unsuccessful defense in 67 CE of the Galilean town of Jotapata (Yodefat), its fall to Roman forces after a forty-seven-day siege, and his initial reluctance to surrender for fear of being executed as a rebel commander. Most of his troops choose suicide over capture, but Josephus attributes his survival to divine providence, as well as to the fact that when brought before the Roman generals Vespasian and Titus (Vespasian's son), he discloses what has been revealed to him in a dream: that father and son will each become emperor of Rome (*War* 3:351–52; 399–401). Of course, we have only Josephus's word for the details of this improbable account, although it is a matter of historical record that Vespasian assumed the title of Caesar Augustus two years later, in 69 CE, while Titus took office upon his father's death in 79. Not surprisingly, says the former commander turned historian, recounting his own experience in the third person, "Vespasian disbelieved it at first, thinking that Josephus was just scheming to save his own life. But after some time he was convinced and believed what he said to be true, when God had raised his hopes of gaining the empire by other signs of his coming dominance."[13] Others have similar reservations: two friends of Vespasian also happen to be present, one of whom wonders aloud "if these words are not a *nonsensical invention* [λῆρος] of the

---

Resurrection, 35.

12. Of many examples in Greek literature, cf. Aeschines, *On the Embassy*, 2 §53; Hippocrates, *De morbis popularibus* [*On Common Diseases*], Epidemics 1 §4; Lucian, *Saturnalia* §8; Plutarch, *De garrulitate* [*On Talkativeness*] §20; Theophrastus, *Characters* §28.3; *Vita Barlaam et Joasaph* 32 §295, etc.

13. Josephus, *War* 3:403–4 (Rogers): http://www.biblical.ie/page.php?fl=josephus /War/ JWG3#08.

prisoner to avert the storm which he has raised."[14] Much as later readers might also be inclined to doubt the details of his story, Josephus can claim that far from being "utter nonsense," his testimony is a matter of divine revelation as well as (in due course) historical fact. Both the situation itself and (no less importantly) the language that he uses are remarkably close to those of Luke, the women at the tomb, and their disbelieving male companions.

In our eyes an intrusive Savior and an unexpected resurrection are both invariably λῆρος, nonsense, for at least three reasons, possibly more. First, because to observers of a more sober and demanding disposition, those who promulgate such silliness are not worth believing. Just so, the pagan Celsus, writing around 178 CE, averred that the Christian gospel was suited only to "the foolish, dishonourable, and stupid, and only slaves, women, and little children."[15] Whether our disdain is directed toward fundamentalists, foreigners, or the generally feeble minded, we know better than to take them at their word. Second, because the event itself cannot be accommodated within our settled vision of the way the world works. If only on a technical point: the Romans were efficient killers, which is how they maintained their grip on power. The *Pax Romana* relied on the power of death, and would do so with great effectiveness for centuries more. When it came to crucifixion, Rome and its military could be counted on to get the job done. Nor does anything in our prior experience suggest that death might be reversible. Third, Christ's resurrection seems like something from the same category as Santa Claus and the tooth fairy (or according to Goulder, UFO sightings and the Sasquatch)[16] because we are too concerned for our standing in the eyes of others to entertain the possibility that we ourselves might, for all our sophistication, be somehow culpable, lacking sufficient insight, or simply mistaken. "Whoever wants to save their life will lose it," said Jesus; only by letting your life go is it possible to get it back (Mark 8:35). By clinging for dear life to all that is safe and predictable, we are left with the safest and most predictable outcome of all: death itself. Resurrection is of another order

---

14. *War* 3:405, in the Loeb translation of Henry St. John Thackeray (emphasis added).

15. Origen, *Contra Celsum* 3:44, 49, in the translation by Chadwick, *Origen: Contra Celsum*.

16. Goulder, "Did Jesus of Nazareth Rise from the Dead?," in Barton and Stanton, *Resurrection*, 61–63.

entirely, and the furthest we normally stretch credulity is to the point of graciously dismissive agnosticism. As David Schlafer observes,

> "New" life—resurrection life—if and when it comes—is likely to be as disorienting to those of us who are charged with preaching today as it was to those who were the initial witnesses to the resurrection. And such words—film clips, tweets—as we are able to craft may well be dismissed as "an idle tale."[17]

Skepticism notwithstanding, the male disciples have no grounds of their own for boasting, and no basis on which to defend their own suitability as witnesses to Jesus' resurrection. Far from being faithful themselves, they too have abandoned their teacher in his hour of need—all, that is, apart from Judas Iscariot, who stands head and shoulders above his fellow disciples for having initiated the betrayal. Generally speaking, their attitude ranges from sadness and regret (Cleopas and a companion on the road to Emmaus) to a wholesale forsaking of their identity as followers of Jesus, indicated by a speedy return to their former lives (hence Simon Peter's announcement in John 21:3, "I am going fishing"). Apart from Judas, Simon himself may be the most obvious example of self-disqualification, with his profound lack of self awareness and his insistence that he alone will be faithful even should the others fall away: "he said vehemently, 'Even though I must die with you, I will not deny you'" (Mark 14:31). But the other ten are no less culpable: "And all of them said the same." Their vacillation will be remedied, of course, by the day of Pentecost, but in the meantime, the Gospels paint a less than flattering portrait of the surviving Eleven.

Incidentally, we should note the implications of this near universal desertion for the lengthy and detailed accounts of Jesus' death. Apart from mention in John's Gospel of the "beloved disciple" (John 19:26) and various anonymous bystanders in Luke (Luke 23:35), the evangelists are unanimous in identifying women as the only followers of Jesus to witness his crucifixion in person:

> There were also women looking on from a distance; among them were Mary Magdalene, and Mary the mother of James the younger and of Joses, and Salome. These used to follow him and provided for him when he was in Galilee; and there were many

---

17. Schlafer, "Anticipating Unpredictable Resurrection," 209.

other women who had come up with him to Jerusalem. (Mark 15:40–41)[18]

In the words of W. D. Davies and Dale Allison, these women are "eyewitnesses to the kerygmatic triad: Jesus died, was buried, and was raised."[19] The implication should not be lost on us: if we do not, in principle, doubt the witnesses—women all—with respect to death and burial, on what grounds may we demur when it comes to resurrection? Nor should it escape our notice that in many parts of the church, a similar situation still obtains today wherever women are not permitted to preach, teach, or testify to their encounter with the resurrected Christ. They are silenced simply on account of their gender. The Gospels are somewhat paradoxical in this regard. In the Synoptic accounts, Simon Peter holds pride of place for being the first to confess Jesus as the Christ (Mark 8:29 and parallels). But according to John, Peter's most explicit confession is simply, "We have come to believe and know that you are the Holy One of God" (John 6:69). In that Gospel, a Samaritan woman (allegedly unreliable on the grounds of gender and religion alike) is the first to speculate as to whether Jesus might be the Messiah (John 4:25, 29), although others in Jerusalem—unnamed but certainly Jewish—come to the same conclusion not long afterwards (John 7:25–26, 31, 41). Although the fact is usually overlooked, the most explicit messianic confession in John's Gospel belongs to Martha, who declares, "Lord, I believe that you are the Messiah, the Son of God, the one coming into the world" (John 11:27).

Nor does later tradition do much remedy to this state of affairs. When the Apostle Paul chronicles the history of Jesus' post-resurrection appearances, he does so in the following terms:

> For I handed on to you as of first importance what I in turn had received: that Christ died for our sins in accordance with the Scriptures, and that he was buried, and that he was raised on the third day in accordance with the Scriptures, and that he appeared to Cephas, then to the twelve. Then he appeared to more than five hundred brothers and sisters[20] at one time, most of

---

18. Cf. Matt 27:55–56; Luke 23:49; John 19:25–27. Marcus (*Mark 8–16*, 1059) observes that "we know virtually nothing about these women," which is extraordinary given their pivotal rôle in the formulation of early Christian tradition (although historical records are similarly limited for many of the male apostles).

19. Davies and Allison, *Gospel according to Saint Matthew* 3:637.

20. The NRSV (like the NIV) inserts this clause, although the Greek reads, simply, ἀδελφοῖς ("brethren" [RSV]; "brothers" [CEV]).

> whom are still alive, though some have died. Then he appeared to James, then to all the apostles. Last of all, as to one untimely born, he appeared also to me. (1 Cor 15:3-8)

The apostle openly acknowledges that he is, for the most part, "handing on" received tradition. As Gordon Fee notes, "it is generally agreed" among commentators that Paul is here "repeating a very early creedal formulation that was common to the entire church, to which he adds other traditions about several resurrection appearances."[21] In obvious contrast to the Gospel accounts, however, there is no mention of any women: the tradition of the early church appears to have either suppressed or forgotten them entirely. The same contrast is present even in Luke. Cleopas and his companion (since Cleopas is a masculine name)[22] relate the women's testimony (with some uncertainty), only to find it true in the one to whom they encounter on the road to Emmaus. Returning to Jerusalem with good news of their own, they discover "the eleven and their companions gathered together . . . saying, 'The Lord has risen indeed, and he has appeared *to Simon*!'" (Luke 24:33-34). Not, that is, to the women at the tomb (Luke 23:54-24:10). Since this is the first we hear of an appearance to Peter (at least in this Gospel), it seems to have supplanted the very testimony that Luke himself earlier highlights. The two situations are thus essentially alike: whether with respect to messianic confession generally or to resurrection in particular, the church still has difficulty hearing (all the more so prioritizing) the testimony of women (and outsiders generally), despite the fact that such testimony furnishes the very basis for the church's existence. Their word must be co-opted and forced to fit within prevailing plausibility structures (sociological or cultural as much as conceptual).

Rowan Williams reasons that the message of the resurrection is by definition subversive and iconoclastic, both as to its content and as concerns those who first conveyed it:

> The story as it stands . . . provides a very clear ground for the primitive sense of the resurrection gospel as a message from outside. The grave is discovered by people outside the apostolic band itself, and it is these "marginal" figures who are charged to go and preach to the community: "Go, tell his disciples and Peter . . ." (Mark 16:7). The very first thing that generates a hope and

---

21. Fee, *First Epistle to the Corinthians*, 718.
22. Fitzmyer, *Luke X-XXIV*, 1563.

wonderment about the possibility of encountering Jesus afresh is the message from an outsider, a *woman* (not only socially marginal for the Eleven but also, of course, one whose evidence could not be adduced in the customary procedures of Jewish law—so that her testimony cannot be assimilated into familiar legal structures), that his body is not to be seen.[23]

That the male apostles have a tendency to fence and limit the power of the Messiah within conventions intended maintain their own preeminence is evident already from the curious episode of "Unknown Exorcist," which survives intact only in the Gospel of Mark: "John said to him, 'Teacher, we saw someone casting out demons in your name, and we tried to stop him, because he was not following *us*'" (Mark 9:38). Neither the objection itself nor its preservation in early Christian tradition are unusual, given the pivotal rôle of the Twelve and the need for strong social boundaries in a minority, sometimes persecuted church. But contrary to all such instincts, Jesus' answer affirms that the name and power of the Messiah are entirely self-authenticating: "Jesus said, 'Do not stop him; for no one who does a deed of power in my name will be able soon afterward to speak evil of me. Whoever is not against us is for us'" (Mark 9:39–40). The same principle applies in that instance as for the resurrection: testimony to the power of Jesus' name does not require institutional approval or authorization (even that of the apostles!). Again: the church (and the structures by which it maintains its identity) do not authenticate testimony to the Messiah; rather, it is testimony to the Messiah that constitutes and authenticates the church.

Whether they are judged by the standards of their own day or by those of readers today, what unites all the various witnesses to the resurrection is a consistent lack of qualification for the rôle. The same is true for Saul of Tarsus and those of whom he writes. Paul, as he is subsequently known, refers to himself as "the least of the apostles, unfit to be called an apostle, because I persecuted the church of God" (1 Cor 15:9). In fact, he describes himself in decidedly unflattering terms, as an ἔκτρωμα (1 Cor 15:8: "one untimely born" [NRSV]; "one abnormally born" [NIV]), a word that more commonly applies to miscarriage or abortion. When, in the same passage, he reports that the Risen Christ "appeared to more than five hundred" at one time (1 Cor 15:6), no mention is made of their qualifications either. Since this is the only surviving record of such a group, we

---

23. Williams, *Resurrection*, 105–6.

may further conclude that they are witnesses only in the limited sense of having beheld Christ, but likely not by virtue of having passed on the good news to others.

Whether, then, for women, Samaritans, waffling apostles, or others whose identity is now lost, it is a matter of theological principle that inadequacy, insufficiency, cultural disqualification, and failure as witnesses—of whatever form or on whatever grounds—are intrinsic to the message of the gospel. Paul is referring to the power of Christ's resurrection at work in human lives when he explains that "we have this treasure in clay jars, so that it may be made clear that this extraordinary power belongs to God and does not come from us" (2 Cor 4:7). Whether referring to his own experience or that of Christians generally, says the apostle, Christ's resurrection is the supreme manifestation of divine sufficiency, precisely on account of human inadequacy (including the human inadequacy of the witnesses and their testimony to God's provision of new life).

Articulating the theological implications of Jesus' resurrection, Williams reflects at length on the significance of his appearance to the very same disciples who had abandoned him only a few days prior.[24] Returning to Galilee, the male disciples attempt to resume the life they had previously known, but Jesus will not let them do so: in John's Gospel, he confronts them with his own disturbing reality over a charcoal fire, much as Peter had attempted to deny his discipleship over a charcoal fire in the courtyard of the high priest (John 18:18; 21:9).[25] The usual reading of Jesus' subsequent challenge, "Simon son of John, do you love me?" (John 21:16, 17), and especially "Do you love me more than these?" (that is, more than the other disciples, v. 15) is that Peter must learn that love for Jesus implies a willingness to serve the Lord's "flock." Hence the reply, "Feed my lambs ... Tend my sheep," etc. But there is a deeper implication here: until he knows that the real answer to these questions is in the negative, and that he has already demonstrated the poverty of his devotion by denying his Lord, Peter is not ready to care for Jesus' other sheep. Like so many of us, Peter initially has great confidence in his love for Christ, but what he really loves is his own prominence and self-preservation. Until he knows this, he does not really love the Lord, no matter how much he may feel aggrieved at being doubted and called to account. As with the woman who interrupts a dinner party to anoint Jesus for burial (Luke

---

24. Williams, *Resurrection*, 7–36, and passim.
25. Williams, *Resurrection*, 34.

7:47), only in recognizing that Christ's love for him is vastly more sufficient than his own love of Christ will Peter be able to care for all the other sheep who do not love their Shepherd nearly enough either.

Still, Jesus confronts the survivors in the very place of their failure so as to demonstrate, in definitive fashion, that not even their betrayal can succeed in bringing his ministry to an end. In this sense, the risen Jesus represents the failure of their failure. All that has changed is the illusion of their own piety: by encountering him anew just as they try to resume normal lives, the disciples are confronted by the awkward fact that not even the poverty of their faith and faithfulness has been sufficient to defeat him. Paradoxically, looking beyond sufficiency and insufficiency alike is the basis on which they will engage in new ministry and establish the fledgling church:

> If the disciples are to be sent *now*, it is as men who have encountered afresh the Lord who sends them; and he comes now to men whose history is one of initial hope and promise, followed by betrayal and emptiness. They are called now and sent now as forgiven men: their apostasy does not alter God's purpose . . . On the far side of the resurrection, vocation and forgiveness occur together, always and inseparably.[26]

In this way, the message and content of the Christian gospel, which concerns a definitive divine-human reconciliation and the disciples' experience of the Risen Christ, are inextricably linked. As Willimon remarks, "Forgiveness and reconciliation are linked to resurrection because Jesus wasn't just raised, he didn't just reappear—any old god could have done that. He appeared to the very ones who so betrayed and disappointed him in the first place—the same losers with whom he shared his last meal before execution."[27] What the apostles will soon preach is not, therefore, an abstract set of principles or religious ideals, much less a new and improved version of the religious life, but a breathtaking, life-giving reality that they have already encountered, face to face, in the person of Jesus, post-crucifixion and in the aftermath of their own abject personal failure. The value of their testimony will consist in the substance of the testimony itself, rather than in the quality or qualifications of those who offer it.

Accordingly, with respect to preaching today, if the resurrection is to have an impact on our hearers it will not do so simply because of our

---

26. Williams, *Resurrection*, 35.
27. Willimon, "Preaching after Easter," 38.

words, or because our sermons succeed in making sense of it. If the New Testament accounts provide any kind of precedent, our quality as witnesses is more liable to impair than to commend our testimony. Again, we are not the ones who make sense of Jesus' resurrection; it is Jesus' resurrection that makes sense of us, fashioning us into witnesses by virtue of its ability to create a coherence and vitality that we would otherwise lack.

The Message of the Resurrection: "He Is Not Here"

> After the Sabbath, as the first day of the week was dawning, Mary Magdalene and the other Mary went to see the tomb. And suddenly there was a great earthquake; for an angel of the Lord, descending from heaven, came and rolled back the stone and sat on it. His appearance was like lightning, and his clothing white as snow. For fear of him the guards shook and became like dead men. But the angel said to the women, "Do not be afraid; I know that you are looking for Jesus who was crucified. He is not here; for he has been raised, as he said. Come, see the place where he lay. Then go quickly and tell his disciples, 'He has been raised from the dead, and indeed he is going ahead of you to Galilee; there you will see him.' This is my message for you." (Matt 28:1–7)

As Matthew tells it, the women come not to wash or anoint the body (as is the case in Mark and Luke), or even to contemplate it, but simply "to see the tomb" (Matt 28:1). This is the approximate equivalent of bringing flowers to the graveside: it is a gesture of grief, finality, and defeat, of conceding that death has had the last word. Although the two Marys are inspired by the most pious of motives—to grieve for one whom they have loved and lost—Jesus evades and frustrates them. Where others have rejected or abandoned him, they simply want to accord him, if only in death, the honor he is due. But he is nowhere to be found.

At this point, there is no proof yet of anything unusual having taking place, no evidence other than the evidence of absence: the body that was once Jesus is not where by rights it should be, although failing to find a corpse in the proper place is the most minimal of indicators. This is, in the most concrete sense possible, an argument from silence. The women must take the word of an angelic witness, much as the other apostles will (initially, anyway) have only the words of the women to rely on. Depending second hand on the testimony of a heavenly messenger seems dangerously close to what Paul will later warn against in his Letter to the Colossians, which is the error of "insisting on . . . worship of angels; taking one's stand on visions [ἃ ἑόρακεν]" (Col 2:18). Although Luke's language is distinct (despite the apparent similarity of English translation), this is surely what prompts uncertainty and skepticism on the part of the two travelers on their way to Emmaus. The women, they report, "came back saying that they had even seen a vision of angels [καὶ ὀπτασίαν ἀγγέλων ἑωρακέναι]" (Luke 24:23).

What, then, is their testimony, and the testimony of the angel at the tomb? "He is not here" (Matt 28:6). This is non-testimony, bearing witness at most to emptiness and absence. They have, quite literally, lost track of the Messiah: he is lost to them both as to his whereabouts and in the fact of his death. Rational explanations spring to mind: the gardener has shifted him (John 20:15); grieving disciples have hidden him (Matt 28:13); grave robbers have stolen him. But rationalization cannot accommodate Mark's young man in bright clothing or Matthew's angel with a face like lightning, seated where the dead Messiah should be. "He is not here." Death could not hold him. Nor, indeed, can we.

It is not that Jesus is nowhere to be found (as modern skeptics, scholars among them, contend); rather, according to the angelic messenger, "he is going ahead of you to Galilee; there you will see him" (Matt 28:7). Or as the bright young man in Mark has it, "he is going ahead of you to Galilee; there you will see him, *just as he told you*" (Mark 16:7). He is, in short, exactly where he said he would be; henceforth he will be where he fulfills his promises, and nowhere else. He will show up even as the defeated apostles cower in the Upper Room, trying to decide what to do with their interrupted lives. But his absence apart from these promises means that from now on he will turn up on his own terms, in his own time and way. He will choose the moments of his own self-revealing, and (having done their utmost in this regard already) no one else will henceforth be able to constrain him. As far as we and the other disciples can tell, "He is not here," but that does not mean that he may not choose to reveal himself, even to strangers and enemies, or those inclined to doubt.

In assessing this testimony, the women must weigh two sources of information: the word of one whom death (so they are certain) has now defeated, and the word of an angel: "He has been raised, *as he said* . . . This is my message for you" (Matt 28:6–7 NRSV); "Now I have told you" (NIV). In other words, the evidence is itself equivocal. All Jesus' accomplishments would seem to be contradicted by the irrefutable fact of his death, yet the heavenly messenger tells them otherwise—contradicting the contradiction—and they have no further indication to the contrary. In the face of conflicting evidence, it appears that the women must make their decision on other grounds. Whether, as the angel indicates, the resurrected Jesus has now gone ahead of them to Galilee, and they will encounter him there, remains to be seen—quite literally so. Only time will tell. In the meantime, three other factors enter into play, all of which operate in the angelic testimony. We may, for the moment, set aside the messenger's "appearance . . . like lightning" and his effulgent robes (Matt 28:3). These are certainly persuasive, especially so for the guards who have been knocked into a stupor at the sight. But since preachers cannot rely on anything similar taking place, angelic light shows are of little assistance to the average sermon.

Parenthetically, the purpose of the guards and their lethal weapons (whatever we imagine these to be) is to threaten death against any who dare disturb the one who is already dead. Such power, according to Matthew, is intended to countermand a possible claim that "he has been raised from the dead" (Matt 27:62–66). It seems fitting, therefore, that the guards themselves are promptly incapacitated, on which point Matthew's language is precise: for fear of the angel, he reports, "the guards shook and became *like dead men*" (Matt 28:4). Which is to say, those who defend the dead with the power of death find themselves unexpectedly subject to death.[28] That the only power they wield is turned against them, rendering them impotent, seems a fitting *entrée* into the new order that Jesus' resurrection has inaugurated, one ruled instead by the power of life.

For his resurrection to make sense, the women must first remember what Jesus once taught, in this case the promise, repeated three times, that he would "be killed, and on the third day be raised" (Matt 16:21; cf. 17:22–23; 20:18–19).[29] Upon reflection, they will remember what they had either forgotten, misunderstood, or dismissed outright as impossible and absurd. Surviving the terrible efficiency of Roman crucifixion is unprecedented, so the women (along with all the other disciples) have reverted to a more normal way of thinking: "I know," says the angel, "that you are looking for Jesus who was crucified." But for the women (and

---

28. Their circumstances, and Matthew's wording of it, seems an unwitting fulfilment of Jesus' aphorism in Matt 26:52.

29. From Mark 8:31; 9:31; 10:33–34; cf. Luke 9:22, 44; 18:32–33.

the others in their turn), Easter faith begins by remembering what Jesus taught, and taking him at his word.

What encourages them to do so is, second, a recognition of his reliability. Jesus was never one to toy with credulity or abuse trust: quite the contrary, in fact. So the women must weigh what they recall of his teaching together with the character of the one who taught it. Despite speculation and the legends that have emerged to supply missing background information, we know very little about these women: Matthew mentions "Mary Magdalene and the other Mary" just three times: as having been present at Jesus' crucifixion (27:56), as witnessing his burial (27:61), and as returning to the tomb at dawn on the first day of the week (28:1). Yet the personal risk that identifying with a condemned criminal would have entailed suggests both courage and profound devotion on their part. In contrast to the male disciples who—to a man—are nowhere in sight, these women not only knew Jesus well, but love him sufficiently to remain with him in death. The reminder of what he said, together with what they know of the one who said it, begins to change their minds.

There is also a third factor: although the angel's message is brief (forty-eight words at most in Matthew's Greek), he repeats one point twice. Just as Jesus himself foretold that he would be crucified and "raised" (ἐγερθῆναι, Matt 16:21; cf. 17:23, 20:19), so the angel reiterates that Jesus has indeed been "raised" from death (ἠγέρθη). And lest the frightened women miss his meaning, he says so twice (28:6–7). Whatever language the angel spoke (what language do angels speak, anyway?), Matthew's vocabulary makes it clear that the messenger is echoing Jesus' promises verbatim. More precisely, in Matthew's account the angel repeats the passive voice: he has *been raised* from death. Since this turn of phrase implies divine action, the angelic announcement is not only deferential and circumspect but also—most importantly—theologically potent. So the two Marys must, first, recall what Jesus had taught regarding his own death and resurrection. Second, they must take his character into account, weighing the likelihood that he misled them or was himself mistaken. Third, knowing what to make of the empty tomb and the testimony of the shining messenger comes down to acknowledging divine power. Everything they have learned from Jesus has been about his Father and his Father's kingdom. The angel does not say, in so many words, "God did this; don't you get it?" His indirect language is as respectful of their freedom (and ours) as it is deferential toward Almighty God.

It might have been simpler for Jesus himself to appear in place of angels. If he wanted the women as his witnesses, would it have been so difficult for him to wait a few more hours until they showed up to anoint his body? Doing so would have overcome much uncertainty at the outset, as well as obviating centuries of extraneous theological deliberation. To complicate matters, this is closer to how events unfold in the Gospel of John (John 20:14–17). But as Matthew tells it, testimony comes prior to encounter. Remarkably, it is at this point that Jesus unexpectedly materializes:

> So they left the tomb quickly with fear and great joy, and ran to tell his disciples. Suddenly Jesus met them and said, "Greetings!" And they came to him, took hold of his feet, and worshipped him. Then Jesus said to them, "Do not be afraid; go and tell my brothers to go to Galilee; there they will see me." (Matt 28:8–10)

This pattern will recur in the book of Acts: first there is testimony, then its acceptance—in effect making witnesses of those who receive the testimony of others—then Jesus appears, in one way or another, to confirm that what has been said about him is true.

Preachers typically wish that the process were less complex: a direct line to God, with the authority to invoke divine affirmation, would make the preparation and delivery of sermons considerably simpler. But if preachers are, in their own small way, witnesses to the power of God, Matthew has much to teach us about our craft. To bear witness to the risen Christ on the model that Matthew indicates begins when we, in essence, receive the testimony of others by means of the biblical text. Codified and canonized, to be sure, and set in place long before our day, Scripture bears witness to the ways of God, above all in the person of Jesus of Nazareth and his resurrection following death. Much like the two Marys at the tomb, preparing sermonic testimony of our own requires that we begin by weighing testimony that concerns Jesus, recorded in the biblical canon, in light of his character, all in the broader context of what Scripture has to say and what we ourselves (perhaps over a long process of trial, failure, and rescue) have learned to be true of God.

As a personal aside, one colleague of my acquaintance made a habit, Sunday by Sunday, of explaining from the pulpit how any supernatural or miraculous elements recorded in the biblical text could not possibly be credible for those of more modern sensibilities. He was correct, of course, that modernism is unapologetically reductionistic, refusing to consider anything outside the bounds of a narrowly conceived version of scientific rationalism. But Scripture by definition (along with spirituality in general, mysticism in particular, and God above all) calls us beyond ourselves, inviting us not to encounter but to be encountered by something, Someone, whom we can neither co-opt nor command, much less reduce to that which is comfortable or convenient. Only when we are seized with "fear and great joy" by the immeasurable "otherness" of God to which the text bears witness, will we have something worth preaching about, something that is capable of drawing us beyond the anxious theological lethargy that so often characterizes our sermons and our lives.

Just so, says Matthew, Mary Magdalene and the other Mary hasten from the tomb "with fear and great joy" (Matt 28:8). They are fearful yet exultant because according to the angel, they have been wrong about Jesus. Evidentiary logic suggests that they should not pass on their findings prior to verification. In this regard Thomas the Twin (to whom we will return in due course) is undoubtedly correct: "Unless I see the mark of the nails in his hands, and put my finger in the mark of the nails and my hand in his side, I will not believe" (John 20:25). Yet whether from faith, credulity, or simple foolishness, the women now run "to tell his disciples" despite having nothing to report but a report. Only then does Jesus appear, confirming what they have chosen to believe. The logic of Matthew's narrative is thus very specific, for it seems to indicate that trust in the power of God (bound up with Jesus' promises, which the women had temporarily forgotten) takes priority over hard-headed persuasion and the normal rules of human experience. More subtly: whereas we are preoccupied with details of the narrative (and their various contradictions), Jesus affirms the women's preoccupation with the one whom they still love by coming forward himself even before they have a chance to speak.

Before they can fulfill their task—bearing witness to the angelic witness and joining their voices with his—Jesus stops them with a word of his own. Translating this acclamation is more difficult than at first appears. "Greetings" (NIV; NRSV) is hardly a modern way of speaking; "Hail!" (RSV) or "All hail" (KJV) are even worse, and "Good morning!" (MSG) is simply painful. In other contexts, the verb in question refers to rejoicing or gladness (Matt 5:12; Phil 4:4, etc.), although it is a familiar and conventional form of personal or literary greeting (Luke 1:28; Acts 23:26; James 1:1, etc.). Louw and Nida comment that it implies "a wish for happiness on the part of the person greeted . . . In traditional English one might employ an expression such as 'long live!'" (LN §33.22). This is a wonderful (if not exactly idiomatic) suggestion for the present passage: the One who has been restored to life wishes long (eternal!) life upon those he greets. Although there is no good modern equivalent and we don't normally talk this way either, we get some additional sense of what this form of address entails if we imagine Jesus telling the women, "Rejoice!" or "Be glad!" Without making too much of a single word, Jesus' simple greeting is the counterpoint both to the crushing disappointment of recent days and to their immediate alarm at learning of his resurrection. Apparently not daring to look him in the face, they fall down, grasp his feet, and worship him.

At least in Matthew, the words of the angel and the message of Jesus are substantially the same. "*Do not be afraid*," says the angel, "Go quickly and tell his disciples he has been raised from the dead, and indeed he is going ahead of you to Galilee; there you will see him"; "*Do not be afraid*," says Jesus, "Go and tell my brothers to go to Galilee; there they will see me" (Matt 28:7, 10). The difference between the two admonitions is that the first does not fully dispel their fear, since in the following verse the women are still afraid ("they left the tomb quickly with fear and great joy"). By contrast, there is no further mention of apprehension when the women finally take leave of their Lord (Matt 28:11).

It is one thing to be told that Jesus is somehow "alive" and quite another to be encountered by someone more concrete than metaphorical; having an idea in mind (however unconventional) is not nearly as disruptive as being confronted by it in the flesh. By analogy, much as we may pray for a friend to be healed, we are still shocked when it happens: we search for some explanation just shy of the miraculous and divine. That Jesus himself waylays them, just when they are about their Master's business, reminds us that the message they bear is no substitute for the one whom it concerns. Where we would make much both of the resurrection message and of its messengers, proclaiming the risen Christ is simply a prelude to encountering Jesus for ourselves. Jesus reiterates as much, telling the women to direct the male disciples to Galilee, where they will see him for themselves. The irony here is perhaps unintended: that the men will disregard both the messengers and their message is nothing unusual. For that very reason, they must judge for themselves, and in order to do so must believe and obey the women anyway. That Jesus calls them "brothers" is remarkable because they have treated him the same way they treat the two Marys, and not even meeting him in person will entirely dispel their doubts. For all these various reasons, testimony to resurrection must take its cue from the resurrected one, not the other way around.

Might it be that resurrection preaching—preaching that takes account of resurrection, and therefore the resurrection of preaching itself—pursues a similar path? Even the most theologically conservative preacher will confess that Jesus' resurrection confounds all human understanding. The job description for most preachers includes conducting funerals; for the aging congregations that many of us serve, funerals are about as close as we will get to a growth industry. Yet not a single funeral will end like this. We may be visionaries in the pulpit, but at the graveside or the crematorium we are unapologetic pragmatists. Once the parishioner is dead and the funeral finished, there will be no further revision of their status. He or she can safely be removed from the parish rolls.

Preaching resurrection therefore begins with an admission that we have simply been wrong. This is neither a normal death nor a normal victim, and our normal rejection of the miraculous—our essentially flat-footed, hard-nosed refusal of the absurd—must be overturned by the recollection of Jesus' promises, our experience of him in Scripture and the course of discipleship; above all by knowledge of God. To state the matter more bluntly: we are reluctant witnesses of Jesus' resurrection because (much like the Sadducees whom Jesus once rebuked in similar terms) we "know neither the Scriptures nor the power of God" (Mark 12:24).[30] Normally, we know better, but on this occasion, our epistemological self-assurance must be overturned by an awareness that we are well beyond our depth, theologically speaking.

So resurrectional preaching, on the model that Matthew's narrative implies, will likely be characterized by careful attention to Jesus' identity and teaching alike; it will "lean not on its own understanding" (Prov 3:5) as it considers the life-giving power of God, and it will have to reckon with the limits of its own method in light of the one whom it proclaims. It will point beyond itself and the preoccupation with their own importance that bedevils preachers, as it awaits the unconstrainable initiative of the Risen Christ, who encounters those who wait for him and are willing to speak even before they are fully certain. Such preaching will not imagine that it is either the first or the last word on whatever theological issue is at hand, but will simply take its place in a long line of testimony

---

30. On this comment as key to understanding Jesus' teaching, see Knowles, *Of Seeds and the People of God*, 7–17.

to Christ that depends upon Christ himself confirming its veracity with testimony of his own.

Responding to Resurrection: The Necessity of Doubt

> Now the eleven disciples went to Galilee, to the mountain to which Jesus had directed them. When they saw him, they worshiped him; but some doubted. And Jesus came and said to them, "All authority in heaven and on earth has been given to me. Go therefore and make disciples of all nations, baptizing them in the name of the Father and of the Son and of the Holy Spirit, and teaching them to obey everything that I have commanded you. And remember, I am with you always, to the end of the age." (Matt 28:16–20)

To understand what ails the church in our age—preaching in particular—we need look no further than this passage. To be sure, it has inspired much good, motivating ecclesiastical pilgrims and missionaries to "make disciples of all nations, baptizing them . . . and teaching them to obey everything that [Christ has] commanded." But while I have no quarrel with the principle or *fact* of making disciples, the *manner* of our doing so has not always been Christlike. In general, it would seem that we have frequently taken Jesus' assertion of his authority as a warrant for our own. The authority of the Risen Christ has been seen to devolve on those whom he authorizes to act on his behalf. And there is a direct line from such reasoning to authoritarian preaching from the pulpit. Yet a closer reading of the passage reveals a far more complex state of affairs.

Although an explanation intervenes to account for rumors that the disciples of Jesus stole his body while the guards slept (Matt 28:11–15), we must assume that "Mary Magdalene and the other Mary" have fulfilled their task. In obedience (reluctant or otherwise) to the instructions that these women convey, the eleven disciples journey north (five days or so by foot, depending on their pace) in anticipation of meeting their Lord. There, true to his word, Jesus appears to them. Like the two women, they worship. But unlike the women, some of them (Matthew is mercifully silent as to which) have their doubts. The key verb here (unique to Matthew)[31] has turned up once before in the account (also unique to this

---

31. The verb διστάζειν does not occur in the Septuagint, although it is central to Plato's discussion of how the gods sometimes inspire fine poetry and music even in

evangelist) of Peter stepping out of the boat in the early morning hours and walking on water:

> Early in the morning [Jesus] came walking toward them on the sea. But when the disciples saw him walking on the sea, they were terrified, saying, "It is a ghost!" And they cried out in fear. But immediately Jesus spoke to them and said, "Take heart, it is I; do not be afraid." Peter answered him, "Lord, if it is you, command me to come to you on the water." He said, "Come." So Peter got out of the boat, started walking on the water, and came toward Jesus. But when he noticed the strong wind, he became frightened, and beginning to sink, he cried out, "Lord, save me!" Jesus immediately reached out his hand and caught him, saying to him, "You of little faith, why did you *doubt* [ἐδίστασας]?" When they got into the boat, the wind ceased. And those in the boat worshipped him, saying, "Truly you are the Son of God." (Matt 14:25-33)

This passage bears more than a passing resemblance to Synoptic accounts of the resurrection yet to come: the disciples think that they are seeing a spirit (cf. Luke 24:37, 39); their first response is holy terror; Jesus answers, "It is I [ἐγώ εἰμι]" (cf. Luke 24:39) and "Do not be afraid" (so Matt 28:10, etc.). Nonetheless, they acclaim him as "Son of God" (like the centurion at the cross), and worship him. In other words, their faith is far from absolute. Much less is it a sufficient qualification for discipleship, even that of Peter. True to form, Peter will subsequently acclaim Jesus as "The Christ, the Son of the living God," only to turn around at once and question both his authority and the wisdom of his plans (Matt 16:16, 22-23). In both earlier and later episodes, acclamation and uncertainty—to the point of doubt and outright fear—go hand in hand. Yet none of this causes Jesus to expel the disciples from his inner circle or, in the case of Peter, to withdraw his gift of "keys" (i.e., authority) or his words of affirmation about building the future church (Matt 16:18-19).

Recalling Matthew's initial use of the same infrequent verb (διστάζειν; to doubt or waver) and the numerous parallels to resurrection in that earlier account invites a more careful reading of Jesus' apparent

---

those of negligible human talent, "to be a sign to us that we should not *waver or doubt* that these fine poems are not human or the work of men, but divine and the work of gods; and that the poets are merely the interpreters of the gods, according as each is possessed by one of the heavenly powers" (*Ion* 534e [trans. Lamb; LCL 164], accessed via Perseus. http.//data.perseus.org/citations/urn:cts:greekLit:tlg0059.tlg027.perseus-grc1:534e).

"authorization" in chapter 28. "All authority... has been given to me," he explains; "Go therefore and make disciples." Whether we direct the force of the conjunction (οὖν) toward the preceding verb ("going, therefore") or the one that follows ("therefore... make disciples"), it is clear that these instructions are a direct consequence of the authority to which the previous sentence refers. Our instinct is to assume that since Jesus has been given authority (by God—another use of the passive voice), that fact authorizes disciples and the church in turn, who act on his behalf and "in his name." But it is equally legitimate to understand Jesus' declaration of authority as the justification for the command itself, rather than as the basis for the disciples' ministry: "Since I have been given authority, heed my command to make disciples." Even allowing that authority devolves upon them by virtue of sending itself (so *m. Ber.* 5:5: "A man's emissary [*shaliaḥ*] is like himself"), nothing in this commissioning is equivalent to, for instance, the language of an ordination service: "Take thou authority to preach the Word of God, and to minister the holy Sacraments, in this Congregation."[32] If the apostles are authorized to teach and make disciples, the authority for doing so rests in and remains with the Messiah himself. This is all the more necessary since not even seeing the risen Christ face to face is sufficient to dispel the doubts of some. Their uncertainty would suggest that Jesus' climactic promise, "Remember, I am with you always, to the end of the age" is not so much an affirmation of their special status as a concession to their inadequacy for the task. Since some, at least, are not quite sure about him anyway, and all of them abandoned him in his moment of need, it is just as well that he remain with them "to the end of the age," for how else will they manage to make disciples, instruct new converts, or establish the church? What else will prevent them from claiming his authority for themselves?

The question of authority is critical to the identity of the church and its preaching of the Christian gospel. Generally speaking, human authority operates by virtue of sanction—sanctioning approved forms of conduct (in the positive sense of the word) while also sanctioning (that is, penalizing) disapproved forms. The "force" of such authority lies in its ability to employ force and—if necessary—coerce obedience or conformity. As Paul explains (to those in Rome!), the state "does not bear the sword in vain! It is the servant of God to execute wrath on the wrongdoer" (Rom 13:4). Even nations that do not impose the ultimate penalty

---

32. Although with spelling modernized, this phrase is from 1550 revision of the First English Prayer Book of Edward VI (1549).

on their own citizens undertake to defend their own interests by threat of war and death against the citizens of other nations. Jesus, by contrast, inaugurates a radically different social and political order:

> "You know that among the Gentiles those whom they recognize as their rulers lord it over them, and their great ones are tyrants over them. But it is not so among you; but whoever wishes to become great among you must be your servant, and whoever wishes to be first among you must be slave of all. For the Son of Man came not to be served but to serve, and to give his life a ransom for many." (Mark 10:42-45)

Rather than accruing power—wielding the power of "life and death" over others—Jesus yields to death and bids his followers do the same. He can only ask this of them in anticipation of resurrection—both his own and theirs—as he establishes a new human order that functions not on the basis of power, fear, coercion, and death, but by appeal to grace and the gift of new life. Their own encounter with this new order is what impels the twenty-four elders in the heavenly throne room to throw down their crowns in symbolic fashion and cry out, "'You are worthy, our Lord and God, to receive glory and honor and *power* . . .'" (Rev 4:11). While there is certainly a place in New Testament theology for "godly" fear ("Fear God; honor the emperor" [1 Pet 2:17]), 1 John articulates the essence of this alternative dynamic: "There is no fear in love, but perfect love casts out fear; for fear has to do with punishment, and whoever fears has not reached perfection in love" (1 John 4:18). Thus whereas the order of death is an order of command, constraint, and control, operating by coercion ("The sting of death is sin, and the power of sin is the law" [1 Cor 15:56]), Jesus frees humanity from the power of condemnation and opens the way for at least the possibility, if not yet the full implementation, of an ethic based on God's gift of new life.[33] His resurrection inaugurates and demonstrates this new order.

Viewed in this manner, the theological character and content of the Christian gospel has profound implications for preaching. Instinctively, preachers want their sermons to persuade, to delight, to convict, and above all to *enact* the message of the gospel: we want our words to prove compelling and to that end employ whatever strategies or methods we find either theologically congenial or operationally effective. More

---

33. This helps to explain how Paul can affirm both that "knowing the fear of the Lord, we try to persuade others" and at the same time that "the love of Christ urges us on, because we are convinced that one has died for all" (2 Cor 5:11, 14).

precisely, our disposition toward power in the pulpit has at least three closely linked dimensions. With respect (first) to our own identity, we desire to be, and to be seen as, capable and effective speakers. Otherwise, why speak in the first place? Particularly when we are unsure whether or not God will show up, relying on our own strength seems a much more reliable manner of proceeding. With respect (second) to our sermons, we therefore make instrumental use of various rhetorical strategies, literary devices, or forms of delivery in a bid to communicate more effectively. Willimon sees rhetorical self-reliance of this sort as a direct failure of faith in Jesus' resurrection:

> That many of us preachers still use essentially secular (i.e., godless) means of persuasion borrowed uncritically from the world is testimony to our failure to believe that God raised Jesus Christ from the dead, thus radically changing everything. In so doing we act as if Jesus were still sealed securely in the tomb, as if he did not come back to us, did not speak, and cannot, will not speak to us today.[34]

Accordingly, third, with respect to the congregation, our whole purpose in preaching is to initiate, encourage, or sustain allegiance to the reign of God, since nothing is more frustrating than a sermon that falls on deaf ears or fails to make any difference to its hearers. Even if the preacher is simply attempting to liberate, enlighten, and empower the congregation, he or she will assume responsibility for such outcomes and employ whatever means are necessary in order to accomplish this goal. It is deeply paradoxical that any form of Christian address—even that which expressly abjures authoritarian speech—should nonetheless operate as an efficacious instrument geared to a specific end. One way or another, we want to preach with power and authority (that is, ἐξουσία).[35] But the embrace of efficacy itself—trying to "do things with words"—belongs in principle to the old order of coercion and death by virtue of the fact that (whatever their goal) our words intend to be agential and we ourselves remain in power as primary agents of change.

Humanly speaking, for Paul to concede the charge of his detractors that he is personally weak, frequently defeated, and a poor speaker (1 Cor 2:3; 2 Cor 10:10; 11:6, 30, etc.) is incomprehensible. Yet he does so because he is convinced—on the basis of Jesus' death and resurrection—that

---

34. Willimon, "Preaching as Demonstration of Resurrection," 14.
35. On the semantic range of this term, see L&N §76.12.

despite the Corinthian's love of traditional rhetoric and its ability to persuade, the "authority" and authenticity of the gospel does not rest with him and, more importantly, does not function like any other form of human agency:

> My speech and my proclamation were not with plausible words of wisdom, but with a demonstration of the Spirit and of power, so that your faith might not rest on human wisdom but on the power of God. Yet among the mature we do speak wisdom, though it is not a wisdom of this age or of the rulers of this age, who are doomed to perish. But we speak God's wisdom, secret and hidden, which God decreed before the ages for our glory. (1 Cor 2:4–7)

It is not that Paul's own preaching, or preaching of the Christian gospel generally, is ultimately powerless or ineffectual; the apostle himself unmistakably insists otherwise (2 Cor 13:3–4). The difference is that the authority—ἐξουσία—of such preaching derives not from the preacher's use of efficacious words (however delightful or insistent these may be), but from God alone: "Our confidence," says the apostle, "is from God, who has made us competent to be ministers of a new covenant, not of letter but of spirit; for the letter kills, but the Spirit gives life" (2 Cor 3:5–6). Preaching that conforms theologically (and therefore methodologically) to the conditions of the Good News does not trade on the power of condemnation and death by insisting on its own validity and commanding assent. Rather, it appeals simply to God's gift of new life, as demonstrated by Jesus' resurrection, inviting God to authenticate words that are faithful and true. This is Paul's defense when disgruntled converts challenge his ministry: "You yourselves are our letter . . . to be known and read by all; you show that you are a letter of Christ, prepared by us, written not with ink but with the Spirit of the living God, not on tablets of stone but on tablets of human hearts" (2 Cor 3:2–3). The proof of his preaching lies in neither its occasional forcefulness nor its apparent futility, but in its powerful consequences, especially among those who have their doubts about his ministry.

Because it is essentially noncoercive, preaching of the gospel must always allow for doubt, whether as concerns the gospel message itself or those who are commissioned to preach it. Not simply out of respect for its hearers, but because in the new order of a new creation that operates by the power of God alone, the preacher does not possess any means of compelling assent.³⁶ In one sense, this is highly ironic, because doubt normally calls into question the very basis for transcending doubt itself. Nonetheless, preaching that conforms to resurrection and the new divine order of which it is the first expression entails the same three dimensions. First, with respect to our own identity, preaching turns attention away from ourselves, even in the very act of speaking: "we do not proclaim ourselves; we proclaim Jesus Christ as Lord and ourselves as . . . slaves for Jesus' sake" (2 Cor 4:5). As noted already, painful awareness of our personal limitations will make it obvious, both to ourselves and to our hearers, "that the transcendent power belongs to God and does not come from us" (2 Cor 4:7). In fact, confidence in divine agency is what makes it possible for the apostle confess that his own theological apprehension and spiritual gifts are equally incomplete ("For we know only in part and we prophesy only in part" [1 Cor 13:9]). Second, with respect to our sermons, we may employ any number of communicative strategies (which are, in any event, integral to human speech), but we will do so in full awareness of their native inability either to bestow or to sustain the gift of new life in Christ. Third, with respect to the congregation, we refuse to claim the rôle of intermediaries, inviting our hearers to respond independently of us so as to be enfolded instead within Jesus' response to God. Thus, if we follow the example of both Jesus and Paul, preaching will always be an exercise in weakness, yielding to divine prerogatives and power rather than attempting to wield power for ourselves. At the same time, it will be marked by hope, mercy, and forgiveness, in the assurance that Christ himself makes "all things new." And it will testify, above all, to the transformative power of grace, which can only be offered and received as an unconstrainable gift.

In a striking reversal of audience expectation, Paul famously asserts that "God chose what is foolish in the world to shame the wise; God chose what is weak in the world to shame the strong; chose what is low and despised in the world, things that are not, to reduce to nothing things that are, that no one might boast in the presence of God" (1 Cor 1:27–29). A comprehensive listing of all that is "foolish," "weak," "low," and "despised" would have to include not only the cross itself (along

---

36. Along the same lines, Gorman ("Preaching and Living the Resurrection Today," 4) points out that whether in Athens at the Areopagus (Acts 17:32) or among the converts in Corinth, there appears to have been widespread skepticism concerning the resurrection of the dead. Yet that same skepticism is what occasions the apostle's most comprehensive apologia for resurrection itself, in 1 Cor 15.

with the one who chose to die there) but also the women whose vital testimony was scorned, the men who knew better than to believe them, the disciples who doubted Christ to his face in Galilee, the former zealot and convert from Tarsus, the message that he preached, and the cantankerous sceptics (whether in Athens, Corinth, or elsewhere) who heard him proclaim it. The same, of course, will be no less true for those who preach today, those who receive the disruptive, counterintuitive message of death and resurrection, and those who reject its "Good News" as either partially or wholly implausible. These are simply the conditions under which proclamation of the Christian gospel invariably takes place. Hence the importance of Jesus' resurrection and the principle of irreplaceable divine validation that resurrection entails. Whether as a matter of historical record or for those who hear of it today, his resurrection affirms that "God's foolishness is wiser than human wisdom and God's weakness is stronger than human strength." Quite independently of its uncertain reception, therefore, the resurrection of Christ reveals him to be both "the power of God and the wisdom of God" (1 Cor 1:24–25). It is this conviction that first gives rise to preaching rather than preaching that first gives rise to such convictions.

Where the present chapter has considered the problem of inadequate, unreliable, or otherwise impotent witnesses in relation to preaching, we now turn to reflect on theodicy and the question of resurrection as the improbable and unexpected reversal of human suffering.

4

Turning Back from Emmaus

> My life is like a faded leaf,
>   My harvest dwindled to a husk;
> Truly my life is void and brief
>   And tedious in the barren dusk;
> My life is like a frozen thing,
>   No bud nor greenness can I see:
> Yet rise it shall—the sap of Spring;
>   O Jesus, rise in me.
>
> —Christina Rossetti (1830–1894), "A Better Resurrection" (1862)[1]

JESUS' CROSS AND RESURRECTION present the preacher with two impossible dilemmas. First, if Jesus truly was God's Son, how could he die? In the world of the early church, this was simply a contradiction in terms: either he died or he was divine, but not both, since mortality and divinity were mutually exclusive categories.[2] For preachers today, the challenge is more subtle and diffuse. Metaphysics aside, if the purpose of Jesus' ministry was to deliver us from suffering and death, what place remains for the cross in Christian discipleship? Because we are both emotionally and culturally disposed toward success and well-being, we find it difficult to accommodate suffering within our vision of God's plan for our lives. Preaching on the subject is particularly awkward, since the very real trials of human existence (even in the affluent West) and gospel-based promises of blessing seem to cancel one another out. This is the second dilemma: because resurrection represents the absolute reversal of human suffering,

---

1. Rossetti, *Goblin Market and Other Poems*, 137–38, lines 9–16.
2. See further discussion in Knowles, *We Preach Not Ourselves*, 86–90.

suffering itself would appear to make resurrection irrelevant in present experience. In particular, preaching about resurrection risks minimizing adversity and (as sometimes happens with funeral sermons) appearing to make light of grief and loss, as though there were no place for it in the life of faith. All these issues come to the fore in post-resurrection accounts from Luke and John.

We begin with the curious question of Sabbath observance in relation to resurrection. Sabbath rest codifies and enforces a theological principle that is basic to the self-understanding of God's people, namely that human life is neither granted nor sustained by human effort alone. By abstaining from all the many activities that life normally demands, they acknowledge that life itself is ultimately the gift of God. However, the women who must wait to anoint Jesus' body for burial find themselves unexpectedly poised between alternative, and oddly competing expressions of this gift.

Worst Sabbath Ever

In its original form, the biblical commandment is both simple and straightforward:

> Remember the Sabbath day, and keep it holy. Six days you shall labor and do all your work. But the seventh day is a Sabbath to the LORD your God; you shall not do any work—you, your son or your daughter, your male or female slave, your livestock, or the alien resident in your towns. (Exod 20:8–10; cf. Exod 23:12; Deut 5:13–14)

Equally absolute is the penalty for transgression: "Six days shall work be done, but the seventh day is a Sabbath of solemn rest, holy to the Lord; whoever does any work on the Sabbath day shall be put to death" (Exod 31:15). In contrast to the simplicity of the general principle, the Mishnah (with voluminous expansion in the Palestinian and Babylonian Talmuds)[3] devotes an entire tractate (*Shabbat*) to discussion of how this

---

3. The names of these texts and the relationship between them can be confusing for non-specialists. The foundational document is the Mishnah, final redaction of which is traditionally attributed to Rabbi Yehudah ha-Nasi ("Judah the Prince"; ca. 135–217 CE); the Tosefta, from about the same period, is a "Supplement" to the Mishnah (which is the meaning of its name). The main body of commentary (or "Gemara") on the Mishnah appears in two forms: the earlier Palestinian Talmud (after 350 CE) and the longer, more definitive Babylonian Talmud (around 500 CE). The Mishnah is divided

commandment applies in particular cases, most famously in specifying 39 categories of generative or creative labor that are forbidden (*m. Šabb.* 7:2). Of course, Sabbath rest and grief rituals are different matters, but the two unavoidably overlap.[4]

Although other teachers will find precedent for a full seven days of mourning in the mention of seven days prior to the Flood (Gen 7:10; so *t. Soṭah* 10:3; *y. Moʾed Qaṭ.* 3:5 [82c]; *b. Sanh.* 108b), as well as in Joseph's manner of grieving the death of Jacob (Gen 50:10), the Talmud of the Land of Israel attributes to a rabbi of the late second century the view that mourning should not be conducted on the day of rest (*y. Ber.* 2:8 [5b]; cf. 3:1 [6a]).[5] Yet according to the Mishnah, care for the deceased takes precedence over Sabbath prohibitions: "They prepare all that is needed for a corpse. They anoint and rinse it, on condition that they not move any limb of the corpse" (*m. Šabb.* 23:5; cf. *t. Šabb.* 17:18-19). But it is difficult to know what stipulations were in force in first-century Jerusalem. What is unmistakable, in any case, is that the women who wish to care for Jesus' body are sufficiently devout that they interpret Sabbath observance with a degree of strictness that prevents them even from visiting Jesus' burial site until the day following—let alone carrying the embalming spices or applying them to the corpse:

> It was the day of Preparation, and the Sabbath was beginning. The women who had come with him from Galilee followed, and they saw the tomb and how his body was laid. Then they returned, and prepared spices and ointments. On the Sabbath they rested according to the commandment. (Luke 23:54-56)

---

by subject area into sixty-three tractates grouped in six divisions, many (but not all) of which are addressed in the other three works. See further Strack and Stemberger, *Introduction to the Talmud and Midrash*, 109-18; 150; 164-68; 191-92.

Because of their later dating, not even the earliest of these compilations can provide direct evidence for interpreting the New Testament. While all four incorporate earlier material, how much earlier is a matter of debate. At best, similarities between New Testament and Mishnaic materials can suggest common trajectories of interpretation and/or continuity of custom and practice within a conservative social context.

4. Carrying spices would amount to bearing a burden and touching a dead body would impart ritual uncleanness, but simply visiting the tomb to grieve (the situation envisaged, for instance, in John 11:31, with Mary weeping for Lazarus) entails neither of these. There remains, however, a concern for uncleanness being imparted indirectly in the presence of the dead, on which see Instone-Brewer, *Feasts and Sabbaths*, 72-73.

5. See further Kraemer, *Meanings of Death*, 87-88.

Mark and Luke include the detail that the three women (Mark 16:1 names them as Mary Magdalene, Mary the mother of James, and Salome) came to the tomb with "spices and ointments" (Luke 23:56) in order to anoint Jesus' body. According to Jewish custom, washing the body and anointing it with aromatic oils are part of a normal preparation for burial (*m. Šabb.* 23:5). As John tells it, this vital task has already been undertaken by Joseph of Arimathea and Nicodemus, whom Pilate entrusts with Jesus' lifeless body (John 19:38–42). John also suggests that Jesus has been anointed, wrapped, and sealed away in haste, on the grounds that all work must cease at sundown when the Sabbath commences (so Luke 23:54). In Mark and Luke, on the other hand, preparation for burial is left to the women instead. Matthew offers a still more minimal account, making no mention either of spices or of anointing.

There is, of course, a certain theological irony in the women's scrupulousness: at least in their view (and whatever one makes of the rabbinic guidelines that later govern such concerns), one may not minister to the deceased on a Sabbath, for to do so might contravene God's covenant. The further irony, however, is that the restraint they demonstrate is death's last small victory. Understanding this rather complex dynamic takes us back to Paul's explanation of sin and Torah. "The sting of death is sin," he says, "and the power of sin is the law" (1 Cor 15:56). Death, as a consequence of sin, exercises its power by spelling out the limits of what is either permissible or punishable in human conduct, according to the contours of God's holy decree. Death, which for the moment holds sway over Jesus, holds sway over the women also by dictating what they can and cannot do on the day that follows his crucifixion. Yet even though they are prevented from visiting his tomb or ministering to his body, they cannot be prevented from grieving, and therefore must do so alone and at a distance from the one they love.

All this is about to change—grief, Sabbath, death, and the power of sin—because when they finally get to the tomb, it will be vacant, its short-term occupant arisen. In the meantime, however, we can only imagine this to have been the most painful Sabbath ever, as the power of prohibition, which is the power of death, has kept the women from returning to care for the one whom death has also claimed. It was love of God—and God's love for them—that first drew them to him, and love of God that now keeps them away. Sabbath, intended as a source of delight and rest (modern Jews speak of "Queen Sabbath") is on this particular day a source of torment, multiplying their sorrow with sanctions of its own. The sign of this inner conflict is the fact that they arrive at the tomb just as dawn is breaking, at the earliest possible moment—one of the few details on which all four Gospels agree. "Very early . . . when the sun had risen," writes Mark (16:2); "As the first day of the week was dawning," according to Matthew 28:1, or "at early dawn" (Luke 24:1). For John, "it was still dark" (20:1). Fleeing the constraints of a commandment that threatens them with death, they must have set out from home in the dark, only to discover, as dawn begins to break, that Jesus himself has been set free from the same constraint.

There is much to be said for envisaging discipleship as an extended experience of waiting for the Sabbath to conclude. In one sense, we are bound by the commandment of God in its condemnation of our sin, at least in the sense that Jesus' crucifixion in our place has validated the sentence against us. To this we have no answer; truly, someone had to die. Yet Jesus is no longer dead: in his vindication lies the promise and prospect of our own. Although Paul can rejoice that for followers of the Messiah, "the night is far gone, the day is at hand," so that "salvation is nearer than when we first believed" (Rom 13:11-12 RSV), stating the matter in these terms concedes the incompleteness of our present experience. While our grief is not that of the two Marys, we nonetheless "groan inwardly while we wait for adoption, the redemption of our bodies" (Rom 8:23).

Preaching, likewise, must come to terms with sin, death, religious discipline, and the promise of new life—not simply as fitting topics for the Sunday sermon, but in terms of the principles that they imply for the manner and conduct of preaching itself. If, that is, Christian preaching proceeds on the theological basis of Jesus having been raised from death, it can only do so in a matter appropriate to resurrection itself. It will depend for its power and authority not on the prospect or threat of death as the just consequence of disobedience to God's covenant, but by appeal to God's gift of new life. Exploring the manner in which this is so will require us to pursue a lengthy route through various resurrection appearances in Luke 24 and elsewhere, beginning on the road that leads from Jerusalem to Emmaus and back again.

Their Eyes Were Kept from Recognizing Him

> Now on that same day two of them were going to a village called Emmaus, about seven miles from Jerusalem, and talking with

> each other about all these things that had happened. While they were talking and discussing, Jesus himself came near and went with them, but their eyes were kept from recognizing him. (Luke 24:13–16)

Apprehension and uncertainty are consistent features in all four Gospel accounts of the resurrection and its aftermath. Luke's account of two disciples (one, strangely, never named) on the road both to and from Emmaus pivots ultimately on a recognition scene reminiscent of eucharistic celebration, and as such might seem an unlikely source of homiletical theory. But for praxis that looks to the power of God, wrestling as it does so with anxiety, doubt, and the unavoidable reality of human suffering, it has much to offer, especially concerning the ways of the risen Christ.

While the two disciples are leaving Jerusalem, headed away from the place of disappointment and defeat, Jesus comes to them as an inquisitive stranger. Not only does he intrude on their company and their sorrow, he insists on interrogating them about it as well. At least to this point, the defeat of their hope has been a matter for internal discussion only, an awkward subject because despite their earlier faith, hope, and love for him, they appear to have been proven wrong. Those who refused to believe in him and all who fell away before it was too late seem to have been vindicated. So the reason for their long faces is not a topic to be shared with a random stranger who is unlikely to be sympathetic. They are ashamed.

Without reducing the gesture to mere symbolism, it nonetheless seems fitting that they stop: "They stood still, looking sad" (Luke 24:17). They have been called to account for the hope that is no longer in them. Because they must speak publicly, their flight from disillusionment cannot proceed as planned: they are frozen between what has already happened and an uncertain future. Strangely, the one thing they get half right is that they fail to see their uninvited companion for who he is: "Their eyes were kept from recognizing him" (24:16). They see him only as a stranger, a visitor to Jerusalem, one who does not know and cannot understand the way things are because he is not from around here. And that is certainly the case: the Son of God is not from around here. All the more so now that he has defeated death, Jesus is truly a stranger: he is other, foreign, different, and no longer subject to the lethal tyranny of a dysfunctional creation. No wonder they do not recognize him, for he is risen. Paul captures this perspective exactly: "Even though we once knew

Christ according to the flesh (κατὰ σάρκα), now we no longer know him that way" (2 Cor 5:16).

Equally blunt in response, Cleopas verges on rudeness: "Are you the only visitor to Jerusalem who does not know the things that have happened there in these days?" (Luke 24:18). Jesus' answer, however brief, is no less momentous than any of his other post-resurrection sayings. "What things?" he responds, no more than a single word in Greek (24:19). This is like God, walking in the garden in the cool of the evening breeze and calling out—as if God were somehow both ignorant and blind—"Adam, where are you?" (Gen 3:9). The question is not what it seems, for it is about Adam's knowledge, not God's. "Adam, do you know where you are? I know, but do you? Do you know that hiding is futile? Do you see where disobedience has led you both?" Just so, Jesus' question is, from a certain perspective, absurd. He does not need to be reminded of where betrayal and abandonment have led; of his own suffering and death. Or of the infidelity and failure of his disciples, perhaps even the two now standing before him. But *they* have to be reminded. It is a forced review of events that have crushed all hope of deliverance and vindication: "What things?"

Their recital is a model of evasion. "Our chief priests and rulers delivered him up to be condemned to death, and crucified him." Of course this is not quite accurate, by Luke's own account. Technically, it was Pilate who pronounced the sentence of death, then delivered Jesus to his cross (Luke 23:24). Crucifixion—both the decree and its execution—lay solely within the jurisdiction of Rome (cf. John 18:31). But the sad companions' account is more theological than narrowly historical: they are looking for someone else to blame. In their own eyes, they are liable only for being gullible, too hopeful, too easily misled: "We had hoped that he was the one to redeem Israel" (24:21). They fail (not surprisingly) to mention the passivity of the onlookers (23:35) and the wholesale flight of Jesus' closest friends. Even in reporting the testimony of the women, the two disciples choose their words with care: "Some women of our company amazed us, left us astonished" (24:22). Which, of course, is not quite how it happened either. As we have seen, when the women reported their terrifying vision of two messengers in dazzling apparel, the men dismissed their words as "nonsense," silliness, fluff, the kind of thing one would expect women to say: "and they did not believe them" (24:11).[6] The ex-disciples

---

6. A cultural conviction as to the ostensible unreliability of women—in this case, old women—is encoded lexically in the adjective γραώδης (derived from γραῦς, "old

on the road to Emmaus are simply doing what we always do: telling matters in such a way as to present themselves in the best possible light. A disappointing outcome is best explained as someone else's fault. Buttrick calls it "a confession of past-tense faith now shattered."[7]

Wrapped in excuses, their response is nonetheless painfully accurate. Testimony to the resurrection will always sound like an old wives' tale—the foolishness of those who are simply not smart enough to know better—because we are too interested in making ourselves look good and too committed to a world that continues uninterrupted in all the ways we have come to expect. Death and suffering are lamentable, but at least they are predictable. So Jesus rebukes them: "How foolish [ἀνόητοι] you are, and how slow of heart to believe all that the prophets have spoken!" (Luke 24:25). It is an extraordinarily rude comment for a stranger to make, but Jesus is no ordinary stranger. What seems striking is that he does not chide them either for failing to recognize him (that comes later, in the company of the Eleven: "Why are you frightened, and why do doubts arise in your hearts?" [24:38]) or for failing to heed the assurance that death would not hold him ("The Son of man must . . . be killed, and on the third day be raised" [9:22]). Rather, Luke's choice of vocabulary is again precise. As with Paul's sense of obligation "both to the wise and to the foolish" (Rom 1:4) or, in particular, his rebuke of "foolish" Galatians (Gal 3:1, 3), this word does not imply mental incapacity, but quite the opposite: that having the capacity to understand, they simply refuse to accept an uncomfortable truth.[8] It is hardly a flattering adjective. In Proverbs, it is the opposite of wisdom (Prov 17:28: "Even *fools* who keep silent are considered wise"); in the New Testament, it describes the folly of the godless and immoral, the essence of all that converts have ostensibly left behind: "For we ourselves were once *foolish*, disobedient, led astray, slaves to various passions and pleasures" (Titus 3:3). The implication is that from Jesus' perspective, far from being irrational or an intellectual embarrassment, his resurrection should be fully comprehensible in light of Scripture, to say nothing of God, all that he has taught, and who his followers have believed him to be. This is equally the sense of his second insult: he calls them "slow of heart." While in classical Greek the adjective

---

woman"), which means "characteristic of old women—'like old women say, like old women do'" (L&N §9.38). This term occurs only once in the NT, at 1 Tim 4:7: "keep away from godless myths such as old women are likely to tell."

7. Buttrick, "Easter Preaching," 59.

8. So L&N §32.50; more fully, Behm and Würthwein, s.v. ἀνόητος, *TDNT* 4:961–62.

βραδύς can mean either "slow" or "tardy," it also indicates mental sluggishness, applied in particular to the illiterate (LSJ, s.v.). But its use here is even more precise, since in Jewish thought the "heart" is the seat both of deliberation ("You shall love the Lord your God with all your heart" [Matt 22:37]) and of volition ("by your hard and impenitent heart you are storing up wrath for yourself" [Rom 2:5]).[9] The implication is that they are not only "slow on the uptake," as we would say, but deliberately reluctant as well.

Having pinpointed the source of their disbelief, Jesus now addresses them in terms they will recognize, appealing to the accepted authority of the sacred text: "beginning with Moses and all the prophets, he interpreted to them the things about himself in all the Scriptures" (Luke 24:27). It may be that Cleopas and his companion were not, in fact, close followers during Jesus' lifetime; possibly they were not even aware of the Passion predictions. Perhaps the Twelve had known better than to divulge what they themselves did not fully grasp. But Jesus expects his hearers to acknowledge the meaning of the text as he now expounds it "concerning himself." Still, the larger premise should not be overlooked. From a certain perspective, Jesus intends only to explain a particular scriptural expectation concerning a particular historical experience—his own. But the scope of this account ("things about himself in all the Scriptures") hints at a broader principle. The claim of scriptural inspiration is axiomatic within the world of Jewish thought and, notwithstanding certain demurrals regarding the cessation of prophecy, Jewish scribes were viewed as guardians of the prophetic tradition and experts in authoritative exegesis.[10] That is, they understood the biblical text and, more to the point, did *not* understand it as referring to or being fulfilled by Jesus of Nazareth. Nor, evidently, has Jesus himself previously offered such an interpretation of "*all* the Scriptures." Only now that he has completed his messianic ministry does he expound the biblical text with reference to himself.[11] If we follow the logic of this account, the proper meaning of the sacred text therefore emerges 1) only after God has raised Jesus from

---

9. So L&N §26.3; further, Baumgärtel and Behm, s.v. καρδία §A, D, *TDNT* 3:605–7; 611–13.

10. On the equivocal claims regarding cessation of prophecy in Second Temple and subsequent Judaism, see Aune, *Prophecy in Early Christianity*, 103–6.

11. So Longenecker, "The Messianic Secret in the Light of Recent Discoveries," 213: "From the strictly theological point of view no man can be defined as a messiah before he has accomplished the task of the anointed."

death and 2) only as Jesus himself expounds its sense. Counterintuitive as this may seem in the world of our day, such convictions are basic to the New Testament reading of Hebrew Scripture and to its use of fulfilment citations in particular, as was equally the case for the messianic community at Qumran.[12] Indeed, what Luke here describes in principle, Matthew provides in practice, adducing scriptural citations at key moments in the biography of Jesus in such a way as to correlate details of the sacred text with the life of the Messiah.[13] Luke's narrative and Matthew's exegesis both indicate that from the resurrection onward, Christian exegesis is in principle unavoidably messianic. From their perspective, Jesus' resurrection demands as much.

For the travelers on the road to Emmaus, this premise has unanticipated implications. As his explanation unfolds, Jesus expects them to recognize that suffering is unavoidable, even for the Messiah: "Was it not *necessary* that the Christ should suffer these things and enter into his glory?" (Luke 24:26). Here we encounter the *crux* of the matter; the cross. If God is to intervene in human affairs—so the argument goes—it must mean power, triumph, and the crushing of evil. In particular, divine intervention must entail the defeat of death, "the last enemy," for the domain of death and the reign of life, whose source is God, must be mutually exclusive. Here we are close to the first century Greco-Roman distinction between non-overlapping domains of mortality and divinity. This is the expectation of Palm Sunday, as adoring and exultant onlookers cry out, "Blessed is the one who comes in the name of the Lord! Blessed is the coming kingdom of our ancestor David!" (Mark 11:9–10). As they see it, God's chosen champion is about to take back his throne by force. Stated more simply, in the language that Jesus himself employs, "suffering" and "glory" do not overlap. Just so, we ourselves cling to life, desperate for deliverance from the power of death.

But only in our own view κατὰ σάρκα must God have no truck with death. Jesus boldly asserts the opposite: not only is death the route to glory, and not only is it so even for the Messiah, but it is necessarily so. It is God's intended way, and—according to his altogether alarming interpretation of the text—that intention has been evident in Scripture all

---

12. See Knowles, *Jeremiah in Matthew's Gospel*, 20–27.

13. Colin Hickling observes ("The Emmaus Story and its Sequel," in Barton and Stanton, ed., *Resurrection*, 25–26) that the preaching of Peter (Acts 2:14–36; 3:22–26; 4:11; 10:43) and Paul (Acts 13:32–41) in Acts operates on the same principle, explicating the biblical text with reference to Jesus.

along. Whether post-Enlightenment readers are disposed to see Hebrew Scripture quite so is beside the point, because Jesus is not here concerned to address post-Enlightenment reading strategies. He is appealing to and applying a thoroughly Jewish, Second Temple approach to the text. "Turn it over and over, for everything is in it," says the delightfully named Ben Bag Bag (apparently a convert to Judaism from the first century CE; *m. 'Abot* 5:25). According to Jesus, the text conveys necessity, and the necessity of suffering in particular, even for the Messiah, as the one and only way for him to enter into his rightful glory. More trenchantly: in his view, only willful foolishness and hardness of heart prevents us from seeing that this is indeed the testimony of Scripture and the outcome that God has intended ever since humanity went astray in Eden.

Against all expectation, Jesus concurs with the inevitability of death by submitting to it, and in submitting to it rises above it. No doubt what we hate about this manner of proceeding is that it seals the inevitability of our own suffering and death, when the one thing we desire most from God is to be delivered from such things. But if the Messiah must suffer, and "the servant is not above the Master" (John 15:20), then we know what our own fate will be. Not, of course, that we are likely to take such news lying down: what good is God anyway, we ask, or the Son of God, if all he does is lead us down the very path that we have been seeking to avoid all along?

Recognition

Two of the most famous scenes in all of ancient Greek literature hinge on recognition of one's Master or "Lord" by way of healed scars. The first and oldest of these is from Homer's *Odyssey*, which enjoyed near-scriptural status in the Hellenistic world.[14] Composed on the basis of oral tradition around the eighth century BCE, it tells the story of King Odysseus' arduous journey home from the Trojan War (the subject of Homer's other, equally famous work, the *Iliad*). Arriving in Ithaca after a ten-year journey and an absence of some two decades, he finds his putative (and still faithful) widow, Penelope, being pursued by a host of eager suitors. Partly in order to gain enough time to plot revenge, Odysseus initially keeps

---

14. "By the time the New Testament was written, familiarity with Homer was taken for granted by authors and readers in the Greco-Roman world"; so Taylor, "Recognition Scenes in the Odyssey and the Gospels," 248 (citing debate on the extent of evidence for such awareness on the part of NT authors).

his identity hidden, pretending to be a wandering beggar. But his plan begins to unravel when Penelope assigns Euryclea, his former wet-nurse and now an old woman, the task of washing the wanderer's feet. Odysseus seems to have survived ten years of warfare and ten more of an adventurous homecoming largely unscathed, but above one knee is a visible scar where he had been gashed by a boar while hunting on Mount Parnassus, many years prior:

> ...the old woman took up a glittering basin
> which she used in foot washing and poured in plenty of water,
> cold to begin, then added hot to it. Meanwhile Odysseus
> stayed in his seat by the hearth; then quickly he turned to the darkness,
> for in his heart he suddenly thought that as soon as she touched him,
> she would discover his scar and the facts of the case would be open.
> Coming up close, she was washing her master and quickly discovered
> that very scar which a boar inflicted on him with its white tusk...[15]

A long explanation of the original injury ensues, but eventually we learn the old nursemaid's response:

> Pleasure and sorrow at once laid hold of her mind, so that both eyes
> filled with the tears she shed; and her vigorous voice became silent.
> Taking his beard in her hand, she spoke these words to Odysseus:
> "Certainly, dear child, you are Odysseus; but not even I could
> recognize you before every part of my lord I had handled."
> (Book 19, lines 471–75)

Although Euryclea tries to communicate her discovery to Penelope, a combination of threats from Odysseus and intervention by the goddess Athena prevents this from happening. Four books later, once the returning king has slaughtered those who sought to sway his wife's fidelity, Euryclea herself tells Penelope of the scar (Book 23, lines 73–77), just as Odysseus himself reveals the scar when his aged father, Laertes, asks him for a "sign" (Book 24, lines 327–35).

After Homer's *Odyssey* and *Iliad*, the next most famous work of Greek literature today is undoubtedly *Oedipus the King* by Sophocles of Athens (ca. 496–406 BCE), due in part to Freud's ambitious identification of its plot line as characteristic of identity development in children. Freud aside, the story revolves around another king, this one in search of his true identity and lineage. To his horror, King Oedipus discovers that as an

---

15. Homer, *Odyssey*, 339–40 (Book 19, lines 386–93). Subsequent references to this edition are included in the body of the text.

infant he had been left for dead on account of an oracle that he would one day slay his father and bed his mother. By the time we meet him in the play, however, both deeds are already done, and all that remains is for Oedipus to discover how firmly he is held in the grip of the gods: everyone's efforts to spare him such a terrible fate—his own included—have only succeeded in fulfilling it. This plot, too, hinges on recognition of a scar: the aged messenger who carries news of Oedipus's father, Laius, having been murdered in an ancient version of road rage turns out to be the shepherd who rescued Oedipus as an infant and subsequently gave him up for adoption. For as long as he can recall, Oedipus has had scarred ankles; the messenger reveals this painful disfigurement to have been the work of Oedipus's own father, who pierced and bound the baby's feet to render him immobile in the wilderness:

> Oedipus: A herdsman, were you? A vagabond, scraping for wages?
> Messenger: Your saviour [σωτήρ] too, my son, in your worst hour.
> Oedipus: Oh—
> When you picked me up, was I in pain? What exactly?
> Messenger: Your ankles . . . they tell the story. Look at them.
> Oedipus: Why remind me of that, that old affliction?
> Messenger: Your ankles were pinned together. I set you free.[16]

Aristotle mentions both scenes (along with several others) in order to highlight the importance and widespread use of recognition as a literary device in ancient Greek drama (*Poetics* 1452a–b; 1454b–55a).[17] New Testament scholars, in turn, have begun to explore similarities between this larger set of traditions and the way in which the evangelists recount post-resurrection meetings between Jesus and his disciples. But their respective purposes seem to be different. While both literatures concern the involvement of God or the gods in human affairs, and both are interested in questions of perception, hidden identity, and the difference between appearance and reality, we have already seen that a more central consideration in the resurrection accounts is that of suffering. In a world for which God (or the gods) cannot, by definition, possibly suffer, Jesus' scars are more than simply tokens of his true identity. Recognition of his healed wounds amounts to acknowledgment that the Son of God has

---

16. "Oedipus the King," lines 1028–33, in Sophocles, *Three Theban Plays*, 219–20.

17. See further Larsen, *Recognizing the Stranger*, 25–72, to which the present discussion is indebted.

indeed suffered, even to the point of death, but that his unexpected suffering has been dramatically reversed.

As the two disciples make their way toward Emmaus, according to Taylor, "recognition" unfolds "in two stages: an increase of understanding as the Scriptures are explained on the road, then full and personal recognition at the table."[18] But recognizing that Luke may have crafted his account in light of ancient literary conventions (however indirect their influence) suggests at least a three stage process: the first literary, the second liturgical, and the third by way of personal signs or tokens. The first, as we have seen, entails messianic exegesis: "he interpreted to them all the things about himself in all the Scriptures" (Luke 24:27). The second comes at the insistence of the disciples, who (in keeping with Middle Eastern custom) press hospitality upon their guest while he politely declines. It is not difficult to see here a reference to the Lord's Supper: "when he was at table with them, he took bread, blessed and broke it, and gave it to them. Then their eyes were opened, and they recognized him" (24:30–31). Even more clearly in translation than in the original Greek,[19] the wording of this passage is closely similar to that of ten days prior: "Then he took a loaf of bread, and when he had given thanks, he broke it and gave it to them, saying, 'This is my body, which is given for you'" (Luke 22:19). Preachers from more liturgically oriented traditions might deduce from this passage that recognizing what Scripture has to say about Jesus—even should Jesus himself be the teacher—requires participation in the sacrament, at which Christ himself presides. As Taylor rightly observes, "There is a moment of recognition for the reader too, for we realize that this is the first Christian communion service, the first re-enactment of the Lord's Supper."[20] Pentecostals and Pietists, on the other hand, are more likely to emphasize the need for direct revelation: unless God opens the eyes of the hearers, they will not understand what is being said—even should Jesus himself expound the sacred text.

---

18. Taylor, "Recognition Scenes in the Odyssey and the Gospels," 256.

19. While it is possible (indeed likely) that Luke has intentionally coordinated the language of the two passages, one difference stands out: the account of the Lord's Supper employs the verb εὐχαριστέω, "to give thanks" with reference to the bread (21:19), where for the meal at Emmaus, Luke uses εὐλογέω, meaning "to bless" or "praise" (24:30). Where Mark 14:22–23 and Matt 26:26–27 employ both verbs (one for the bread and the other for the cup), Luke's use of εὐχαριστέω alone (as in 1 Cor 11:24) is usually cited as evidence of a distinct tradition. In any event, both are translation variants of the Hebrew/Aramaic verb *barakh*.

20. Taylor, "Recognition Scenes in the Odyssey and the Gospels," 256.

Might there also be a more universal principle at play, one that is incumbent upon all traditions and schools of interpretation? For all the similarities of language in this later episode, a key command from the Upper Room is missing: "Do this in remembrance of me." Whereas later disciples will make obedience to this command a centerpiece of the church's identity, here, in the first such meal following his resurrection, Jesus himself initiates their table fellowship (as is also the case in Luke 24:41–43 and John 21:13). Cleopas and his companion have been headed in the opposite direction, away from Jerusalem, in an effort to put aside the brutal crushing of their hopes. In order, that is, to prevent remembrance both of his suffering and of their own, if only by putting distance between themselves and the site of their misunderstanding. By making himself known to them in this fashion, Jesus challenges them to return (with all that returning implies). His initiative implies that full recognition of the risen Christ (with or without strangely warmed and burning hearts) comes only in conjunction with remembrance of his death.

The third stage of recognition in Luke's Gospel is perhaps closest of all (in formal terms) to Hellenistic literary convention, since Christ now invites the disciples to handle his scars directly. But the evangelist again introduces distinct features. If one characteristic of the resurrection appearances is doubt, holy terror is even more frequent. This might be one reason why we have so little experience of resurrection in our own lives: the risen Christ is so radically "other"—so very unearthly—that we will substitute almost anything else in his place, so long as doing so leaves us a modicum of safety and control. Luke, never at a loss for vocabulary, uses a range of different terms to describe the disciples' response: they are "startled [πτοηθέντες] and terrified [ἔμφοβοι]" (24:37); "frightened [τεταραγμένοι]" (24:38); "disbelieving [ἀπιστούντων] and ... wondering [θαυμαζόντων]" (24:41). To get a sense of what the evangelist intends, it helps to review similar vocabulary elsewhere in the New Testament. To be "startled" or "alarmed" is the proper response to hearing of war and insurrection as history draws to an end, when social order descends into chaos and violence (as in Jesus' description of the last days from Luke 21:9). One is rightly "terrified" by the glory of angels (Luke 24:5; Acts 10:4), by the prospect of final judgement (Acts 24:25), and all the more so by the calamities that appear to presage it (Rev 11:13). Jesus' description of the disciples in Luke 24:38 as being "frightened" or (more precisely) "troubled" is the same language that John uses to describe Jesus' own response to the prospect of betrayal by one of his disciples (John 13:21), or that Luke later employs for pious outrage sufficient to incite rioting (Acts 17:13). Doubt and disbelief, of course, are the order of the day in the aftermath of resurrection; "wondering" or "marveling" is the way Luke himself (in Stephen's fateful last sermon) describes Moses's response to the burning bush (Acts 7:31). But the language in Luke 24:38 ("Why are you frightened and why do doubts [διαλογισμοί] arise in your hearts?") "suggests sharp controversy."[21] Indeed, beginning with 2:35 ("This child is destined to cause the falling and rising of many in Israel, and to be a sign that will be spoken against, so that the *thoughts* of many hearts will be revealed" [NIV]), Luke's use of this term consistently indicates "evil, critical, or antagonistic thoughts."[22]

Of course, particular words may convey somewhat different meanings in different contexts, but we nonetheless get a sense that Luke is pulling out all the stops in his desire to describe the disciples' uncontrollable fear and perplexity. This feature sets the New Testament resurrection accounts apart from Hellenistic literature. For what concerns the evangelists is not recognition of a homecoming hero or tragic protagonist whose unveiling will bring the tangled narrative to a tidy resolution, but the acknowledgment of one whose identity upsets and transcends all human plot lines. Notwithstanding similarities to other contemporary literature, this is "recognition" like no other.

In some ancient manuscripts, Jesus greets the terrified disciples with the words, "Peace be with you";[23] that the status of this phrase is less than fully certain seems fitting given the fact that they are not sure of him either, and are very far indeed from being at peace. In their accounts of the crucifixion, none of the evangelists make mention of Jesus' wrists or feet having been pierced. Yet here as elsewhere, this detail is key to recognizing his true identity: "See my hands and my feet; that it is I myself. *Handle* [ψηλαφήσατε] me and see" (Luke 24:39 RSV). This particular verb appears only one other time in Luke's two volume work—in Paul's famous missionary sermon at the Areopagus of ancient Athens:

---

21. Hickling, "The Emmaus Story and its Sequel," in Barton and Stanton, ed., *Resurrection*, 22; cf. Schrenk, s.v. διαλογισμός §B.1, *TDNT* 2:97: "In view of the more flexible LXX usage, it is striking that the NT uses διαλογισμός only in the negative sense for evil thoughts or anxious reflection."

22. Fitzmyer, *Gospel according to Luke I-IX*, 430, citing Luke 5:22; 6:8; 9:46–47; and 24:38.

23. See Metzger, *Textual Commentary on the Greek New Testament*, 160.

> God who made the world and everything in it, he who is Lord of heaven and earth, does not live in shrines made by human hands, nor is he served by human hands, as though he needed anything, since he himself gives to all mortals life and breath and all things. From one ancestor he made all nations to inhabit the whole earth, and he allotted the times of their existence and the boundaries of the places where they would live, so that they would search for God and perhaps *grope* for him and find him ... (Acts 17:24–27)

Returning for a moment to the adventures of Odysseus, this is the term that Homer uses to describe the man-eating monster Polyphemus (a "Cyclops") fumbling about in darkness after Odysseus and his companions have blinded him with a glowing stake (*Odyssey* Book 9, line 416). The Septuagint employs the same verb to describe a blind and aged Isaac grasping at the hands of Jacob as his younger son pretends to be Esau (LXX Gen 27:12, 22).[24] In Luke's Gospel, however, it is the panicked disciples who have difficulty seeing the one who reveals himself before them. Handling his scars—the unmistakable tokens of his crucifixion—will prove his identity. To be clear: resolution of their terror and doubt comes only in the assurance—or "recognition"—that Jesus has triumphed over the worst of human suffering.

This same dynamic is central to John's well-known account of "Doubting Thomas," the disbelieving Twin:

> The other disciples told him, "We have seen the Lord." But he said to them, "Unless I see the mark of the nails in his hands, and put my finger in the mark of the nails and my hand in his side, I will not believe." A week later his disciples were again in the house, and Thomas was with them. Although the doors were shut, Jesus came and stood among them and said, "Peace be with you." Then he said to Thomas, "Put your finger here and see my hands. Reach out your hand and put it in my side. Do not doubt but believe." (John 20:25–27)

As John tells it, hearing alone is not enough; neither is seeing (even without the obstacle of divinely inspired obtuseness, which was Luke's initial

---

24. The relevant entries in LSJ indicate that the verb ψηλαφάω ranges in meaning from "touch" or "handle" (as in Luke 24:39; Heb 12:18; and 1 John 1:1) to "grope," "fumble" (LXX Deut 28:29; Judg 16:26 [the blinded Samson]; Isa 59:10; Acts 17:27), or "test" (although not with this sense in the canon of Scripture). Without implying that all of these senses apply in every context, Luke's use of this verb nonetheless suggests a sense of ignorant fumbling.

explanation). Whatever the evidence of his other senses, here too Jesus invites Thomas to touch him. We might easily imagine Thomas to be the author of 1 John, with its testimony to "what we have heard, what we have seen with our eyes, what we have looked at and touched with our hands" (1 John 1:1). John the Evangelist made much of the soldiers piercing Jesus' side with a spear, in fulfilment of Scripture (John 19:34–37; cf. Zech 12:10). But this detail only serves to highlight the reference in John 20:27 to Jesus' *hands*, of which, as in Luke, there has been no previous mention.

Elizabeth Goodman speaks of the "annual shaming of Thomas," one whose ostensibly inexcusable doubt is held up to public scrutiny in contrast—as if!—to our own obedient belief.[25] She proposes, instead, that his uncertainty is only to be expected, for Thomas sees no evidence to persuade him otherwise. Stan Harstine goes further. Juxtaposing nine recognition scenes in John's Gospel with those of Odysseus's homecoming and reviewing the use of similar language to describe Odysseus's wife Penelope (as well as from elsewhere in Hellenistic literature), he proposes that Jesus' challenge to Thomas, "Do not be ἄπιστος but πιστός" (John 20:27) would for first-century hearers "not have been related to religious faith but to personal loyalty and/or trustworthiness."[26] Far from lacking faith, he argues, "it is probable that Thomas's presentation in the Fourth Gospel would be understood by a first-century reader as that of a loyal and faithful servant, a servant who is waiting for a sign of recognition that only his true master can provide."[27] Thomas needs, and waits, to be shown the truth of resurrection, for which he must see the once-wounded Lord with his own eyes.

Incidentally, this episode does not speak well of the apostles' esteem for each other. They evidently know one another to be self-interested cowards who haven't the courage to stand up publicly for what—and who—they say they believe. Knowing that none of Jesus' inner circle (one of whom has already committed suicide) are to be trusted with the Truth—himself included—Thomas may have little reason for believing this latest news to be anything more than a self-exculpatory fantasy. Neither does Goodman think of Thomas as doubting that his fellow disciples have seen Jesus, whether in a vision or otherwise. Clearly they all accept the reality of supernatural apparitions, having mistaken Jesus for a ghost

---

25. Goodman, "Preaching the Easter Texts," 4.
26. Harstine, "Un-Doubting Thomas," 439–46; here, 444.
27. Harstine, "Un-Doubting Thomas," 447.

at least once before (Mark 6:49; Matt 14:26). It seems more likely, then, that Thomas is simply a pragmatist: "Unless I see the nail marks" implies that he has been around too long to think that suffering is so easily reversed. "What I hear," writes Goodman, "isn't that Thomas demanded proof of the Resurrection, but that he needed proof of the Crucifixion. I don't think Thomas doubted the Resurrection; I think he doubted the Resurrection of one crucified."[28] Anyone can have a vision ("You may be an undigested bit of beef, a blot of mustard, a crumb of cheese, a fragment of an underdone potato," says Scrooge to the ghost of Jacob Marley),[29] but hallucinations, however entertaining, cannot resolve suffering, much less death. This, surely, is the theological crux of resurrection: that it cannot be divorced from the suffering that it redeems. Even resurrected, Jesus is still scarred. It is, surely, the recognition that Jesus has survived horrific suffering that causes Thomas to cry out, "'My Lord and my God!'" (John 20:28). Just as with the disciples in Luke 24, John makes no mention of Thomas having actually touched Jesus, as he is invited to do.[30] Simply seeing the healed scars is evidently sufficient to convince him.

Still, it is vital that we not over-simplify the situation: although Jesus' wounds have been healed, they have not been erased.[31] Scars are evidence that although the wounding is past, its impact is still visibly present: the experience of suffering is now integral to Jesus' identity, even—perhaps especially—in resurrection. He will carry the marks of his wounding into the very presence of God. Just so, John of the Apocalypse sees in his vision a lamb that has been "slaughtered" standing beside the throne of God (Rev 5:6). No less importantly, Thomas himself has yet to be healed: whatever wounds he may bear, they will certainly end in death. Handling Jesus' scars orients him back to the reality of suffering and forward to the promise of healing: touching and being touched, Master and disciple stand poised between the two.

---

28. Goodman, "Preaching the Easter Texts," 5.

29. Dickens, *A Christmas Carol*, 27.

30. So Beasley-Murray, *Preaching the Gospel from the Gospels*, 79. These two accounts are all the more arresting in that the interaction they report seems the exact opposite of what Mary Magdalene experiences in her own encounter with the "gardener" just a few verses earlier in John's Gospel: "Jesus said to her, 'Do not hold on to me, because I have not yet ascended to the Father'" (John 20:17).

31. Although my own study does not engage with her analysis in any greater detail, I owe this important insight to Rambo, *Resurrecting Wounds*.

If there is a fourth stage in the process of "recognition" (at least in Luke), it is a repetition for the benefit of "the eleven and their companions" of Jesus' earlier explanation on the road to Emmaus:

> Then he said to them, "These are my words that I spoke to you while I was still with you—that everything written about me in the law of Moses, the prophets, and the psalms must be fulfilled." Then he opened their minds to understand the Scriptures, and he said to them, "Thus it is written, that the Messiah is to suffer and to rise from the dead on the third day, and that repentance and forgiveness of sins is to be proclaimed in his name to all nations, beginning from Jerusalem. You are witnesses of these things." (Luke 24:44–48)

Here, Luke includes a critical term that was also central to the earlier accounts. When Jesus blesses bread in their home and gives it to the two travelers, "their eyes were opened [διηνοίχθησαν], and they recognized him . . . They said to each other, 'Were not our hearts burning within us . . . while he was opening [διήνοιγεν] the Scriptures to us?" (24:31–32). As so often elsewhere, Luke's use of the passive voice implies divine agency. In addition, Fitzmyer draws attention to identical language in LXX 4 Kgdms (i.e., 2 Kings) 6:17, where Elijah prays that God would open the eyes of his servant, who is terrified at the sight of the armies of the King of Aram: "the Lord opened his eyes, and he saw, and behold, the mountain was full of horses, and there was a chariot of fire all around [Elijah]" (NETS).[32] Similarly, in Luke 24:45, recognition of his messianic identity comes directly from the Messiah himself: "he opened [διήνοιξεν] their minds to understand the Scriptures."

Thus while it might seem simpler to situate biblical exposition, dogmatics, or christological apologetics under the category of Lukan pneumatology, the evangelist himself accords Christ a more prominent epistemological rôle. Without reducing the post-resurrection appearances (whether in this Gospel or elsewhere) to mere doctrinal tableaux, the details of this presentation suggest Christ's own active involvement in revelation of the Christian gospel. On the one hand, that the disciples' failure to comprehend is sometimes reported in the passive voice makes it seem not entirely their own fault. When Jesus first announces his imminent betrayal, "its meaning was concealed from them, so that they could not perceive it" (Luke 9:45); a more detailed explanation of this

---

32. Fitzmyer, *Luke X–XXIV*, 1568.

prospect meets with the same response: "they understood nothing about all these things; in fact, what he said was hidden from them, and they did not grasp what he said" (18:34). Just so, when the companions encounter Jesus on the road to Emmaus, "their eyes were kept from recognizing him" (24:16). But the opposite seems not less true, as in the case of Lydia at Thyatira ("The Lord opened her heart to listen eagerly to what was said by Paul"; Acts 16:14) and, more particularly, the words of the one who knocks Paul to the ground on the road to Damascus: "I am Jesus whom you are persecuting . . . I will rescue you from your people and from the Gentiles—to whom I am sending you to *open their eyes* so that they may turn from darkness to light and from the power of Satan to God" (Acts 26:15, 17–18). Elsewhere in Acts, Luke depicts Paul and the apostles preaching in a manner that directly echoes the content and theology of Jesus' exposition in Luke 24, as for example at the synagogue in Thessalonica: "Paul went in, as was his custom, and on three sabbath days argued with them from the Scriptures, explaining [διανοίγων, 'opening'] and proving that it was necessary for the Messiah to suffer and to rise from the dead, and saying, 'This is the Messiah, Jesus whom I am proclaiming to you'" (Acts 17:2–3; cf. 3:18; 26:22–23). Although this sort of dogmatic or expository preaching has fallen out of favor in many pulpits, not least because post-modern congregations do not share the kind of assumptions regarding biblical authority that it requires, the underlying principle remains in force: that the authority or efficacy of preaching rests with the one who is proclaimed, rather than with those who proclaim him. The fact that as preachers we instinctively prefer to maintain a grip on verbal efficacy (sometimes even while claiming not to) argues strongly for the validity of this premise rather than against it.

In Luke, all three stages or dimensions of the disciples' recognition of the risen Christ focus directly on his suffering. First, the burden of his scriptural exegesis concerns the necessity of the Messiah's death as the prelude to his vindication by way of resurrection. Second, and even without benefit of a more fully developed sacramental theology, Jesus' breaking of bread recalls his broken body: the one who is now restored enacts a memorial of all that made restoration necessary. Third, the clearest tokens of failed death take the form of scars now unexpectedly healed. In stark contrast to consistent expressions of doubt, terror, and simple obtuseness on the part of various disciples, Christ himself directs all three aspects. And all three militate against a dogmatic or doctrinaire approach to preaching on the subject, both because the preacher does not possess the necessary power to command "recognition" and because intellectual hesitation and holy terror alike seem intrinsic to the process of acknowledging the identity of the risen Lord. That being said, there is also a larger theological and operational principle at stake, as was indicated at the outset of the present chapter.

Two Ways of Preaching

In his inaugural sermon on the day of Pentecost, the Apostle Peter quotes an extended excerpt from Psalm 16 as a scriptural testimonium in defense of Jesus' resurrection. The key verse, according to Peter, is "You will not abandon my soul to Hades, or let your Holy One experience corruption" (Acts 2:27, 31, citing LXX Ps 15:10), which he interprets with reference to the Messiah. Although it receives no direct comment, Luke's quotation of the psalm continues on to the next verse: "You have made known to me the ways of life; you will make me full of gladness with your presence" (Acts 2:28; LXX Ps 15:11). Expanding the figurative sense of the original metaphor, the Septuagint (which Luke cites directly) refers not to a particular "way of life," as does the Hebrew text,[33] but—somewhat unusually—to "ways" in the plural (ὁδοὺς ζωῆς). From Jeremiah comes God's challenge to his people, "Thus says the Lord: See, I am setting before you the way of life and the way of death" (Jer 21:8; cf. LXX Prov 6:23; Didache 1:1). But the translators' choice of the plural noun is more typical of passages such as Prov 15:24, "The thoughts of the intelligent person are *ways of life* in order that one turn aside and escape from Hades" (NETS; cf. LXX Prov 5:6). This wording hints at a larger perspective or orientation, suggesting a manner of conduct that coheres more broadly with life as God intends it.

Just so, in the context of Peter's sermon and its quotation of Psalm 15, the language of Acts 2:28 speaks of "ways of life" that correspond to resurrection.[34] Whereas the "ways of death" involve a contest that trades on mortality and the certainty of human finitude, resurrection expresses God's intention to bestow life on those who know themselves to be defeated and dead already. The subject is far too large to pursue at length

---

33. As at Prov 2:19; 5:6; and 15:24, "'*orach* is normally used for the way of life"; so Koch, s.v. דֶּרֶךְ *derekh** [etc.], §III.9, *TDOT* 3:281.

34. Cf. the comment of Keener (*Acts*, 1:950), recalling Jer 21:8 and Matt 7:13–14, that "Luke might envision the 'ways of life' as the 'ways of the Lord' (Luke 1:76; 3:5; Acts 13:10)." For other NT uses of the plural noun, see Acts 13:10; Heb 3:10; Rev 15:3.

here, but whether in terms of executive and judicial power (which, in Paul's memorable phrase, "does not bear the sword in vain" [Rom 13:4]), military force, contract theory, or the agonism of professional sports, much of human society is governed by rules of contest, balances of power, and the warrants of penalty, punishment, or defeat. Perhaps this is a condition of the fall, in which trust itself must be conditional and sanctions are required as provisional or proleptic enactments of death that is the ultimate consequence of sin. By contrast, resurrection is not imposed on us as though it were a punishment. On the contrary, it is the reversal of punishment, obviating the "ways of death" by rendering them obsolete. In Jesus' resurrection, God makes humanity a free and noncoercive offer of life, leaving us at liberty, if we so choose, to remain enmeshed in the "ways" of sin and death. Only in these terms is it possible to understand the mutually exclusive universalisms of 1 Cor 15:22: "as in Adam all die, so in Christ shall all be made alive" (RSV).

Might it be, therefore, that for homiletics as for the biblical wisdom tradition, we should distinguish between the "ways" of death and life, respectively? The one form of preaching relies for its effect on compulsion and demand, if only in covert form. Such preaching makes assertions that demand assent—not directly threatening the hearers, in most cases, but nonetheless seeking to impose on them (as if "from above") a certain vision, perspective, or set of convictions. Such preaching is overtly assertive or intentionally directive, even while sometimes claiming not to be, in a manner that warns of and is governed by the dire consequences of disbelief. It leaves its hearers poised and paralyzed, like the women who waited in darkness for the Sabbath to end, fearful lest their pursuit of the one they love bring punishment instead. Somehow such preaching fails to grasp the deeper implication of Jesus' death: that by this means God comes to us, not to impose death from on high but to suffer it in our place. It is difficult to imagine a less coercive means of persuasion than that of self-sacrifice that intentionally substitutes for obligations owed by others.[35] No more than this may preaching participate in the "ways of death."

---

35. "Far from being a neutral, impersonal force, distant and external to the world, God sends his glory into the world in the form of slavery, humiliation, suffering, and death on the cross. Far from imposing, God draws near, invites, and enters into communion. Far from demanding service from others for enhancing his influence, God generously gives and expends his life in service to others for their enhancement" (Pasquarello, *We Speak*, 32).

Its converse is a form of proclamation that endeavors to invoke rather than to impose or impel, relying for affirmation solely on God's own gift of life. Its proper mode is that of noncoercive testimony, in which the inherent authenticity of the events to which the preacher bears witness take definitive precedence over the character of the witness or the rhetorical form of the testimony. Its power and authority reside with God—the One to whom the preacher testifies—rather than with the one who testifies or the testimony itself. Above all where such preaching directly concerns the resurrection of Jesus, making known "the ways of life" in a manner that is informed by that same gift leaves hearers wholly free, allowing room for doubt, uncertainty, or (however paradoxically) godly terror. Hearers may accept such testimony at face value; they may interrogate, curtail, or correlate it with some less demanding point of view, or reject it altogether. As we have seen, much scholarly writing falls into these latter categories, which only proves the point: testimony to the resurrection of Jesus is noncoercive, its acceptance non-compulsory. Just so, preaching that conforms to the "ways of life" will leave hearers free to respond as they themselves see fit.

While the dynamic of belief or non-belief involves the One to whom a preacher testifies, testimony itself is governed by the events that provide its content. At the opposite end of the moral and metaphysical scale, if the witnesses to a murder are either justifiably confused or intentionally evasive when questioned by police, or if their testimony in court does not agree in certain important details, it does not change the fact that someone has been killed. The victim is still a victim, whatever the circumstances of her untimely death. With luck and a measure of rhetorical skill, a clever defense lawyer may raise doubts about the reliability of certain witnesses, perhaps even winning acquittal for a client who is "guilty as sin." The accused will smile at having gotten away with murder. Yet no one thinks to cancel the victim's funeral or abandon the court system, all on account of uncooperative, forgetful, or otherwise imperfect witnesses. So, by analogy, in the economy of God: there is sufficient variation in the accounts of the empty tomb and the events between Good Friday and Pentecost as to leave room for doubt, thereby preserving the freedom of subsequent hearers. But that does not change the fact that Jesus was raised from the dead or absolve preachers from responsibility for situating that resurrection at the center of the Christian gospel. It simply means that preachers must reckon both with the absolute freedom with which they offer testimony to the ways and acts of God and with the absolute freedom of their hearers to reject such testimony. Perhaps more precisely: Jesus' resurrection is *sui generis*, an eschatological event for which we cannot account in merely human terms; biblical testimony to it is therefore equivocal and multivalent, while yet remaining foundational for Christian faith. This is one of the senses in which testimony to the resurrection is governed by the character of resurrection itself. Given the initial and definitive testimony of Scripture (in keeping with the distinction advocated by Barth), preachers offer subsequent and secondary testimony in a similar manner, referring hearers back to God as the source of new life and relying on the "force" of this gift to prove persuasive on its own terms.

Thus to preach in a manner consistent with the "ways of life" is to do so in the same manner that God offers resurrection itself—by offering rather than imposing it, presenting it as a free and gracious gift rather than demanding acceptance or resorting to other forms of coercion. In terms of epistemology and intellectual apprehension, hearers have the choice either to remain in the realm of "death"—the realm of duress and submission, which imposes its views by force and thereby compels assent—or to embrace all that Christ's resurrection implies, whereby the ways of God only become clear in direct relation to God. Only God can be the guarantor of any speech that claims to be (even remotely, or by extension) "the word of God." In this regard we fall back once more on Luther's succinct dictum: "We have the right to speak but not the power to accomplish." Or, to adopt a more rabbinic manner of expression, in proclamation as in resurrection proper, the "keys of life" are not in the hands of the proclaimer, but in the hands of the One proclaimed.

All this being said, at least two qualifications seem necessary. First, it is important to acknowledge Luther's critical distinction between the "alien" and "proper" work of God, which correspond to the cross and resurrection of Christ, respectively:

> God's alien work . . . is the suffering of Christ and sufferings in Christ, the crucifixion of the old man and the mortification of Adam. God's proper work, however, is the resurrection of Christ, justification in the Spirit, and the vivification of the new man . . . conformity with the image of the Son of God includes both of these works. (*LW* 51:19)[36]

---

36. Echoing Luther (and, like Luther, quoting the reference in Isa 28:21 to God's *alienum opus*), Philip Melanchthon (1497–1560) writes that the prophet "calls it an alien work of God to terrify, because the proper work of God is to make alive and console. But he terrifies, he says, in order to make room for consolation and vivification

In simple terms, this means that God must first convict the unrighteous of their sin, disobedience, and spiritual alienation; only then does the offer of forgiveness and salvation appear as "good news." Luther explains further:

> The proper office of the gospel is to proclaim the proper work of God, i.e., grace, through which the Father of mercies freely gives to all men peace, righteousness and truth, mitigating all his wrath . . .
>
> But the strange work of the gospel is to prepare a people perfect for the Lord, that is, to make manifest sins and pronounce guilty those who were righteous in their own eyes by declaring that all men are sinners and devoid of the grace of God . . .
>
> So the gospel sounds exceedingly harsh in its alien tones, and yet this must be done, in order that it may be able to sound with its own proper tones. (*LW* 51:20)[37]

Just so in the fifty-eighth of his famous *Ninety-Five Theses*, Luther contends that the merits of Christ "always work grace for the inner person and cross, death, and hell for the outer person."[38] As Paul Scott Wilson observes, "God's Word is dual-edged; it both binds and frees, condemns and liberates, demands and enables, it is both trouble and grace."[39]

So it cannot be said that God never convicts of sin, that death has no place in the divine economy, or that the injustice of Jesus' crucifixion is not integral to God's saving purpose. Luther reminds us that the ways of God accommodate, even incorporate, the "ways of death" and the "ways of life" alike. These are dialectical rather than binary opposites, existing in necessary tension. According to Barth, such paradox is integral to the message of Scripture as a whole, as it presents God's response to the questions of human existence:

---

because hearts that do not feel the wrath of God loathe consolation in their smugness" ("Apology of the Augsburg Confession" XII.5, cited in Wengert, "'Peace, Peace . . . Cross, Cross,'" 200).

37. Cf. Thesis 18 of the *Heidelberg Disputation*: "It is certain that one must utterly despair of oneself in order to be made fit to receive the grace of Christ" (cited from Dennis Bielfeldt, "Heidelberg Disputation, 1518," in Wengert, *Roots of Reform*, 83).

38. Wengert, "[The 95 Theses or] Disputation for Clarifying the Power of Indulgences, 1517," in Wengert, *Roots of Reform*, 42; cf. *LW* 31:212; WA 1·605

39. Wilson, *Four Pages of the Sermon*, 22.

> One simply cannot ask or hear the "question" without hearing the *answer* ... *This* No is really Yes. *This* judgment is grace. *This* condemnation is forgiveness. *This* death is life. *This* hell is heaven. *This* fearful God is a loving father who takes the prodigal in his arms. The crucified is the one raised from the dead. And the explanation of the cross as such is eternal life.[40]

But that the ways of God include the "ways of death" does not authorize God's messengers to follow suit, as if they might wield its power over those in their care. Paul, in fact, takes pains to preclude such an inference. That he proclaims Jesus as Κύριος, "Lord," he says, does not give him the right, even as an apostle, to "lord" it (κυριεύειν) over the congregants entrusted to him. Even with the fractious saints of Corinth, some of whose members are certainly in need of correction, he explicitly draws back from imposing himself on them: "I call on God as witness against me: it was to spare you that I did not come again to Corinth. I do not mean to imply that we lord it [κυριεύομεν] over your faith; rather, we are workers with you for your joy" (2 Cor 1:23–24). Thus, although he speaks of being "conformed to the image" of Christ (Rom 8:29) and calls upon his converts to imitate him as he himself imitates Christ (1 Cor 11:1; cf. 1 Cor 4:16; 1 Thess 1:7), such imitation extends only as far as abasement, not exaltation or the exercise of human forms of authority.[41]

As pertains to preaching, the Lutheran concept of God's *opus alienum*, which threatens divine "wrath," "death," and "hell" for a sinful humanity, might seem an outright contradiction to any notion of gracious, noncoercive testimony, or to preaching that accords with the "ways of life." Yet the distinction intended here is not between conviction and consolation in principle, but rather between the prerogatives of God and the responsibilities of the preacher. Since preachers are as much subject to divine justice as their hearers, they are hardly in a position to pronounce judgment against anyone else. On this score, although he finds it necessary to defend himself against his detractors, the Apostle Paul refrains even from self-assessment, let alone the condemnation of others:

> I am not aware of anything against myself, but I am not thereby acquitted. It is the Lord who judges me. Therefore do not pronounce judgment before the time, before the Lord comes, who will bring to light the things now hidden in darkness and will

---

40. Barth, *The Word of God and the Word of Man*, 120.
41. Further, Gorman, *Cruciformity*, 291–98, and Knowles, *We Preach Not Ourselves*, 175–77.

> disclose the purposes of the heart. Then each one will receive commendation from God. (1 Cor 4:4–5)

That God is holy and demands justice in all spheres of life is theologically foundational, and preaching should not shy away from saying so. But whereas the preacher can do no more than call for righteous conduct (in herself as much as others), the Spirit of God enables it. However imperfectly he may have implemented this proposal in the course of his own preaching, Luther's point is that just as crucifixion and resurrection are each integral to God's purpose, so conviction and consolation alike are the work of God alone: "That is the twofold work and performance of Christ in us: He kills us, and He resurrects us; He humbles us, and He exalts us, each in His good season."[42] As Luther and Paul both insist, the Sunday morning preacher has neither the authority nor the ability to attempt anything similar. What remains, instead, is the prospect of a deferential withdrawal, as the preacher draws back from presuming too much, leaving the Spirit of God free to do what only the Spirit is able.

Second, lest this proposal appear to open the door to a doctrinal free-for-all (an all-too-familiar scenario in some seminaries and congregations), the distinction proposed here is not between firm theological convictions, on the one hand, and unbounded perspectivism, on the other—a kind of radical theological egalitarianism. Rather, it is a matter of distinguishing between human authority and divine; between hearers acquiescing intellectually because the preacher (or denomination or magisterium) insists on submission and being persuaded by the breathtaking reality of the Risen Christ and the power of the Holy Spirit that attends him. If the sermon is true, it is true because it bears faithful witness to that which is true of God; if it proves persuasive, it is so because the Spirit of God testifies in the hearts and minds of the listeners to the authenticity of what has been said. The evangelists themselves intend just such a distinction when they report that Jesus taught "as one having ἐξουσία [authority, force], and not as the scribes" (Mark 1:22; cf. Matt 7:29; Luke 4:32).

At least for human speakers, the converse of assertive or authoritarian speech is not abdication from any assertion whatsoever (whether doctrinal, ethical, rhetorical, or otherwise), but rather theological and operational contingency in the form of wholesale reliance on "God who

---

42. "Psalm 68: About Easter, Ascension, and Pentecost," trans. Martin H. Bertram (on Ps 68:6), *LW* 13:8; *WA* 8:9.

raises the dead." This is the stance that Paul exemplifies in 2 Cor 1:9. To be sure, such an orientation requires us to trust in God, imitating Jesus as we do so. But—as implied already—it also requires us to draw back, not simply refraining from rhetorical, intellectual, or methodological presumption, but intentionally leaving room and making space for God to act. In terms of the categories crafted by Austin and Searle, a sermon may perhaps be *rhetorically* assertive, directive, commissive, expressive, and/or declarative. Yet whatever its form of expression, it awaits and relies upon *theological* assertion, direction, commitment, expression, or declaration of a sort that only God and the Spirit of God can provide. Our further exploration of this proposal will be guided in one respect by the theology of Karl Barth and in another by the sociocultural theories of Homi K. Bhabha, following which we will return to the three species of testimony and recognition noted above: literary, liturgical, and as concerns personal encounter with the scarred and Risen Lord.

> Nicht das Wort „Christus," nicht irgendwelche Beschreibung Christi, sondern allein das Geschehen von Gott aus mit uns in Christus, das Immanuel, Gott mitt uns—dies ist der Mittelpunkt aller Predigt.
>
> Not the mere word "Christ," not a mere description of Christ, but solely what God has done with us in Christ, Immanuel, God with us—this is the central point of all preaching.
>
> —Karl Barth (1886–1968)[43]

---

43. Barth, *Homiletik*, 36 (ET 51).

5

Third Space; Third Voice

> But as it is, they desire a better country, that is, a heavenly one. Therefore God is not ashamed to be called their God; indeed, he has prepared a city for them.
>
> —Hebrews 11:16

> The Spirit descends. Out they go to preach the resurrection—and in the process their preaching is resurrected.
>
> —David Schlafer[1]

Contesting Christian Space

IN CHAPTER 16 OF Acts, Luke recounts how, compelled by his dream of a man from Macedonia who pleads for assistance, Paul travels to Philippi, "a leading city of the district of Macedonia and a Roman colony" (Acts 16:12). This last detail is especially significant for our understanding of his ministry, and of Christian identity in principle. Philippi (now a UNESCO World Heritage site)[2] had been the location in 42 BCE of the last two battles of the Roman Civil War, pitting as many as 200,000 combatants against each other. By defeating Marcus Brutus and Gaius Cassius, the forces of Marcus Antonius and Gaius Octavius avenged the assassination

---

1. Schlafer, "Anticipating Unpredictable Resurrection," 214.
2. See http://whc.unesco.org/en/list/1517/

of Octavius's adoptive father, Julius Caesar, and brought the revolt of the Eastern provinces to an end. Their triumph set in motion the events that would establish the Roman Empire and inaugurate a long period of relative calm known as the *Pax Romana*. Little more than a decade after the battle, Octavius himself would be given the title *Caesar Divi Filius Augustus*: "Caesar Augustus, Divine Son." In honor of this pivotal victory, the adjacent settlement was refounded as a prosperous Roman colony—*Colonia Victrix Philippensium* ("Colony of the Conquering Philippians"), later *Colonia Augusta Iulia Philippensis* ("Colony of the Philippian Julius Augustus")—with retired soldiers forming the core of its society and civic structure. A wealth of surviving inscriptions and archaeological remains provide ample evidence of the city's thoroughly Roman character.[3]

Entering Philippi from the east along the Via Egnatia, Paul and his companions would have passed through the Neapolis Gate, a *propylaea* or monumental portico bristling with imperial imagery and statues of Roman deities.[4] Given the commemorative character of the colony as a whole and the conventions of Augustan civic architecture in particular, there can be little doubt that this would have been a triumphal arch, intended to symbolize the theological as well as military supremacy of Rome.[5] Stephen Johnson notes that "city walls and gates were always *res sacrae*, under public ownership and the tutelage of the gods. They were thus, particularly in the earlier periods, as much civic monuments as functional passageways and might be expected therefore to have been highly ornamented."[6] In this case, ornamentation intentionally signaled

---

3. For brief histories of the city, see Chaido Koukouli-Chrysantaki, "Colonia Iulia Augusta Philippensis," in Bakirtzis and Koester, eds., *Philippi at the Time of Paul and after His Death*, 5–10, and the Archaeological Receipts Fund, *Archaeological Site of Philippi*, 154–56; cf. 267–71.

4. Koukouli-Chrysantaki, "Colonia Iulia Augusta Philippensis," 13–15 (with n52). Still surviving is a niche in the city wall, adjacent to the Neapolis Gate, where in 1920 archaeologists uncovered a Roman altar dedicated to "Isis Regina"; so Roger, "L'enceinte basse de Philippes," 29–30 ("La porte paraît avoir reçu dès les premiers temps un caractère religieux, qui s'est longtemps perpétué"). Although the current remains date from the Byzantine era, they provide an approximate sense of scale, with flanking bastions set some 8.5m (28 ft) apart to create a structure more than 31m (102 ft) wide (p. 26).

5. See further Knowles, "'Wide Is the Gate,'" 187–90, with the examples and literature cited there, especially Richmond, "Commemorative Arches," 172–74; cf. also discussion of the typical dimensions of Roman city gates, 190–94.

6. Johnson, *Late Roman Fortifications*, 13.

ideology. As Sze-kar Wan observes, "This was Rome's favorite colonial strategy: inscribing an imperial discourse on the colonized space."[7]

For any Roman city, the encircling walls were not merely defensive, but liminal: they marked the boundaries of consecration and colonial domain. Accordingly, to enter Philippi, passing through an arched gateway guarded by the figures of tutelary deities, was to cross a threshold into sacred space—into the realm and dominion of the Roman pantheon. That Paul would have been fully alert to the theological challenge that this implied cannot be in doubt (cf. Acts 17:16). Indeed, it helps to explain his bold assertion in Phil 3:20 that for the followers of Jesus, "our place of citizenship is in heaven."[8] The apostle's choice of vocabulary is telling, although the word he uses (πολίτευμα, appearing only here in the New Testament) can have a range of meanings. It can refer to a government department, a constitution or state, to citizenship, or (as with the large Jewish population of Alexandria) to a "colony" of foreigners accorded "specific political rights."[9] First Peter 2:9 describes believers as "a chosen race, a royal priesthood, a holy nation [ἔθνος], God's own people," on the one hand, yet as "foreigners and exiles" (2:11–12 NIV; cf. 1:1) among the Gentiles, on the other. Conversely, in Ephesians, those who were formerly "foreigners and strangers" (2:19 NIV) are now said to be "fellow citizens with the saints and members of the household of God" (2:20 RSV; cf. 2:12). But where Ephesians and 1 Peter (which also counsels submission to Rome) each describe the church in language denoting citizenship and political affiliation, Paul's claim in Phil 3:20 is more precise.

Notwithstanding overlapping theological identities and the incorporation of non-Roman deities under the broader *aegis* of Roman religion, to walk through Philippi's Neapolis Gate would be to pass from the primary domain of Thracian or Macedonian gods into the overarching dominion of Roma, the personification and protectress of Rome.[10] To

---

7. Wan, "'To the Jew First and Also to the Greek,'" 140, citing Anchises's charge to Aeneas in Book 6 of Virgil's *Aeneid*: "Roman, remember by your strength to rule the earth's peoples—for your arts are to be these: to pacify, to impose the rule of law, to spare the conquered, battle down the proud" (140n31).

8. So L&N §11.71; cf. RSV: "commonwealth."

9. Strathmann, s.v. Πόλις §A.I.5, *TDNT* 6:519–20, whose apolitical reading of Phil 3:20 (§C.II.4, p. 535) expressly precludes the interpretation proposed here.

10. Roman policy favored absorption of local practice wherever possible, a strategy at odds with the exclusivist outlook of Jewish and Christian faith. Archaeological evidence attests the vitality of both Roman and non-Roman cults within the Roman walls. Extant temple remains indicate that "the cult of Augustus, as also of his

be baptized into Christ, by contrast, and to be made mystically one with him, was to become a citizen of the "kingdom of God" (1 Thess 2:12, etc.). This is a directly contrary claim, not an overlapping one. It is all the more remarkable since Paul himself is clearly in custody (and thus under the tangible jurisdiction of Rome) at the time of writing, perhaps detained by the elite Praetorian Guard (Phil 1:13). That he is not alone in having to negotiate the competing claims of Christ and Empire is evident from the fact that he sends greetings from fellow believers in the "household of Caesar" (Phil 4:22). Indeed, in this regard Paul's situation is similar to that of the congregants whom he addresses. To join the tiny fellowship of Philippian believers, likely in a private house or villa, would have involved not one but two sets of competing theological claims: where Roman deities had initially conquered or absorbed the native gods of Macedonia, Christ now supplanted them all. The place where these converts meet for worship is therefore sacred space within sacred space, a sanctuary consecrated to a victim of Rome within a civic domain consecrated to the power that had crucified him. Confirming this interpretation, what Paul declares concerning the saints of Corinth can be no less true for those at Philippi, which is that both individually (1 Cor 6:19) and especially in their corporate gatherings, the believers represent "the temple of the living God" (2 Cor 6:16; similarly, 1 Cor 3:16).[11] As such, the Christian assembly is an embodied refutation of Rome's claim to assert dominion over its members' lives and theological destinies.

Some five centuries later, well after Constantine's nominal "Christianization" of the Roman Empire, a different series of texts is inscribed

---

adopted sons Gaius and Lucius Caesar, already existed in Philippi when Paul arrived. The cult of Livia [Augustus' deified wife] had been introduced by Claudius in 44 CE" (Koukouli-Chrysantaki, "Colonia Iulia Augusta Philippensis," 16). Similarly, "On the slopes of the [acropolis] hill are open-air shrines with more than 140 bas-reliefs of the gods, including the Thracian deity Bendis (who was equated with the Greek Artemis) as well as Cybele and Bacchus, and a sanctuary of the Egyptian Gods (Isis, Serapis, Harpokrates)"; so Finegan, *Archeology of the New Testament*, 102a.

11. In "Contested Spaces in 1 Corinthians 11:17–33 and 14:30" (in Balch and Weissenrieder, eds., *Contested Spaces*) Weissenrieder takes the unusual reference in 1 Cor 14:30 to worshippers "sitting" as a clue to the theopolitical character of the Christian worship assembly: "the Corinthian *ekklēsía* not only possessed a space, but rather *was* this space; the gathering place is the remembrance of the humiliating death of Jesus Christ in that it embodies and represents it physically. A gathering place of the *ekklēsía* in 1 Corinthians is therefore also always the spatial expression of christological forces" (106; emphasis original).

on white marble and set into the city wall adjacent to the Neapolis Gate.[12] This new inscription is an ambitious fabrication, excerpted from an apocryphal exchange of first century correspondence in which an ailing King Abgar of Edessa begs Jesus of Nazareth for healing.[13] In return, Abgar offers to provide the Savior a new home and refuge from whatever difficulties he is currently facing! Of interest here is not the altogether dubious historical character of the legend itself, but rather its sociopolitical, theological, and thus apotropaic intent.[14] As clearly as the Romans had claimed the territory within the city walls on behalf of the gods to whom they looked for power, so in a later generation the church, having assumed power of its own, does the same for Philippi in the name of Christ. More precisely, the new inscription affirms that what Christ had apparently accomplished on behalf of King Abgar and Edessa, he will surely bring about for the benefit of the Philippians also.

For Paul and the Philippian church, Christian space is always contested: it must be actively claimed in the face of competing assertions. In like manner, Christian identity is itself contested, always hybrid and subject to negotiation. Accordingly, the situation at Philippi is instructive for the church of every age, which must continually work out its identity by negotiating between the claims and counter-claims of rival obligations (whether these be theological, political, or ideological in nature). Recognizing this dynamic allows us to see Christian identity, Christian ministry, and the preaching of resurrection in a new light. In the language of postcolonial theorist Homi K. Bhabha, followers of Jesus inhabit a "Third Space," an interstice of perpetual tension that is characteristic (as the title of Bunyan's famous allegory has it) of "The Pilgrim's Progress from this World to That Which Is to Come."[15] As with Paul's equivocation on the matter in Phil 1:23, disciples are forever "torn between the two" (NIV). It is characteristic of Christian faith, he tells the saints at Corinth, that so long as "we are at home in the body we are away from the Lord," even

---

12. Picard, "Un texte nouveau."

13. Also reported by Eusebius, *Hist. Eccl.* I:13.2.

14. Picard, "Un texte nouveau," 56–57, noting that a similar inscription, of similar purpose, survives at Edessa itself (58–59), with further discussion 59–63.

15. Its full title is equally telling: *The Pilgrim's Progress from This World to That Which Is to Come Delivered under the Similitude of a Dream, Wherein Is Discovered the Manner of His Setting Out, His Dangerous Journey, and Safe Arrival at the Desired Countrey*. The enduring popularity of this work over the course of three centuries attests to its viability as an overarching metaphor for Christian experience.

though "we would rather be away from the body and at home with the Lord." Hence, he says, "we walk by faith, not by sight" (2 Cor 5:6–8). These spatial metaphors are the equivalent of Barth's contrast, recast in eschatological terms, between the "unconditional 'whence'" and "unconditional 'whither'" of preaching itself.[16] Not unlike the resurrection of Jesus, both metaphors situate the life of faith at a point of critical intersection between the human and the divine, between rival domains that each claim exclusive allegiance.

To minister in this place of dual citizenship, divided loyalties, and incomplete attachment is to recognize the need for an intentionally crafted Christian identity that is suited to the process of pilgrimage, risking alienation from our first homeland before we have fully arrived in the "better country" that is our destination. In much the same way, to preach in this theological "Third Space" requires a different way of speaking, one that claims neither too much nor too little, invoking the language and thought forms of our adoptive community in accents that still betray the places from which we have come. Along these lines, the ensuing discussion will first review certain key concepts from Bhabha and their possible implications for Christian identity, then turn to consider what it might mean to preach and speak of resurrection in a "Third Voice."

Homi K. Bhabha and Third Space

Bhabha is a complex and demanding theorist. As David Huddart rightly observes, "reading him can be initially confusing": "His essays are complex, fragmented mosaics of quotation, neologism, poetry, and cultural analysis. Further, they are not coherent mosaics in which all the pieces fit together harmoniously: their pieces often have jagged edges. They are mixed critical texts that use concepts or quotations in a patchwork critical form."[17] His topics of address range from cultural analysis to psychology, philosophy of language, hermeneutics, racism, the history of India, contemporary art and literature, and social identity theory (to name only a few more prominent subjects). Yet his allusive, fluid form and frequent appropriation of ideas from other theorists and authors coalesce around a consistent focus on "the negotiation of cultural difference in a way that

---

16. Barth, *Homiletics*, 51–55.
17. Huddart, *Bhabha*, 14.

is liberating for those caught in oppressive situations."[18] In a key move, Bhabha focuses on the formation of the modern nation state, observing that its emergence as an expression of democratic, "Enlightenment" values coincides with the despotism of colonial conquest. Indeed, one is a mirror of the other, since the "master narrative" of Western civility and civilization implies the denigration of all other stories and histories, relegating them to inferior rank or allegedly primitive status. In practice, the colonial enterprise acts out an ideology of cultural supremacism:

> The Western, metropolitan histories of progress and *civitas* cannot be conceived without evoking the savage colonial antecedents of the ideals of civility and the mythology of "civilization" ... In other words, the postcolonial perspective ... insists that cultural and political identity is constructed through a process of "othering."[19]

Just so, in the Roman Empire, the negotiation of imperial identity requires the colonial "other" as an ideological foil, as a contrasting geographical and political landscape against which Roman identity may be asserted, and from which it must be distinguished. In Bhabha's more complex formulation, "Hegemony requires iteration and alterity to be effective."[20] Just as the ancient Philippians perceive the need to erect walls for social and ideological as much as defensive purposes, so Rome must erect statues of its gods and inscribe those same walls with imperial propaganda not only to remind the Macedonians of who is now in charge but also as a means of consolidating Roman identity on otherwise "foreign" soil.

Bhabha's concern is as much philosophical as social or political, for he proposes that even the process of formulating binary categories (us/them; colonizer/colonized; European/non-European; modern/postmodern) does violence to the freedom, particularity, and individual identity of those it describes in such terms. For Bhabha, identity is never fixed, but is constantly in flux, requiring constant negotiation and compromise. Accordingly, "people cannot ... be addressed as colossal, undifferentiated

---

18. Runions, *Changing Subjects*, 75; cf. 78.

19. Bhabha, "The Third Space," 218–19. Similarly, Bhabha, *Location of Culture*, 32–35 (further developed in the concepts of "mimicry," 85–92, and "hybridity," 111–18, etc.); "The objective of colonial discourse is to construe the colonized as a population of degenerate types on the basis of racial origin, in order to justify conquest and to establish systems of administration and instruction" (70). For a succinct summary of the ideology of colonialism, see Travis, *Decolonizing Preaching*, 23–29; 78–85.

20. Bhabha, *Location of Culture*, 29.

collectivities of class, race, gender or nation"; rather, the social identity of each group is always individual, always crafted and reinforced through the recitation of communal narratives and life stories that are constantly challenged and contradicted by countervailing narratives on the part of other constituencies.[21] This is particularly the case for colonized, immigrant, minority, or otherwise notionally "subaltern" peoples. To explain what he means, Bhabha quotes from an essay on cultural identity published by T. S. Eliot more than twenty years after the poet had left the United States to take up British citizenship. Eliot reflects on the fact that new immigrants always leave some part of their identity behind:

> The people who migrated have never represented the whole of the culture of the country from which they came, or they have represented it in quite different proportions ... The people have taken with them only a part of the total culture in which, so long as they remained at home, they participated. The culture which develops on the new soil must therefore be bafflingly alike and different from the parent culture: it will be complicated sometimes by whatever relations are established with some native race and further by immigration from other than the original source.[22]

In "Imaginary Homelands," his own essay on the same subject, Salman Rushdie ponders the nature of his identity as an Anglo-Indian:

> The Indian writer, looking back at India, does so through guilt-tinted spectacles ... I am speaking now of those of us who emigrated ... and I suspect that there are times when the move seems wrong to us all, when we seem, to ourselves, post-lapsarian men and women ... Our identity is at once plural and partial. Sometimes we feel that we straddle two cultures; at other times, that we fall between two stools.[23]

It is, he says, an "ambiguous and shifting" but "not ... infertile territory for a writer to occupy."[24] The potential for new expression, and new identity, emerges from the fact that geographical and cultural displacement requires constant translation between different worlds of meaning. As Rushdie notes in a literary aside, "The word 'translation' comes,

21. Bhabha, "The Third Space," 220.
22. Eliot, *Notes*, 64, partly quoted in Bhabha, "Culture's In Between," 30.
23. Rushdie, *Imaginary Homelands*, 15; quoted in part by Huddart, *Bhabha*, 71.
24. Rushdie, *Imaginary Homelands*, 15.

etymologically, from the Latin for 'bearing across.' Having been borne across the world, we are translated men. It is normally supposed that something gets lost in translation; I cling, obstinately, to the notion that something can also be gained."[25] What is gained in "translation," says Bhabha, is a new and wholly unique sense of personal as well as corporate identity. "We should remember," he writes, "that it is the 'inter'—the cutting edge of translation and negotiation, the *in-between* space—that carries the burden of the meaning of culture."[26]

Whereas colonialism seeks to subsume all other identities within the overarching framework of a dominant culture and new immigrants are, in similar fashion, sometimes tempted to abandon their cultures of origin, Bhabha sets the powerful and disempowered on a more equal footing, proposing that each must renegotiate their identity in light of the other. So, he says, "The non-synchronous temporality of global and national cultures opens up a cultural space—a third space—where the negotiation of incommensurable differences creates a tension peculiar to borderline existence."[27] Bhabha returns repeatedly to the concept of an interstitial "Third Space" as the location in which authentic identity emerges. His most influential work to date, *The Location of Culture*, opens with a discussion of this critical principle:

> These "in-between" spaces provide the terrain for elaborating strategies of selfhood—singular and communal—that initiate new signs of identity, and innovative sites of collaboration, and contestation, in the act of defining society itself . . . This interstitial passage between fixed identifications opens up the possibility of a cultural hybridity that entertains difference without an assumed or imposed hierarchy.[28]

In another essay, aptly named "Frontlines/Borderposts," he writes,

> These spaces provide the terrain for elaborating strategies of selfhood and communal representations that generate new signs of cultural difference and innovative sites of collaboration and contestation. It is at the level of the interstices that the

---

25. Rushdie, *Imaginary Homelands*, 17.
26. Bhabha, *Location of Culture*, 38.
27. Bhabha, *Location of Culture*, 218.
28. Bhabha, *Location of Culture*, 1-2, 4.

intersubjective and collective experiences of nationness, community interest, or cultural value are negotiated.[29]

For Bhabha, it is critical that no one culture, perspective, or worldview may claim to provide the framework for interpreting others (since this is a key characteristic of the moral, military, and intellectual hegemony that colonialism entails): "The difference of cultures cannot . . . be accommodated within a universalist framework."[30] Bhabha repeatedly speaks of "hybridity" and the "incommensurable" character of cultural differences—the fact that different cultures simply do not "speak the same language." Hence a difficult negotiation is required, with neither "majority" nor "marginal" cultures in a position to dictate the terms of their encounter. Writing in light of the controversy over Salman Rushdie's novel *The Satanic Verses*, Bhabha is particularly concerned with attempts on the part of religious authorities to suppress perspectives other than their own.[31]

While thoroughgoing relativism constitutes an obvious challenge to the unitary truth claims of Christian faith, Bhabha's critique of social, cultural, and political domination is nonetheless wholly compatible with an understanding of Jesus' resurrection as the means by which God relativizes all human cultures and perspectives, radically reorienting them around the inbreaking of a new creation. Thus, within Christian discourse, the initial and more obvious negotiation between Jew and Gentile (those whom Eph 2:17 describes as formerly "near" to God and "far off," respectively) is quickly resolved because both positions are subsumed within a larger negotiation of identities between "Christ" and "culture." H. Richard Niebuhr's proposed resolution of this tension is well known: in place of the moderating positions "Christ against culture," "the Christ of culture," "Christ above culture," or "Christ and culture in paradox," he proposes "Christ the transformer of culture," whereby Christ converts people who are inextricably rooted within their cultural situations, and in the process transforms culture itself.[32] However, the extent to which two millennia of Christian confession have succeeded in transforming culture is unclear at best, not least because (as Bhabha reminds his readers)

---

29. Bhabha, "Frontlines/Borderposts," 269.
30. Bhabha, "The Third Space," 209.
31. Rushdie, *Satanic Verses*; cf. Bhabha, *Location of Culture* 33–34, 86–87; "The Third Space," 213–15, 219, etc.
32. Niebuhr, *Christ and Culture*, passim.

Christian mission and cultural hegemony have often gone hand in hand. In fact, this failure to "convert" culture underscores the appropriateness of Bhabha's theoretical model, since the church's persistent inability either to fully embrace or to fully separate from its social and political environment demonstrates that Christian identity cannot be expressed either in solely cultural or in purely theological terms. To the extent that it looks to Christ as the true source of its identity, the church is always more than a simple expression of culture, but always less than the full manifestation of God's reign. Its genuine failures and limited but still real successes situate it in an indeterminate "Third Space" between the two, perpetually praying "May your kingdom come" because the signs of God's reign are ambiguous (even in its own life) and the manifestation of that reign as yet incomplete.

The writer to the Hebrews explains that "as it is, we do not yet see all things in subjection [to him], but we do see Jesus."[33] In the context of the present discussion, we may take this to mean that even prior to the theological exposition of Jesus' human and divine natures that will occupy theologians well into the fifth century and beyond, we see in his life, death, and resurrection the embodiment of an interstitial "Third Space" that successfully negotiates between the positions of colonizer and colonized, and more importantly between "the kingdoms of this world" and the "kingdom of heaven." Jesus of Nazareth is born into a nation under military occupation in which the structures of colonial polity dominate every aspect of life. Whether governed by a client king such as Herod Antipas or (as was subsequently the case) by Roman administrators, the Jews are a subaltern people. Throughout his life and public ministry, Jesus cannot avoid interaction with colonial officials and military personnel; by way of response, he counsels what Bhabha terms "sly civility"[34]—turning the other cheek, performing double the legal requirement of forced labor (Matt 5:39, 41), repaying Caesar in his own coin (Mark 12:17)—even while welcoming those among the occupying forces who acknowledge his authority (Matt 8:5–13/Luke 7:1–10). Against all expectation,

---

33. Heb 2:8–9. As a result of textual uncertainty (on which see Metzger, *Textual Commentary*, 594), the subject of the protasis is either God or Jesus (ESV, NASB, RSV), or else angelic powers (NIV, NRSV).

34. Cf. Bhabha, *Location of Culture*, 93–101, and Huddart, *Bhabha*, 58–59. Ironically, the deferential resistance to colonial rule that he describes is exemplified in Bhabha's own work by intransigence toward Christian missionaries (further, 102–6, 116–22, etc.).

Jesus advocates neither active resistance nor wholesale acquiescence to the colonial forces, at least on the part of his disciples (Matt 26:52-53). Refusing to engage the misuse of power on its own terms, Jesus' closest disciples include a former collaborator (Levi the tax agent [Mark 2:14]) alongside at least one former resistance fighter (Simon the "Cananaean" [Mark 3:18] or "Zealot" [Luke 6:15]).[35] Yet having been betrayed into the hands of his enemies, he is eventually tried by the Roman judiciary and crucified by Roman military machinery. Facilitated in this case by members of the religious establishment, Jesus' death represents the triumph of colonial administration, which suppresses all forms of disorder or dissent in order to maintain its grip on power. However, by allowing himself to be executed he also demonstrates the injustice of corrupt power (religious, military, and political alike), ultimately overturning it by refusing to remain dead. His resurrection robs the oppressors of their most potent weapon.

Whereas Bhabha (and postcolonial discourse inspired by his work) focuses on psychology, sociology, economics, cultural identity, and the politics of power—all "horizontal," anthropological, or sociological considerations—our own concern extends also to the "vertical" and eschatological dimensions of human existence. Considered in light of Paul's assertion that the Philippians' true πολίτευμα (citizenship, allegiance, commonwealth) is in heaven, rather than within the sacred precincts of the Roman colony in which they live, we may think of Jesus' incarnation as the definitive reassertion of God's reign in human affairs. Yet he is no invader, for as John 1:11 insists, "he came to his own home" (RSV: τὰ ἴδια) or "that which was his own" (NIV). However, rather than imposing divine rule or enforcing compliance with the ways of God, Jesus does the opposite: he assumes the rôle of a slave (Phil 2:7), choosing to suffer violence instead of inflicting it. In his own person, Jesus embodies interstitial existence, bridging the distance and erasing the difference by embracing both poles of the metaphysical antithesis of human and divine. His strategy—if it may be called that—is to absorb rather than to impose violence, whether by this we mean the holy violence of divine wrath (John 3:36; Rom 1:18, etc.) or the frequently arbitrary, unjust violence of political dominion and military domination. Contrary to expectation, he takes the place of the conquered and the colonized, entering the space that they occupy in order to transform it from within. In colonial discourse, this is

---

35. So Marcus, *Mark 1-8*, 264. Perhaps also Judas "Iscariot," if his cognomen reflects the Greek σικάριος ("assassin"); cf. Davies and Allison, *Matthew* 2:157.

the ultimate betrayal, an erasure of the distinction between powerful and powerless that undermines the identities of both.[36] Yet Jesus' reconfiguration also manifests both identities in their truest form: that of a holy and life-giving divine in concert with humanity situated in full creaturely dependence on the ultimate source of life.

The argument proposed here is therefore two-fold. Its first contention is that the incarnation, death, and resurrection of Christ have together "broken down the dividing wall" that would otherwise separate Jew from Gentile (so Eph 2:11–20), but also male from female and oppressor from oppressed, whether in social, political, or economic terms. This is the full scope of Paul's revolutionary assertion in Gal 3:28 that "there is no longer Jew or Greek, there is no longer slave or free, there is no longer male and female, for you are all one in Christ Jesus." Stated in simplistic (or proleptic and eschatological) terms, the work of Christ has, in fact, resolved the problems of "difference" that preoccupy Bhabha, reconciling these antitheses within the framework of a larger negotiation that bridges the still more challenging distance between humanity and God. This is the second dimension of the present argument, and its primary focus. That the reconciliation of which Paul speaks is often lamentably absent in practice does not diminish the force of his theological vision. Although Paul states the matter in maximal terms ("there is no longer male and female," for instance, being in equal measures unappealing and impracticable), his point is that new identity in Christ relativizes and subordinates all other sources of identity. Again, this is the force of the handwritten codicil that he appends to the Letter to the Galatians: all that matters, the apostle insists, is "a new creation" (Gal 6:15).[37] This is the domain of resurrection, beyond the reach of our most ambitious social initiatives, as Christ reconciles our differences by remaking us in his own image, transforming those who look to him "from one degree of glory to another" (2 Cor 3:18). That is, those who look *to* him are made to look *like* him.

---

36. Huddart, *Bhabha*, 58–70 (esp. 65: "the phenomenon of 'going native' was recognized, feared, and anatomized from the beginning of the colonial enterprise").

37. The radical extent to which "new creation" in Christ redefines cultural as well as religious origins underlies the Patristic concept of Christians as a "third race," on which see Wright, *Paul and the Faithfulness of God*, 1445–48 (with Gal 6:25 cited p. 1447). For a contrary perspective, cf. Wan, "'To the Jew First and Also to the Greek,'" 134–35.

Still, this solution brings with it difficulties of its own, since the risen Christ problematizes human identity even in the process of refashioning it. At this juncture Bhabha's discussion of difference and interstitial existence becomes especially critical for his post-resurrection disciples. In the wording of the Chalcedonian formula of 451 CE, Jesus of Nazareth is himself τέλειον . . . ἐν θεότητι καὶ τέλειον . . . ἐν ἀνθρωπότητι ("perfect in deity and perfect in humanity").[38] But the same cannot be said for his followers, much as he represents them and their lives are mystically bound up with his, even to the point of sharing his heavenly exaltation (Col 3:1–3). To the extent that we are already "in Christ, a new creation" (2 Cor 5:17), we may speak of having been "translated" (Col 1:13 KJV) into a new realm and mode of discourse; yet to the extent that we still "groan, and long to put on our heavenly dwelling" (2 Cor 5:2 RSV), the "difference" between ourselves and our Savior looms large. We are between times and between realms, creatures simultaneously of the already and the not yet. Even though his own most immediate concerns are not theological, Bhabha helps to clarify this tension.

Horizons Near and Far

In *The Blue Mountains of China*, novelist Rudy Wiebe chronicles the wanderings of a devout Mennonite family in search of safety and a home. In the course of several generations, various members of the extended clan travel east from the Ukraine to the region beyond Lake Baikal, west to the Manitoba and Saskatchewan prairie, or south to Paraguay and back again, often to escape persecution but always looking for a place to belong. The title of the book is a visual metaphor for an unattainable horizon: gazing southward from their isolated settlement in the Russian Far East, members of that colony can see "the faint blue straggle of the Great Khingan, distant as a whiff of oriental scent, a world that lay afar and tempted."[39] Even though they have settled in a place with fertile soil, political upheaval is such that their entire community must flee by night, and even though they head south toward the distant mountains, death still stalks them. Their flight grinds to a halt in the foothills: "And a quick burial by the side of the road (Far over yonder sea of stars there is a better

---

38. Schaff, ed., *Creeds of Christendom* 2:62.
39. Wiebe, *Blue Mountains of China*, 129.

land). And sputtering on the steep turns of the Lesser Khingans till gasp and stop and immobility..."[40]

Wiebe (whose work has not been well received in Mennonite circles) questions our tendency to map spiritual destinies and destinations onto physical geography. The colonists, for all their desire, cannot shake their restlessness; none of the places they have chosen proves secure, so within a few years they must move on. The novel ends with a roadside conversation between two Mennonite pilgrims, one of whom has lost his faith while the other is carrying a wooden cross along the highway in the summer of Canada's centenary. "You know the problem with Mennonites?" he asks;

> "They've always wanted to be Jews. To have land God had given them for their very own, to which they were called; so that even if someone chased them away, they could work forever to get it back..."
> "They came close in Russia."
> "Closest there, I think. Unfortunately. But they are still trying to find it, and it isn't anywhere on earth."[41]

Beneath more obvious needs for social, economic, and political security, what Wiebe discerns is an imbalance in the tension between "This World" and "That Which Is to Come." *The Blue Mountains of China* critiques too easy an elision or overlap between the two categories, a premature resolution of the tension that keeps them juxtaposed. As Douglas Burton-Christie observes, to walk by faith is to acknowledge that this tension is essentially unresolvable:

> Can one be simultaneously at home and on the way, secure and unstable, located within clear boundaries and constantly moving across boundaries, attached to place and detached, grounded in the present and yearning toward the future? This seems to be, against all logic, or probability, precisely what is called for. This paradoxical tension signals, I would suggest, the kind of exquisite balance we must maintain in learning to respond to the touch of God upon the soul, in learning how to live in this world.[42]

---

40. Wiebe, *Blue Mountains of China*, 130.
41. Wiebe, *Blue Mountains of China*, 227.
42. Burton-Christie, "Living Between Two Worlds," 428.

Fittingly, Wiebe's account of intermittent pilgrimage does not take the form of a single coherent narrative, but emerges as a series of vignettes and recollections that move back and forth between the voices of those present and past: the novel itself is as disjointed as lives whose story it tells.[43]

If having to negotiate between flesh and spirit, this world and the next, is simply a condition of pilgrimage, then central to the determination of hybrid identity are notions of *dislocation* and *instability*. "Dislocation" refers to the fact that we do not fully belong in the place where we currently find ourselves (or, perhaps, cannot find ourselves). It is not that we are without a starting point in culture, history, and geography, but that having embarked on pilgrimage, we no longer fully belong in the land of our birth. There is no possibility of return because we have, in any number of senses, already "moved on." Again, it is not that allegiance to Christ renders one stateless or culturally indeterminate, but rather that Christian identity cannot be reduced to association with a particular land or nationality (despite the fact that "state" churches employ this strategy as a means of fostering national cohesion). Another term for the dislocation of pilgrimage might be "alienation," in the political sense of being "non-native." Hence Paul's assertion (at least as translated by the NRSV) that "our *citizenship* is in heaven." The other dimension to be considered is instability. Having left behind our place of origin but having not yet arrived at our intended destination, we remain perpetually on the move, following Jesus "on the way" (a motif typical of Mark's Gospel in particular).[44] As Jesus characterizes his own situation, describing the conditions of discipleship to a would-be follower, "Foxes have holes, and birds of the air have nests; but the Son of Man has nowhere to lay his head" (Matt 8:20). In place of "instability," we might instead describe pilgrimage as a form of perpetual (even if provisional) "homelessness."[45]

---

43. As van Toorn (*Rudy Wiebe and the Historicity of the Word*, 67–68) observes, "Each chapter of the text is dominated by the voice of a separate character, who records events from his or her particular position within Mennonite society. Together they form a fragmented, multi-voiced, historical narrative which encodes the plurality of the Mennonites' experience of the past."

44. Barton, *Spirituality of the Gospels*, 58–59.

45. Bhabha prefers different terminology: "To be unhomed is not to be homeless" (*Location of Culture*, 9). He characterizes the interstitial character of both colonial and colonized experience as "uncanny" or "unhomely," echoing Freud's concept of "Das Unheimliche." As is more clearly implied by the German term, Bhabha's language refers to the sense of being at home neither in one's culture of origin nor in an adopted

Yet homelessness has unexpected benefits, as those who acknowledge their yearning for a place to belong gather in communities of fellow pilgrims and exiles on the margins of the majority culture. As a minority culture Parsi and immigrant several times over, Bhabha describes his own experience in terms of "scattering" that leads to "gathering":

> I have lived that moment of the scattering of the people that in other times and in other places, in the nations of others, becomes a time of gathering. Gathering of exiles and émigrés and refugees; gathering on the edge of "foreign" cultures; gatherings at the frontiers; gatherings in the ghettos or cafés of city centres; gathering in the half-life, half-light of foreign tongues, or in the uncanny fluency of another's language; gathering the signs of approval and acceptance, degrees, discourses, disciplines; gathering the memories of underdevelopment, of other worlds lived retroactively; gathering the past in a ritual of revival; gathering the present. Also the gathering of people in the diaspora; indentured, migrant, interned; the gathering of incriminatory statistics, educational performance, legal statutes, immigration status.[46]

For Christians likewise, "not belonging" (felt, perhaps, most keenly by those of non-conformist, non-mainline, or non-state churches) offers an incentive for gathering with others of similar social and cultural indeterminacy. Certainly it will have motivated Paul who, while acknowledging the riches of his own cultural legacy—"circumcised on the eighth day, a member of the people of Israel, of the tribe of Benjamin, a Hebrew born of Hebrews"—goes on to confess that as a consequence of his faith in Jesus of Nazareth, he has "suffered the loss of all things" (Phil 3:5, 8). The social ostracism and personal peril that confessing Christ entailed for Paul (Acts 23, for instance, describes a plot to assassinate him on religious grounds) will be familiar to converts from other tightly knit communities in our own day.

According to Bhabha, finding and forming community is a first step in the negotiation of new identity, or the reformulation of identity in the place to which one has immigrated. Critical to that process is narrative, as Mechteld Jansen explains:

> In Christian theology "place" is ambivalent. The notion of pilgrimage reminds us that place is just a temporary abode. Yet a

---

or displaced culture. See further Huddart, *Bhabha*, 77–100.

46. Bhabha, *Location of Culture*, 139, also cited in Huddart, *Bhabha*, 79.

renewed understanding of the importance of place from a Christian theological perspective can help people become rooted in making their new place their home while acknowledging their ties to other places in the world . . . Place is much more than neutral territory. It is an existential understanding of our place in the world, our place under the sun. Place is storied place.[47]

Drawing on the work of Ajit Maan, Jansen offers a nuanced account of place as a source and expression of identity, acknowledging that individuals may simultaneously inhabit different—even incompatible—ideological "spaces." A single life story may encompass otherwise incommensurate narratives:

> Multiple narratives may be housed in one body. An Indian woman in Europe, for instance, can speak, dress, work, and socialize in complete adaptation to Western standards at the office, while in another space she lives an Indian life with an Eastern dress code, another language, rules of caste and family alliances, without any inner conflict.[48]

Living in more than one narrative, culture, and worldview requires, in effect, the ability to "be in two places at once":

> People who move and migrate to other places make internarrative associations in order to connect incommensurable narratives. They do not obey the rules of one canonical narrative structure but combine narrative identifications with different groups and cultures to which they are related.[49]

The need to re-combine otherwise disparate narratives in itself produces a new and distinctive life narrative, precisely in the way that Bhabha envisages: "the new environment," says Jansen, "makes them map, construct, and inhabit a new space-time."[50] And it is the telling of new stories that transforms the space that newcomers now inhabit: "Storied space makes a house into a home, and a parking lot into a church, just as stories turn a series of events into a life history."[51] Using stories of newcomers and immigrant churches in Amsterdam and Los Angeles as illustrations, Jansen names this process "homemaking," one that applies both to

47. Jansen, "Christian Migrants," 147.
48. Jansen, "Christian Migrants," 149, citing Maan, *Internarrative Identity*, 61.
49. Jansen, "Christian Migrants," 149.
50. Jansen, "Christian Migrants," 153.
51. Jansen, "Christian Migrants," 158.

individuals and to groups that share common stories and common histories. Importantly, she proposes that "homemaking" takes place not just in formally designated spaces such as churches or meeting halls (important as these may be), but in all the in-between places that serve as "metaphors of that kind of liminal existence that combine 'home' and 'road,' roots and routes . . . we often have the best conversations on the doorstep, halfway between being rooted and being en route."[52]

In effect, dislocation and instability demonstrate the insufficiency of fixed cultural definitions and identities, on the one hand, and the value of religious faith, on the other: "The 'inter' is the space where people meet at the boundaries, and boundaries are privileged places that evoke experiences of utter dependence, or relatedness to one another and to God."[53] But given her acknowledgment that "intercultural boundary experiences are not experiences of the divine per se,"[54] it is surprising that Jansen has little to say about the specific *theological* content of the narratives that sustain faith communities, since theology—an awareness of God's presence and power—is a critical ingredient of story-telling among Christians who find themselves far from home. Nonetheless, her analysis is of a piece with Rudy Wiebe's intentionally disjointed narrative, suggesting that unsettled, "Third Space" existence is characteristic of the life of faith, indeed that stories of being "on the way" are an essential feature of the narrative that shapes Christian identity:

> Christian migrants' life stories reflect the ambiguity of "place," combining the need to be at home and on the way, rooted, and detached. Their stories incarnate Christianity in its paradox of always being contextual and a particular faith of certain people attached to certain soil, surroundings, and ties with family and neighbours, yet always being summoned to cross the boundaries, to break with the ties of blood, nation, and fixed identities.[55]

"Whither Must I Fly?"

Complicating matters further is the fact that we have at best an incomplete sense of the destination toward which we are headed. The disciples

---

52. Jansen, "Christian Migrants," 154.
53. Jansen, "Christian Migrants," 157.
54. Jansen, "Christian Migrants," 158.
55. Jansen, "Christian Migrants," 159.

to whom Mark refers know that they are headed for Jerusalem, and are not comforted by the thought because they know it to be a place of deadly opposition (Mark 10:32). Post-resurrection disciples have even less information about their spiritual destination, beyond the metaphor of the "heavenly city" (as in Hebrews or the Apocalypse of John), or Paul's description of the "heavenly dwelling" with its "eternal weight of glory," to which he looks with longing (2 Cor 4:16–5:2). First John states the matter in still simpler terms, both as to the prospect of transformation and our ignorance regarding its precise contours: "What we will be has not yet been revealed. What we do know is this: when he is revealed, we will be like him, for we will see him as he is" (1 John 3:2). John Bunyan's description of Christian as he first sets out for the Celestial City captures the tension between trust and uncertain vision that applies to pilgrimage in principle. Christian (as he will henceforth be known) is addressing the Evangelist who has urged him to leave his wife, children, and home behind. "Whither must I fly?" he asks.

> Then said *Evangelist*, pointing with his finger over a very wide Field, Do you see yonder *Wicket-gate*? The man said, No. Then said the other, Do you see yonder shining light? He said, I think I do. Then said *Evangelist*, Keep that light in your eye, and go up directly thereto . . .[56]

Whatever its cause, Christian's metaphysical myopism is such that he can do no more than keep his eyes fixed on a distant light; it is hardly a detailed description of the way ahead, and offers no hint either of the dangers that still await him or of the city beyond the river that is his eventual goal. This is what it means for him to walk by faith and "not by sight."

We gain a clearer sense (if that is not a contradiction in terms) of imperfect Christian vision in the theological tension that emerges from comparing Paul's metaphors of mirroring in 1 and 2 Corinthians, respectively.[57] On the one hand, the apostle declares that "all of us, with unveiled faces, seeing [κατοπτριζόμενοι] the glory of the Lord as though reflected in a mirror, are being transformed into the same image from one degree of glory to another" (2 Cor 3:18 NRSV; cf. NIV: "who with unveiled faces *contemplate* the Lord's glory"). According to this reading of the passage, transformation is the consequence of contemplation, as believers gaze on "the glory of God in the face of Jesus Christ" (2 Cor

---

56. Bunyan, *Pilgrim's Progress*, 11, 13.
57. For fuller discussion, see Knowles, *We Preach Not Ourselves*, 121–37.

4:6), himself "the image of the invisible God" (Col 1:15). Even so, says the apostle, for the moment "we see in a mirror, dimly [ἐν αἰνίγματι], but then we will see face to face. Now I know only in part; then I will know fully, even as I have been fully known" (1 Cor 13:12). But the more closely we examine this second passage the more enigmatic it appears. Ancient bronze mirrors (for which Corinth was famous) gave back at best a distorted image.[58] But to whose image does the apostle refer? Read in light of 2 Corinthians, Paul might be suggesting a contrast between the mirror image (Christ) and the prospect of seeing (and knowing) God fully, "face to face." A more natural interpretation of the metaphor, however, is that the image in the mirror is that of the beholder, as yet imperfect and in process of change, in which case the intended contrast is between seeing oneself as yet imperfectly and seeing God. That neither interpretation is fully satisfactory seems somehow fitting, since Paul's main point is that whether with respect to ourselves or to God, "our knowledge is imperfect" (1 Cor 13:9). Although we gaze on God's glory in the face of Christ with unveiled faces of our own, we do not see clearly, as a result of which the process of "being transformed into the same image from one degree of glory to another" is incremental, imperfect, and as yet incomplete. As the RSV has it, "we see in a mirror dimly." Only in seeing God will we be able to see ourselves.

Elsewhere, Paul parses the matter more finely: "You have died," he tells the believers at Colossae, "and your life is hidden with Christ in God" (Col 3:3). But of course, they have not died, at least not in any physical sense. The only one who has actually died is the Messiah, in whom their own lives are at present concealed. Christ too is hidden, for as Paul goes on to explain, "When Christ who is your life is *revealed*, then you also will be revealed with him in glory" (Col 3:4).[59] So Christ and his glory are hidden from their eyes, and the saints themselves are hidden in him. Not even their own death is yet visible. The closest they have come to seeing either death or resurrection has been in the preaching of Paul, who sets the public spectacle of Jesus' crucifixion before the eyes of his audience (Gal 3:1). Yet herein lies the paradox of Christian vision, for the debacle of this death is not what it seems. As Paul explains in 2 Cor 5:16, "Even though we once regarded Christ according to the flesh, we regard him thus no longer" (ESV). To regard the Crucified One merely κατὰ σάρκα

---

58. So Fee, *First Epistle to the Corinthians*, 647–48.

59. The variant "our life" does not affect the theological intent of the passage; see Metzger, *Textual Commentary*, 557.

is to perceive, quite literally, nothing more than a dead body, whereas to behold him with eyes of faith is to discern a glorious transformation that is still hidden from their physical sight. Yet seeing Christ this way enables them to see themselves in the same light also: "From now on therefore," Paul reasons, "We regard no one according to the flesh." This leads him to a triumphant conclusion: "If anyone is in Christ, they are a new creation; the old has passed away, behold, the new has come" (2 Cor 5:17 RSV). We might wish to linger, if only for a moment, over the tenses of Paul's verbs: despite their ostensible similarity in translation, "the old *has passed away* [παρῆλθεν]" is an aorist, while "the new *has come* [γέγονεν]" is in the perfect tense. The first of these situates "the old" firmly in the past, as something done and gone, whereas the second describes a reality that continues into the present: all that is "new" is now and always with us.[60] But as pastors and preachers know only too well, our vision is not always this clear. Jesus himself warns that "the coming of the kingdom of God is not something that can be observed" (Luke 17:20 NIV); as he tells Thomas, "Blessed are those who have not seen and yet have come to believe" (John 20:29). Paul expresses the paradox neatly, bidding his readers see what cannot, in fact, be seen: "We look not to the things that are seen but to the things that are unseen; for the things that are seen are transient, but the things that are unseen are eternal" (2 Cor 4:18 RSV).

While these passages concern perception, discernment, and striving to see a destination or transformation that cannot yet be seen, the most compelling New Testament rendition of the interstitial dislocation, instability, and incomplete vision that characterize pilgrimage is the account in the Letter to the Hebrews of Abraham, his family, and their descendants in faith:

> By faith Abraham obeyed when he was called to set out for a place that he was to receive as an inheritance; and he set out, not knowing where he was going. By faith he stayed for a time in the land he had been promised, as in a foreign land, living in tents, as did Isaac and Jacob, who were heirs with him of the same promise. For he looked forward to the city that has foundations, whose architect and builder is God. By faith he received power of procreation, even though he was too old—and Sarah herself was barren—because he considered him faithful who had promised. Therefore from one person, and this one as good

---

60. I am grateful to my colleague Dr. Chris Land for explaining the function of the tenses in this passage.

> as dead, descendants were born, "as many as the stars of heaven and as the innumerable grains of sand by the seashore." All of these died in faith without having received the promises, but from a distance they saw and greeted them. They confessed that they were strangers and foreigners on the earth, for people who speak in this way make it clear that they are seeking a homeland. If they had been thinking of the land that they had left behind, they would have had opportunity to return. But as it is, they desire a better country, that is, a heavenly one. Therefore God is not ashamed to be called their God; indeed, he has prepared a city for them. (Heb 11:8–16)

That a new home and homeland awaits the travelers—a city with solid underpinnings "whose architect and builder is God"—is not in doubt. What is remarkable, however, is that Abraham is said to have set out "not knowing where he was going"; that he did not receive what had been promised, even though he lived within its geographical boundaries; and that his innumerable offspring were as much "strangers and foreigners" as he himself had been. Even more remarkable is the fact that this passage is addressed not to Abraham and Sarah's physical descendants, but to followers of Jesus. The implication is that, having suffered for their faith (Heb 10:32–34), the Christian believers have likewise left behind the lands to which they once belonged, and have no desire to return (11:15). In the next chapter, the author will assure readers that they have already "come to Mount Zion and to the city of the living God, the heavenly Jerusalem, and to innumerable angels in festal gathering, and to the assembly of the firstborn who are enrolled in heaven" (12:22–23). Even so, they have not yet fully entered the "better country" that awaits them, but—rather than resting from their journey—must still "run with perseverance" the race that lies ahead, keeping their own eyes fixed on Christ (12:1–2; cf. 4:11). They too, in the similar language of 1 Peter, are "aliens and exiles" on the earth (1 Pet 2:11; cf. 1:17).

The value of acknowledging both cultural and theological dislocation will differ according to the preferences of those who embrace this dynamic. For some, no doubt, the provisional, interstitial character of lived Christian identity will promise liberation from rigid theological formulas (concepts of God in particular), while others will find relief from stifling cultural patterns or ossified ways of "doing church." But to acknowledge the unsettled, temporal, and temporary nature of Christian self-expression is not the same as denying the possibility of fixed points of reference. An ocean-going vessel must lose sight of its embarkation point (even more so the shipyard at which it was first built) long before it reaches the port that is its destination. Yet navigating a trajectory far from land relies nonetheless on fixed points of geographical origin and arrival. Even the Israelites' proverbial forty years of wandering in the Sinai, for all its temporary indeterminacy, assumes a basic orientation away from bondage in Egypt and toward the land of promise. The position of a wayfarer is only provisional relative to other positions that are less so. In this case, the resurrection of Jesus presents itself in absolute terms; only as such is it capable of disorienting and reorienting us by drawing us toward itself, away from the ambit of our customary perspectives. Bhabha himself insists that the necessity of negotiating interstitial identity "is no plea for unregulated open-endedness or the celebration of pluralism":

> It is, in fact, an argument for recognizing the necessity of that anxious movement of minority enunciation that insists upon the possibility of choice—ethical, aesthetic, political—in those negotiations of culture and identity, where the proximate relation of difference and distance reveals a straitened, precarious path between circling in pale dreams, and entering the deep current.[61]

A more obvious challenge is the likelihood that from both sides of a social, cultural, or theological divide, hybrid identity will be perceived as a form of grave disloyalty. As sociologist Paul Gilroy observes,

> where racist, nationalist, or ethnically absolutist discourses orchestrate political relationships so that these identities appear to be mutually exclusive, occupying the space between them or trying to demonstrate their continuity has been viewed as a provocative and even oppositional act of political insubordination.[62]

In the realm of theology and resurrection, bystanders on the anthropological shore may accuse the pilgrims of being "so heavenly minded that they are no earthly good," while those who prefer to identify with the "cloud of witnesses" from Hebrews 12:1 are more likely to decry what

---

61. Bhabha, "Editor's Introduction," 459.

62. Gilroy, *Black Atlantic*, 1; quoted in part by Huddart, *Bhabha*, 113. Gilroy's own concern is for Black experience and identity in Britain, seeking "to address the continuing lure of ethnic absolutism in cultural criticism produced by both blacks and whites" (3).

they see as a betrayal of doctrinal confidence. Paradoxically, the same fear of uncertainty, contingency, and the elusiveness of absolutes characterizes discourse on either side of this theological debate. What many of the skeptics and critics of resurrection have in common is unwillingness to venture far from a safe epistemological shore, or to risk the possibility of encountering and being encountered by the unfathomable mystery of God. Yet on the other side is an equivalent, equally entrenched reluctance to admit that faith entails trust in God rather than in doctrinal or ethical positions that—even within classic orthodoxy—remain open to debate and recontextualization. Bhabha states the matter bluntly, choosing to do so in theological language: "Hybridity," he says, "is heresy."[63] Yet, he insists, "Such negotiation is neither assimilation nor collaboration": to occupy a "Third Space" is, rather, to be poised in a "dangerous indeterminacy" between the two.[64] In like manner, to follow Jesus is, as much today as in the Gospel of Mark, to be "on the way" toward Jerusalem, where Jesus will declare to Pilate, "My kingdom is not of this world" (John 18:36 NIV), then prove his case by submitting to the powers of this world and promptly rising above them. On this trajectory, the only certainty is that of death, toward which Jesus and his followers advance in the confident conviction that absolute certainty and complete clarity of vision are only to be found on the far side of that boundary.

The Letter to the Hebrews describes Christian faith as "the assurance of things hoped for, the conviction of things not seen" (Heb 11:1). The contradictory illogic of this assertion only makes sense in, yet also makes sense of, the "Third Space" that is Christian discipleship. Although applying in its original context to an analysis of multinational economics and their impact on cultural expression, Bhabha's description of the new identities that arise in such a "Third Space" seems even more relevant to Christian pilgrimage: "Being in the 'beyond,' then, is to inhabit an intervening space, as any dictionary will tell you. But to dwell 'in the beyond' is also . . . to be part of a revisionary time . . . *to touch the future on its hither side*."[65] To be a pilgrim, a person of faith, a follower of the resurrected Jesus, is likewise "to touch the future on its hither side." Pilgrimage is, by definition, a liminal state, a journey undertaken in the direction of the sacred in full confidence that upon arrival, one will be able to touch,

---

63. Bhabha, *Location of Culture*, 32, 225.
64. Bhabha, "Culture's In Between," 32, 34.
65. Bhabha, *Location of Culture*, 7 (emphasis original).

encounter, experience a reality more holy and transcendent than the place from which one first set out.[66] More precisely, as John Inge observes,

> pilgrimage is, firstly, about roots: it reminds the traveller of the Christian heritage of which he or she is a part . . . Secondly, pilgrimage is about journey. It reminds those travelling that their lives are a journey to God . . . [Finally,] biblical images reveal the third ingredient of pilgrimage, an eschatological one, which is about destination and the consummation of all things in Christ.[67]

According to this formulation of pilgrimage, our point of departure is not simply home and family (as, variously, for Abraham and Sarah, Bunyan's Christian, or "the ties of blood, nation, and fixed identities" of which Jansen speaks),[68] nor even human culture generally, but ecclesiastical cultures in particular—"our roots in the Christian faith which give a new relationship to time and place."[69] On this view, pilgrims are called beyond even the best of Christian tradition toward what Paul describes as "the depths of God"—that which "no eye has seen, nor ear heard, nor human heart conceived" (1 Cor 2:9–10). It is in this context that the Word of God bids us listen and on this basis that Christian preaching proceeds. Modelled on the gracious divine Word that is Jesus of Nazareth, the sermon is something other than ordinary human speech (1 Thess 2:13) because it announces a reality that is of more than human origin, and is therefore inexplicable in human terms alone. Like pilgrimage in principle, preaching invites the listeners "to touch the future on its hither side." Accordingly, the sermon does not rely for its force on customary strategies of rhetoric and persuasion (1 Thess 2:3–6), but on the counterintuitive,

---

66. On the liminal character of pilgrimage, see Turner and Turner, *Image and Pilgrimage in Christian Culture*, 1–39; since, in liminality, the individual "passes through a realm or dimension that has few or none of the attributes of the past or coming state, he is betwixt and between all familiar lines of classification" (2); accordingly, "A pilgrim is one who divests himself of the mundane concomitants of religion . . . to confront, in a special, 'far' milieu, the basic elements and structures of his faith in their unshielded, virgin radiance" (15).

67. Inge, *Christian Theology of Place*, 92; as Inge goes on to explain, pilgrimage "speaks about this world and the next. If the destination of pilgrimage is viewed in a sacramental light, it will combine the biblical themes of place and placelessness, reminding us that 'here we have no abiding city' and are continually called to journey forth."

68. Jansen, "Christian Migrants," 159.

69. Inge, *Christian Theology of Place*, 92.

otherworldly, and eschatological character of its subject matter. Neither, of course, does the preacher stand in the place of God or speak directly on God's behalf, not least because this is the prerogative of Christ alone. Rather, the preacher speaks with what we may venture to call a "Third Voice," bearing witness to grace in a manner that coheres with the transformative graciousness that is the hallmark of resurrection.

Third Voice and the Voice of Preaching

If the story of Abraham and Sarah—setting out for an unknown destination, living in tents on promised ground that was never fully theirs—provides a model for the interstitial, "in-between" nature of Christian identity, its counterpart for the task of Christian preaching is Luke's description of the day of Pentecost. The apostles are already successful preachers, however limited their experience. Although Luke initially omits the detail that Jesus appointed the twelve "to be with him, and to be sent out to preach [κηρύσσειν]" (Mark 3:14 RSV; cf. Luke 6:13), he subsequently affirms that Jesus "sent them out to preach the kingdom of God [κηρύσσειν τὴν βασιλείαν τοῦ θεοῦ] and to heal" (Luke 9:2). Accordingly, he writes, "they departed and went through the villages, preaching the gospel [εὐαγγελιζόμενοι] and healing everywhere" (9:6 RSV). But this initial success turns to bitter defeat—for the Messiah and themselves alike. If the other evangelists are to be believed (although Luke himself maintains a deferential silence on this point), it takes a series of appearances by the risen Christ to dissuade the surviving apostles from abandoning discipleship altogether and simply resuming the lives from which he had first called them. Luke's own portrait of the Eleven on the eve of Pentecost is no more flattering: they interrogate Jesus about the timing of his public enthronement (Acts 1:6) and are clearly puzzled when he chooses instead to disappear into heaven (Acts 1:9–11). The spectacular success of their later preaching does not alter the fact that immediately prior to the day of Pentecost, they have little concrete sense of what the future holds beyond an awareness of needing to restore their fellowship to its full complement (Acts 1:15–26).

Without suggesting that Pentecost itself is repeatable, much less that Christian preachers may model themselves directly on the reconstituted Twelve, the events of this day are nonetheless theologically paradigmatic.[70]

---

70. An earlier version of this analysis (contrasting the theological trajectories of

Luke's account is in three parts: a description of numinous experience (Acts 2:1–4), the response of the onlookers (2:5–13), and the explanation provided by Peter in the form of his first post-resurrection sermon (2:14–36). The essential feature of this experience is not its phenomenological details but their attribution to the Spirit of God:

> When the day of Pentecost had come, they were all together in one place. And suddenly from heaven there came a sound like the rush of a violent wind, and it filled the entire house where they were sitting. Divided tongues, as of fire, appeared among them, and a tongue rested on each of them. All of them were filled with the Holy Spirit and began to speak in other languages [ἡτέραις γλώσσαις], as the Spirit gave them ability. (Acts 2:1–4)

The apostles speak with words that are not their own. What is especially striking about this account is that it is unique in the New Testament. Although Paul on one occasion refers to speaking in the language of angels (1 Cor 13:1), an idea also current in Jewish tradition (attributed in *b. Sukkah* 28a to Paul's near contemporary, Yohanan ben Zakkai), nowhere is there any further mention of *heteroglossia*, which is the supernatural ability to speak in human languages other than one's own. At first glance, this experience seems to run counter to the trajectory of Jesus' incarnation, which affirms in principle the specific circumstances of human identity (including details of language and culture). It also runs counter to the hierarchy of social and religious values that orders the world in which they live, since the region from which the Messiah and his locally recruited disciples originate is considered a critical disqualification for any rôle in the purposes of God. Referring to the controversy that arises over Jesus' birth in Bethlehem of Galilee (John 7:41–52), Seán Freyne notes the "Jerusalem/Judean disdain for Galileans as unlettered and ignorant of the Torah."[71] That Yohanan ben Zakkai is reported to have said, "O Galilee, Galilee, you have hated the Torah. You will end up working for tax farmers" (*y. Šabb.* 16:8 [15d]) attests to the dismal reputation of this region among the religiously learned elite. So likewise for the apostles on the day of Pentecost (as with Peter in Matt 26:73), their distinctive manner of speech establishes their place of origin, situating them as "other" and at some distance from the ostensible focus of God's favor, which is

---

Babel and Pentecost) appeared as Knowles, "Cross-Cultural Preaching," 69–84, esp. 89–95.

71. Freyne, *The Jesus Movement and Its Expansion*, 133.

Jerusalem. For the disciples to speak in accents other than their own might seem yet a further denial of their most basic identity. Those who are already considered to be on the margins are impelled by the Spirit of God to speak in the languages of those who are even further from the center.

The second movement of Luke's account addresses this question directly:

> Now there were devout Jews from every nation under heaven living in Jerusalem. And at this sound the crowd gathered and was bewildered, because each one heard them speaking in the native language of each. Amazed and astonished, they asked, "Are not all these who are speaking Galileans? And how is it that we hear, each of us, in our own native language? Parthians, Medes, Elamites, and residents of Mesopotamia, Judea and Cappadocia, Pontus and Asia, Phrygia and Pamphylia, Egypt and the parts of Libya belonging to Cyrene, and visitors from Rome, both Jews and proselytes, Cretans and Arabs—in our own languages we hear them speaking about God's deeds of power." (Acts 2:5–11)

In future, the miracle of heteroglossia will be replaced by the more prosaic expediency of translation, which may explain why it is never repeated. On this occasion, however, it makes an important theological point, as the Spirit of God moves each apostle to announce divine works of power (τὰ μεγαλεῖα τοῦ θεοῦ) in words that affirm the linguistic specificity of the hearers, rather than that of the speakers. In fact, this is the exact trajectory of the incarnation, which foregoes authority and privilege in order to announce divine salvation in terms that are native to its intended recipients.

Notwithstanding the lack of detail in this description, it is reasonable to assume that the subject of their discourse is what God has recently accomplished in and through Jesus of Nazareth, not least because Luke's previous volume begins with similar language ("the Mighty One has done great things [μεγάλα] for me, and holy is his name"; Luke 1:49).[72] As with God's reversal of what Mary calls her own "lowliness" (Luke 1:48 NRSV)

---

72. Although the alternative μεγαλεῖα in some manuscripts makes the parallel more obvious, the original wording of Acts 2:11 is meant to recall LXX Deut 10:21: "He is your boast, and he is your God, who did among you these great and glorious things [τὰ μεγάλα καὶ τὰ ἔνδοξα ταῦτα] that your eyes have seen" (NETS; similarly LXX Deut 11:7); cf. Fitzmyer, *Luke I–IX*, 367–68.

or "humble state" (NIV), so this Spirit-impelled testimony to divine power presumably speaks, as will Peter moments later, of the abasement and exaltation of Jesus of Nazareth (so Acts 2:22–24), much as the act of testifying itself affirms and dignifies the otherwise unauthorized, allegedly ignorant, and culturally unimpressive "Galileans." By the standards of their co-religionists, they are less than fully credible witnesses, and the presence among them of former tax collectors and revolutionaries will not have lessened this impression. Yet rather than abandoning them as they themselves once abandoned Jesus, God anoints them with the Spirit of holiness and empowers them to testify concerning the Messiah. In this way, we see witnesses from the geographical margins speaking in Jerusalem, the traditional center of God's work, of a rejected and vindicated Messiah, in language that affirms the identities of hearers who also hail from a distance, while at the same time directing their attention beyond those identities to the ways and works of God.

Both sides of this equation—center and margins, absolute and contingent, divine and human—are critical to the concept of "Third Voice."[73] On the one hand, that each of those present on the day of Pentecost should hear such testimony in their own "native language" affirms and ennobles the hearers. As Frank Yamada observes, "When the Holy Spirit falls on the disciples, they do not break into a meta-language, a single-tongue . . . The LORD of the earth prefers the plural over the singular, languages over a single-tongue, cultures over one defining culture."[74] Vinoth Ramachandra explains further:

> In many instances, language belongs to the core of what constitutes a cultural identity . . . What has distinguished the Christian movement from, say, the ancient Asian religions or global Islam is the way, from its inception, the church did not sacralize either the language of Jesus [or] the place of his origins. The language that Jesus used in his preaching was quickly abandoned in favor of country (Koine) Greek and "vulgar" Latin as the uniting

---

73. The concept of "Third Voice" thus formally corresponds to the manner in which Third Space itself, reflecting the categories proposed by Emmanuel Lévinas, represents a negotiation between "the general conditions of language, and the specific implications of the utterance" (Bhabha, *Location of Culture*, 37). That is, "the linguistic liminality of the Third Space is an area where neither the general nor the specific hold sway, but any symbolic, cultural or linguistic interpretation is an 'ambivalent' process that needs to be negotiated between the two" (Baker, *Hybrid Church*, 18).

74. Yamada, "The View From 2040," quoted in part in Kwok, "Postcolonial Preaching," 19.

media of communication. The entire New Testament was written in a language other than the one in which Jesus preached. That the eternal counsels of God belonged to the commonplace, everyday speech of ordinary men and women was a view that was, and remains, revolutionary.[75]

This insight is likewise central to the theology of West African scholar Lamin Sanneh, for whom God's commitment to human culture via the incarnate Jesus of Nazareth validates all cultural expressions of the Christian gospel. "Christianity," he writes,

> has felt so congenial in English, Italian, German, French, Spanish, Russian, and so on, that we forget it wasn't always so, or we inexcusably deny that the religion might feel equally congenial in other languages, such as Amharic, Geez, Arabic, Coptic, Tamil, Korean, Chinese, Swahili, Shona, Twi, Igbo, Wolof, Yoruba, and Zulu. Our cultural chauvinism makes us overlook Christianity's vernacular character.[76]

But Sanneh is quick to point out the other side of the equation, which is that while God's commitment to one culture in the person of Jesus of Nazareth implies a commitment to human culture in principle, the fact that this is a divine initiative ultimately relativizes all cultures and all forms of cultural expression:

> The fact of Christianity being a translated, and translating, religion places God at the center of the universe of cultures, implying free coequality among cultures and a necessary relativizing of languages vis-à-vis the truth of God. No culture is so advanced and so superior that it can claim exclusive access or advantage to the truth of God, and none is so marginal or inferior that it can be excluded. All have merit; none is indispensable.[77]

His comments on biblical translation, understood in light of the incarnation, apply in equal measure to the task of preaching (for what is preaching, after all, than a species of contextualized translation?):

> Translation as radical pluralism promotes cultural particularity while affirming the universal God as its relativizing ground . . . Radical pluralism is radical in the boldness with which the word

---

75. Ramachandra, *Subverting Global Myths*, 133.

76. Sanneh, *Whose Religion is Christianity?*, 105.

77. Sanneh, *Whose Religion is Christianity?*, 105–6, quoted in part by Ramachandra, *Subverting Global Myths*, 147.

of God is invested in the vernacular, and pluralist in denying to
any one language an exclusive claim in the "plan of salvation."[78]

In this light, it seems fitting to recall Salman Rushdie's comment, quoted earlier, that "having been borne across the world, we are translated men"[79] alongside the language of the King James Version, which affirms that God has "translated us into the kingdom of his dear Son" (Col 1:13). This fortuitous overlap of language allows us to observe that the "translation" entailed by Christian confession is holistic, existential, and theological in nature before it is specifically linguistic. Christian proclamation is not simply a matter of negotiating between the semantic domains of various different languages or cultures; still less (scriptural inspiration notwithstanding) may it reduce a receptor language to the conceptual categories of a preacher's native tongue. Rather, the prospect (or experience!) of being reconfigured by the reign of God is what impels communication across other, less radical boundaries of culture and language. Accordingly, the more obvious negotiation in Luke's account between centers and margins (Jerusalem vis-à-vis Galilee; Judea vis-à-vis "the ends of the earth"; eventually, Jew vis-à-vis Samaritan, then Gentile) turns out to be provisional (the technical term is "propaedeutic") rather than intrinsic to the gospel of Christ. There is no privileging of the "margins" in Christian faith because the powerful and the disempowered alike are equally disenfranchised and embraced by divine grace. In this regard, it is helpful to recall the universal intent of Paul's insistence in Rom 3:22–23, serving as the climax of his address to Gentiles and Jews alike, "there is no distinction, *all* have sinned and fall short of the glory of God" (cf. Rom 10:12). Or, as the Letter to the Ephesians explains, the consequence of Christ having "proclaimed peace to you who were far off and peace to those who were near" is that all without distinction are now equally "members of the household of God" (Eph 2:17, 19).

This tension between a universalizing divine initiative and the contextualized particularity of its local expression or address is implied already in Jesus' charge to the future apostolic missionaries, which maps the future of their ministry (as well as dictating the literary shape of the book of Acts): "You will receive power when the Holy Spirit has come upon you," he tells, them, "and you will be my witnesses in Jerusalem, in all Judea and Samaria, and to the ends of the earth" (Act 1:8). Jesus'

---

78. Sanneh, *Translating the Message*, 243–44.
79. Rushdie, "Imaginary Homelands," 17.

last words before ascending into heaven indicate that the message of his vindication applies equally everywhere, even "to the ends of the earth." In the same measure that the apostles' message concerns divine vindication of humanity (and not societal reconciliation alone), so the task of proclamation itself relies on divine power as a gift of the Spirit of God.

Thus the subject of apostolic preaching (Jesus of Nazareth), the life histories of those who preach, the language and manner of their speech, and the diversity of their addressees all entail the same cruciform tension that gives rise to the "Third Voice" of preaching.[80] In keeping with the definitive trajectory of Jesus' incarnation, crucifixion, and resurrection, preaching in a "Third Voice" is always poised between cultural particularity and the christocentric relativizing of all cultures; between divine affirmation of our human identity and its transformation by the power of God. It stands at the margins not just of this culture or of that, but of all human cultures, and of humanity itself, in a Third Space that opens to new creation by means of God's gift of life.

Postcolonial Homiletics: Preaching between Departure and Destination

With or without explicit reference to Bhabha, postcolonial theory has provided a helpful framework for the recovery and empowerment of marginalized voices in the context of Christian preaching, as well as, more broadly, the development of homiletical approaches rooted in (for example) Hispanic,[81] Caribbean,[82] Korean-American,[83] and/or

---

80. Cruciformity is essentially binary, envisaging abasement as the prelude to renewal, whereas the manifold languages of Pentecost suggest initial affirmation as the prelude to divinely authored displacement (thus moving toward rather than away from negation). But the difference between the respective trajectories is more apparent than real, for the Pentecostal embrace of culturally specific address corresponds to the specificity of Jesus' incarnation. Both forms of divine address (as the incarnate and the apostolic Word, respectively) anticipate reversal and redemption, with resurrection corresponding to the transcending of all human culture. Accordingly, both are formally "cruciform."

81. González, "Standing at the Púlpito," 57–69; Jiménez, "Toward a Postcolonial Homiletic," 159–67 (esp. 166–67); Jiménez, "The Troublemaker's Friend," 84–90.

82. Valle-Ruiz, "Toward Postcolonial Liturgical Preaching," 28–37; Jiménez, "If You Just Close Your Eyes," 21–27 (asserting that *traditional deductive preaching is colonial preaching*"! [22; emphasis original]).

83. Kim, *Preaching the Presence of God*; Kim, "Possible Selves," 1–17; Kim,

Filipino-American[84] cultural distinctives. No less boldly, Sarah Travis undertakes to consider the implications of postcolonial critique for the beneficiaries of colonialism.[85] Taking the initiative to counter Eurocentric and colonial biases within Western homiletical tradition is wholly consistent with the radical diversity and cultural democracy expressed at Pentecost. As Pablo Jiménez observes, "Postcolonial homiletics challenge those deemed as subaltern by the colonial powers to embrace, claim and proclaim the full humanity that God has given them . . . The postcolonial preacher has the opportunity to shepherd a community of faith to a life of freedom and dignity."[86] According to Travis, preaching that seeks to unmask colonial bias assumes responsibility for examining cultural and historical legacies in light of the priorities of divine justice: "[This] include[s] recognizing difference and diversity within the listening community and beyond, naming colonialism/imperialism as a past and present reality, speaking against the damaging and destructive patterns and discourses that have emerged within colonial/imperial project, and coming to terms with the relationship between Church and empire."[87] Kwok Pui-lan advocates an even more radical approach:

> As both globalization and localization intensify in our contemporary world, it is critical for the preacher as performer to understand multiple subjectivities and belongings among members of the congregation. She must avoid defining identity based on territorial essentialism (e.g., Asia or Africa), cultural essentialism (e.g., Confucian), or racial essentialism (e.g., Black), because identity is fluid, porous, and hybrid, and is constantly shifting.[88]

Kwok conceives of postcolonial preaching "as a locally rooted and globally conscious performance that seeks to create a Third Space so that the faith community can imagine new ways of being in the world and

---

Preaching to Second Generation Korean Americans.

84. Presa, *Ascension Theology and Habakkuk*, 27–37.

85. Travis, *Decolonizing Preaching*, passim; summarized in Travis, "Troubled Gospel," 46–54.

86. Jiménez, "The Troublemaker's Friend," 85.

87. Travis, *Decolonizing Preaching*, 48.

88. Kwok, "Postcolonial Preaching," 10. Similarly appealing for "transcontextual preaching" is Kim, *Preaching in an Age of Globalization*; further, Kim, *Christian Preaching and Worship in Multicultural Contexts*.

encountering God's salvific action for the oppressed and marginalized."[89] Appealing to the work of Austin and Searle, she proposes that "through speech act and gestures, the preacher as performer seeks to act or consummate an action, to construct new realities, and to perform or signal possible new identities."[90] However, our own exploration of speech act Theory has called into question the extent to which it lies within the power of any preacher to "construct" the new reality that is the reign of God. For us to embrace postcolonial theory as an expression of solidarity with the marginalized while at the same time remaining confident of our ability to "construct new realities" rightly makes common cause with the socially and materially disenfranchised yet fails to acknowledge our own theological estrangement from God. However unwelcome the observation, it does not lie within the power of the dying to raise themselves or their hearers to new life—not, at least, the "new creation" that Jesus promises. As Dietrich Bonhoeffer trenchantly observes,

> The despairing cannot be saved by any law appealing to their own strength; this only drives them into more hopeless despair. Those who despair of life are helped only by the saving act of another, the offer of a new life that is lived not by their own strength but by the grace of God. Those who can no longer live cannot be helped by the command that they must live, but only by a new spirit.[91]

In their original context, Bonhoeffer's comments address the vexed question of suicide, yet they are equally applicable to all disciples whom Christ calls to join him in death, which is to participate in a kind of existential, theological "suicide" whereby we look beyond our own strength or vitality for the power that sustains our life.

If Travis is right to question the assumptions of colonial privilege at the level of social, political, or cultural identity, her critique is no less relevant at the interface of human culture and divine initiative. "Preaching is a theological task that names God's action in the world," she insists;

> Thus, postcolonial preaching disputes and/or resists colonizing discourse by casting an alternative vision of human community rooted in careful theological reflection . . . Postcolonial

---

89. Kwok, "Postcolonial Preaching," 10; that is, "the aim of postcolonial preaching is to create a multivocal and dialogical faith community committed to justice" (18).

90. Kwok, "Postcolonial Preaching," 10.

91. Bonhoeffer, *Ethics*, 200.

preaching cannot happen unless preachers are willing to acknowledge to themselves and to their listeners complicity with imperial systems, the first step in bringing to consciousness the reality that all inhabit colonial spaces.[92]

In our case, however, the situation is reversed. Postcolonial theory calls for justice and redress in the face of cultural hegemony; it sides with the colonized. A Christian worldview, by contrast, speaks of a rebellious creation and of wayward creatures who, like the tenant farmers who seize control of their master's vineyard in the parable that Jesus tells (Mark 12:1–8), resist the Lord of creation and refuse to acknowledge his authority, sometimes violently so. On this view of things, it is Christ who sides with the colonized, but only so as to remedy their insurrection by means of resurrection, restoring their true πολίτευμα "in heaven." Accordingly, preachers and congregations at all points on the social, cultural, and political spectrum might do well to acknowledge their own resistance to grace, which is to say, our stubborn insistence that we are perfectly capable of constructing "new realities" and "new identities" on our own, without need of divine aid and without reference to a new creation that is of God's own making.

Taking Kwok's anti-essentialism to its logical (and theological) limit, such a perspective encourages us to read Travis in a new light:

> Postcolonial theories continually question the power and authority of the "colonizer." In that sense, another question arises for affluent preachers. To what extent am I truly "powerful"? While I perceive myself to inhabit a privileged space, I may be suffering from a delusion of power that leads me to believe I have power to change a system over which I am actually entirely powerless.[93]

To be fair, Travis is referring to "the instability of authority and identity in a postcolonial world," rather than to human agency in principle, relative to the reign of God.[94] Nonetheless, she is fully conscious that Christian preaching is rooted by definition in prior divine action, and affirms that "the good news, the gospel claim of this approach is that we are being continually recreated to participate in an alternative discourse that has

---

92. Travis, "Troubled Gospel," 47, 49.
93. Travis, "Troubled Gospel," 50.
94. Travis, "Troubled Gospel," 50.

already been established by the Triune God."[95] Just so, to preach in a Third Voice, in the Third Space that is between departure and destination, is to join "an alternative discourse that has already been established by the Triune God."

In a perceptive analysis that merits extensive review, Sunggu Yang offers an illustration of what this kind of homiletical discourse looks like from an Asian American perspective. "At the core of Asian American preaching," he writes, "is the promise of the Promised Land."[96] In one sense, America itself has proven to be a land of promise, yet it is also one in which Asian Americans often feel marginalized by a predominantly non-Asian culture. In his own discussion of hybrid identity, Wan concurs that it is difficult for Asian Americans to situate themselves within American culture: "In straining at creating 'Asian American' as an acceptable intellectual category, Asians living in the United States have succeeded in constructing—so far, only for themselves—a hybrid space between 'us' and 'them,' a space that has yet to gain official recognition."[97] According to Yang, Christians seek to mitigate this tension by looking beyond an identity construed in binary terms as "Asian-American," to the more radically liminal character of spiritual pilgrimage:

> In other words, the immigrant's spiritual experience of pilgrimage, as the perpetual sojourner walking in a strange world and looking forward to another (heavenly) world, determines the constructs of faith. The metaphoric idea or the promise of the Promised Land best represents the other heavenly reality that Asian Americans perceive as the eventual terminal of their spiritual pilgrimage. What is important here is that the idea or perceived reality of the Promised Land is not really ethereal or purely other-worldly. Rather, the desired Promised Land synthesizes this-worldliness and other-worldliness.[98]

---

95. Travis, "Troubled Gospel," 54. Travis postulates that at the center of social Trinitarianism is "a space made within God's own self for the created order"—a kind of perichoretic, postcolonial "Third Space" that makes possible "relationships characterized by a similar freedom, mutuality, diversity, and openness" (*Decolonizing Preaching*, 127; further, 128–40).

96. Yang, "The Promised Land," 9.

97. Wan, "'To the Jew First and Also to the Greek,'" 138. In this regard, Lee ("Pilgrimage and Home," 51–53) makes a helpful distinction between "liminality or in-betweenness" (a feature of bicultural existence) and marginality, which is "a forced and permanent liminality."

98. Yang, "The Promised Land," 10.

In this sense, "Asian Americans construct their identity by means of *triple consciousness*," which is to say, as "*Asian, American,* and *Christian.*"[99] That is, "faith in Christ enables Asian Americans to envision a third liberative reality as the eventual destination of their faithful lives and the ultimate transformation of the current hostile foreign land."[100] Of particular importance for working out the implications of this interstitial, Third Space identity are biblical accounts (both from Genesis and Hebrews) of Abraham and Sarah, and the pilgrim theology of Saint Augustine.[101] This vision is, moreover, expressly christological, a manifestation of our call to new citizenship in what the Gospel of Matthew terms "the kingdom of the heavens" (Matt 3:2; 4:17; 5:3, etc.). In the words of H. Richard Niebuhr, "Through Christ we become immigrants into the empire of God which extends over all the world and learn to remember the history of that empire, that is of [people] in all times and places, as our history."[102] Central to such a vision is Jesus' resurrection, understood as victory over the marginalizing forces of human existence, the power of death above all. As Sang Hyun Lee explains,

> Jesus' resurrection from death confirmed that the marginalizing forces in the world are not the ultimately real powers, and that the extreme form of marginalization, namely death, is proved to have no ultimate power over the life-creating power of the loving and compassionate God. For Asian American believers who have united with Jesus . . . their social liminality and marginality in the United States have not been changed by their Lord's victory over the marginalizing forces. Their empirical, social situation remains the same as before. But the resurrection of Jesus in another sense has changed everything. Asian Americans who are united with Jesus are now united with the resurrected Jesus, and need not be afraid to face the disorienting and bewildering experience of liminality. They also need not be demoralized by their marginalization by the dominant white society.

---

99. Yang, "The Promised Land," 11; emphasis original. Yang's analysis builds on the work (each with distinctive emphases of their own) of Lee, *From A Liminal Place*; Matsuoka, *Out of Silence*; and Kwok, *Postcolonial Imagination and Feminist Theology*.

100. Yang, "The Promised Land," 15.

101. So Lee, "Pilgrimage and Home," 54–56; Yang, "The Promised Land," 15–22 (with reference to Bhabha pp. 14–15n17).

102. Niebuhr, *Meaning of Revelation*, 116, quoted in Lee, "Pilgrimage and Home," 57.

Dehumanizing marginalization has proven to be impotent in Jesus' victory over death.[103]

Identifying with Christ in this fashion inspires a spirituality of liminal existence between "This World" and "That Which Is to Come," which Yang describes as an "*already-but-not-yet* spirituality of the Promised Land."[104] Construing the preacher as "a fellow pilgrim who knows exactly what it means and how it feels to live as a stranger in the wilderness," with congregants as fellow citizens and "active agents of this grand promise of God," this approach invites "an unequivocal declaration and assurance that the Promised Land will happen (indeed is happening in the present!), but is *detectable* if only we have pilgrim eyes to see it."[105] As to sermon content, he argues, "The preacher's message promises the eschatological *Third Land* existing beyond Asian lands to which the people cannot go back and beyond American lands to which they cannot truly belong."[106]

Self-evidently, faithfulness to the priority of Christ and the otherworldly call of his resurrection (to say nothing of the day of Pentecost) require us to confess that preachers of all cultures and backgrounds are subject to the same conditions. To do otherwise—to cling, that is, to cultural privilege, epistemological prerogative, or claims of linguistic primacy—is to suffer from what Travis calls "a delusion of power," an anthropological absolutism characteristic of too many laborers in the Lord's vineyard. Not only, that is, those who grumble about their wages (Matt 20:1–16), but also those who resent their subaltern status and imagine that the vineyard would serve them better if they themselves owned the means of production (cf. Matt 21:33–41).

It is at this point that orientation to the resurrection of Jesus, Third Space thinking, hybrid identity, and the task of preaching converge. Whether physically, as at ancient Philippi, or in the broader terms of politics, culture, ideology, and world view, Christian existence is in principle liminal, poised in an unresolvable tension between life κατὰ σάρκα, "according to the flesh," on the one hand, and "new creation," on the other. To be "in Christ," mystically made one with him, is both to be affirmed in our essential humanity by his incarnation while at the same time made new by the power of his resurrection. Both are true for Christian pilgrims

---

103. Lee, *From A Liminal Place*, 85–86.
104. Yang, "The Promised Land," 22.
105. Yang, "The Promised Land," 23, 25–26.
106. Yang, "The Promised Land," 24.

as the opposite poles of departure and destination: in practice, we are situated (whether physically, culturally, or theologically) at neither extreme, but look to both as points of orientation relative to which we plot our trajectory and work out an interstitial, pro-tem identity for the life of the church. To preach from such a perspective is to discern in Pentecost the same two poles of orientation, with a robust affirmation of linguistic and cultural specificity that, in all its rich variety, is nonetheless transcended, re-oriented, and repatriated within the larger context of τὰ μεγαλεῖα τοῦ θεοῦ—God's "mighty works" of salvation. Christian preaching does not have the ability to bring this Third Space into being, nor does it directly transport its hearers to the "eschatological *Third Land*" of which Yang speaks. Rather, it names these things as the handiwork of God, telling stories of dislocation, instability, imperfect vision, homemaking while still en route, and promised arrival. In this sense, preaching is a species of joyful surrender; rather than presuming to stand in God's place—standing, we might say, in God's way—preachers and their sermons are exercises in yielding to God's transformative dominion, inviting hearers to yield in similar fashion as God calls us beyond ourselves, into the territory of promise that is the domain of resurrection, new life, and new creation. This is preaching in a Third Voice.

IV.

Waiting

6

God the Last Word

> You are not here to verify,
> Instruct yourself, or inform curiosity
> Or carry report. You are here to kneel.
>
> —T. S. Eliot, "Little Gidding" I.45–47[1]

> προσδοκοῦμεν ἀνάστασιν νεκρῶν
> καὶ ζωὴν τοῦ μέλλοντος αἰῶνος. Ἀμήν.
> We look for the resurrection of the dead,
> and the life of the world to come. Amen.
>
> —Niceno-Constantinopolitan Creed of 381

In 2003, we had the privilege of hosting Barbara Brown Taylor as our speaker for what was then the annual Gladstone Festival of Preaching at McMaster Divinity College. In one of her lectures, she recounted the following story:

> There was a story making the rounds a couple of years ago about a Zen master who visited a Trappist monastery in New England. He was astonished by the discipline he found there: the life of prayer and of silent withdrawal, of reverence. So astonished by it that he offered to lead a traditional Zen retreat for the Trappist monks with the customary ten hours of silent meditation every day, but with Christian *kōans*, or paradoxical sayings, given to the monks to ponder in place of the usual Buddhist ones. When

---

1. Eliot, *Collected Poems*, 215.

the first monk went in for his daily interview with the *Rōshi* ["Master"; "Teacher"], he found the *Rōshi* sitting there in the lotus position with two copies of the New Testament on the floor in front of him. There was a Japanese New Testament and an English New Testament. The *Rōshi* looked at the monk and said, "You know? I like Christianity." "But," he said, looking down at the books in front of him and then looking at the monk again, "I would not like it without the resurrection." Then leaning so close to the Trappist monk that their noses almost touched, the Master said, "Here is your *kōan*. Show me the resurrection." "That is your *kōan*," he said, "Show me your resurrection."[2]

The point of a *kōan* (most famously, "What is the sound of one hand clapping?") is paradox, contradiction, even logical absurdity. At least within Zen Buddhism, to grasp the absurd in this manner is to acknowledge the vanity of purely intellectual apprehension, as a necessary step toward attaining spiritual enlightenment.[3] Even for Christians, the Master's question seems suitably contradictory. How might I demonstrate my resurrection (more problematically still, that of Jesus) when, by definition, to do so is not within my power? All the more so, indeed, when participation in Jesus' resurrection is key to Christian spirituality. For some, as we have seen, the question itself is a logical absurdity, while for others the answer lies in various forms of moral, social, or political activism, whereby believers take primary responsibility for enacting the conditions of God's reign. Without discounting either the intellectual challenges or the ethical responsibilities implied by resurrection, might it be that a more suitable starting point lies elsewhere, in a spiritual posture of disavowal or intentional withdrawal? This proposal can be approached by way of either spatial or temporal metaphors. Each in its own way is an attempt to acknowledge the interstitial character of Christian pilgrimage; each is characteristic of preaching in what we have termed a Third Voice.

---

2. This account is a direct transcript of Taylor's Gladstone address. As Taylor acknowledges, the story is not original to her; its initial source is unclear, since it appears in various places both on the Internet and in print. The earliest source that I have been able to trace (possibly its origin) is Boyer, *A Way in the World*, 82–83.

3. See Schlütter, "Kōan," *EncBudd* 1:426–29.

Saint Augustine's Purse: Making Space for God

In the weeks that follow Easter of 415, the sixty-year-old bishop of Hippo Regius in North Africa, having been a Christian for nearly thirty years and at the height of his abilities as a theologian and exegete, chooses to preach a series of ten sermons on the First Epistle of Saint John.[4] In the course of his fourth homily, Augustine comes to 1 John 3:2: "What we do know is this: when he is revealed, we will be like him, for we will see him as he is." The learned bishop meditates on the soul's longing for God, and on the fact that God withholds fulfillment of our spiritual desire so as to encourage us to yearn even more:

> What has been promised us? *We shall be like him, because we shall see him as he is.* The tongue has sounded how this could be; let the rest be thought through by the heart. For what did John say when compared with him who is, and what can be said by us human beings who are utterly unequal to his merits?
>
> Let us return, then, to that anointing of his. Let us return to that anointing which teaches within what we are unable to speak, and, because now you are unable to see, let your task consist in desiring. The entire life of a good Christian is a holy desire. What you desire, however, you don't yet see. But by desiring you are made large enough, so that, when there comes what you should see, you may be filled. For, if you wish to fill a purse, and you know how big what will be given you is, you stretch the purse, whether it is made of cloth or leather or anything else. You know how much you are going to obtain, and you see that you purse is small; by stretching it you make it that much larger. This is how God stretches our desire through delay, stretches our soul through desire, and makes it large enough by stretching it. Let us desire, then, brothers, because we have to be filled. . . . Let us stretch out to him so that, when he comes, he may fill us. *We shall be like him, because we shall see him as he is.*[5]

Given the obvious fact of his own intellectual prowess, Augustine makes several remarkable assertions. The first is that intellect alone is incapable of appreciating spiritual truths that cannot even be put into words: they must instead be conveyed inwardly, in the heart, by divine anointing. In fact, he says, 1 John speaks of seeing what we cannot even see, let alone understand. All that remains, then, is an intense longing to glimpse

---

4. On the dating of this series, see Burnaby, preface to *Augustine: Later Works*, 14.
5. Augustine, *Homilies on the First Epistle of John*, 69–70; emphasis original.

Christ for ourselves, a desire that God expands and deepens by delaying even further, making us wait. A humble metaphor illustrates his point: just as one must stretch a cloth or leather purse in order for it to hold a large amount of money, so God stretches and enlarges the soul through this process of delay and anticipation. It is, perhaps, an imperfect illustration: the biblical text speaks of being transformed into the image of Christ, not of being filled or enriched. Nonetheless, Augustine insists that the soul must make room for God: even sightless and uncomprehending, it must make itself even more empty in order to receive the magnitude of what God intends.

In similar fashion, says Barth, "The task of the sermon is to create space for the Word of God."[6] In its original context this is no more than an off-hand comment, a parenthetical observation tossed out in the course of discussing the proper length for a sermon, but its implications are profound. Behind it lies Barth's all-important (and all-encompassing) concept of the Word of God itself. As John Webster explains, rather than being reducible either to the words of the biblical text or to a series of theological propositions, for Barth "The Word of God is an act which God undertakes."[7] As a dynamic process by which God makes himself known, the Word of God takes three forms: "the act of revelation itself, its attestation in the prophetic and apostolic words, and the preaching of that testimony in the community." But these three forms are not equivalent in status or force, since Scripture and preaching are both dependent upon the precedent of original divine revelation, in a manner akin to a series of concentric circles:

> The innermost circle is the Word of God in its pure form as divine speech-act; but it is surrounded by and only approachable through the human speech-acts of Scripture and proclamation which are appointed by God to be its bearers and witnesses, so becoming themselves God's word by derivation.[8]

That is, Scripture and proclamation are only truly God's Word by virtue of God's self-revelation in, through, and prior to them. This means, fundamentally, that rather than assuming or appropriating authority, text and preacher alike point away from themselves toward the sole source of

---

6. Barth, *Homiletics*, 122: "Denn es ist Aufgabe der Predigt, Raum zu schaffen für das Wort Gottes..." (*Homiletik*, 102).

7. Webster, *Barth*, 55.

8. Webster, *Barth*, 55.

their inspiration: "Proclamation and Scripture cannot 'bring [the Word of God] on the scene themselves' ([*CD*] I/1, p. 120); both are functions of the fundamental reality: *deus dixit*."[9] Barth himself states the matter bluntly: "In preaching God himself presents what God wills to present, and will present."[10] This revelational priority is a function of unalterable divine sovereignty, which Barth expresses in a single, striking maxim: "God is Lord in the wording of his Word" (*CD* I/1, p. 139).[11] As he explains in his lectures to young seminarians, "Preaching is not a neutral activity. It is not an action involving two equal partners. It can mean only Lordship on God's side and obedience on ours."[12]

For the preacher to "create space for the Word of God" implies surrender to divine sovereignty, in a form of linguistic and theological abdication that intentionally withdraws in order to leave room for God to act.[13] Rather than presuming to do the work of God on God's behalf, the preacher yields to the prerogative of divine agency implied by responsibility for declaring the Word *of God*. As noted earlier in our discussion of the missional church movement, Barth places great emphasis on this point:

> Preaching must conform to revelation. First this means negatively that in preaching we are not to repeat or transmit the revelation of God by what we do. Precisely because the point of the event of preaching is God's own speaking (*Deus loquitur*), there can be no question of our doing the revealing in any way. In all circumstances we must respect the fact that God *has* revealed himself and he will reveal himself as the one who comes again. All the action that takes place in preaching, which lies between the first advent and the second, is the action of the divine Subject.[14]

---

9. Webster, *Barth*, 56.
10. Barth, *Homiletics*, 49.
11. Quoted in Webster, *Barth*, 56.
12. Barth, *Homiletic*, 50.
13. Cf. Thane, "Speech Act Theory," 200: "Understanding . . . proclamation as a human act bound to God's truth and creating a new [i.e., linguistic] reality opens and expects to have this reality filled and actualised by God's sovereign act of revelation."
14. Barth, *Homiletic*, 47.

In short, he says, first, that "preaching cannot try to be a proof of the truth of God [der Wahrheit Gottes]" and, second, "preaching may not try to create the reality of God [die Wirklichkeit Gottes]."[15]

Drawing, presumably, on the ancient motif of God as a Master Builder, as well as Jesus' traditional occupation as a carpenter or craftsman (τέκτων; Mark 6:3), Marianne Gaarden employs the metaphor of preaching as a Third Room, a place and meaning situated neither in the immediate intent of the preacher nor in "the listener's frame of reference," but between the two in a liminal space of new understanding created by God:

> The preacher is not the carpenter who builds the Third Room, yet the Third Room is dependent on the preacher's willingness to participate in the construction of the Third Room as a tool. Preachers are not holding the tool, but are the tool to be held by the real carpenter of the Third Room—namely, God. With this understanding of God, preachers are participating in God, and whether they serve as a tool in the preaching event depends upon their willingness to relinquish themselves to God.[16]

In this she echoes Calvin's metaphor of the preacher as a tool or instrument in the hand of God,[17] effectively resolving the question of human agency in the kingdom of heaven by appeal to spirituality and the preacher's disposition toward God. It is equally the resolution of the challenge posed by Barth, whom Gaarden quotes with approval: "As ministers we ought to speak of God. We are human, however, and so cannot speak of God. We ought therefore to recognize both our obligation and our inability and by that very recognition give God the glory."[18]

---

15. Barth, *Homiletik*, 33 (ET 48).

16. Gaarden, *Third Room of Preaching*, 14–15; more fully, 113–18, although Gaarden conceives of "God" in non-transcendent terms: "God is not a substantial and transcendent reality about which we can preach, external to ourselves, but a reality in which we human beings are always and already participating" (119).

17. Calvin, *Epistle of Paul the Apostle to the Hebrews*, 255; *Institutes* IV.iii.1 (both cited above).

18. Gaarden, *Third Room of Preaching*, 103 and n4 (p. 158), citing the ET of Barth, *The Word of God and the Word of Man*, 186. However, the German original, which Gaarden also cites ("Wir sollen als *Theologen* von Gott reden. Wir sind aber Menschen und können als solche nicht von Gott reden. Wir sollen beides, unser sollen und unser Nicht-Können, wissen und eben damit Gott die Ehre geben") suggests that the opening phrase is more appropriately rendered, "As *theologians*, we should speak of God . . ."

Craig Dykstra contends that intentional abdication is always characteristic of Christian devotion. Having described the core practices of the Christian faith—worship, prayer, encouragement, hospitality, resisting injustice—as "habitations of the Spirit," he explains that these

> are not, finally, activities we do to make something spiritual happen in our lives. Nor are they duties we undertake to be obedient to God. Rather, they are patterns of communal action that create openings in our lives where the grace, mercy, and presence of God may be made known to us. They are places where the power of God is experienced. In the end, these are not ultimately our practices but forms of participation in the practice of God.[19]

Dykstra goes on to consider the question of "excellence." He notes that excellence in most other human endeavors implies the achievement of mastery and control, which are not the characteristics of faith: "excellence has to do with human achievement. But faith is not a human achievement; it is a gift." "So," he concludes, "our basic task is not mastery and control. It is instead trust and grateful receptivity."[20] His final comments concern Christian teaching and learning (which surely include preaching in their scope):

> So what is the implication for Christian teaching and learning? The implication is that teaching and learning are not finally about mastery. Our task in learning is not to master the practices or the subject matter or ourselves. And our task in teaching is not to master our students . . . The practices of faith are not ultimately our own practices but rather habitations of the Spirit, in the midst of which we are invited to participate in the practices of God.[21]

If we may expand on his explanation, the goal of devotional practice is therefore not mastery, but being mastered, as we yield to the grace of Christ. The aim of preaching, we might say, is not so much mastery as mystery.

Barth speaks in similar terms about the interpretation of Scripture, which is at the heart of Christian proclamation:

---

19. Dykstra, *Growing in the Life of Faith*, 66, with a fuller list of forms of Christian practice at 42–43.
20. Dykstra, *Growing in the Life of Faith*, 75–76.
21. Dykstra, *Growing in the Life of Faith*, 78.

> We should not try to master the text. The Bible will become more and more mysterious to real exegetes. They will see all the depths and distances. They will constantly run up against the mystery before which theology is like trying to drain the ocean with a spoon. The true exegete will face the text like an astonished child in a wonderful garden, not like an advocate of God who has seen all his files.[22]

The aim of preaching and exegesis alike, as for all Christian disciplines and devotional practices, is thus to draw us out beyond ourselves toward a fuller encounter with God.

For Barth, Jesus' resurrection is the point at which mystery beckons us forward beyond ourselves. Recalling Bhabha's comment that "to dwell 'in the beyond' is also . . . to be part of a revisionary time . . . *to touch the future on its hither side*,"[23] Barth assures us that by raising Jesus from death, God has already reached out to us from the "other side" of the divine/human divide:

> [Christ] himself as the One raised from the dead is the other side which has invaded this side, and by which life is promised and given as life in and with Him to those who are put to death in and with Him. The possibility of witness to Him as this other side, and the possibility of faith in Him as the One who is this other side, are, as human actions, possibilities within this world and on this side . . . As such they depend on the fact that Jesus Christ has attested and still attests Himself as the other side within this world. (*CD* IV/1, 352)

It is on this basis, for Barth, that preaching proceeds: "Because he has done this, it can be proclaimed and believed" (*CD* IV/1, 353).

Creating "space for the Word of God" is thus an act of withdrawal in the face of mystery, as well as (recalling the example of Saint Augustine's purse) an expression of our longing for transformation that we ourselves cannot effect. It is neither an act of construction nor an act of deconstruction, but rather a gesture of worship. Perhaps it should also be characterized as a gesture of repentance, for yielding to divine agency is an admission of our own failure to accomplish God's purposes. But it is no less an assertion of trust and expectation: trust in Christ to supply our

---

22. Barth, *Homiletics*, 128. Barth's "Advokat Gottes" (*Homiletik*, 107) can mean "advocate" in the general sense of the word or refer to a legal representative in a court of law (in this case, therefore, likely both).

23. Bhabha, *Location of Culture*, 7.

lack, accompanied by a robust expectation that Christ and the Spirit will continue to work out God's purpose in the space we have vacated. Indeed, withdrawal is only possible in the assurance that the space from which we have withdrawn will not remain void, but that God has already acted to redress our insufficiency.

Claiming and Being Claimed: A Disclaimer

In this light (and recalling similar discussion in chapter 1) an important qualification to the previous account of sacred space now becomes necessary. The example of the Philippian Christians meeting within the walls of a Roman colony suggests that Christian space is always contested, explicitly asserted in the face of rival claims to allegiance and theological sovereignty. But if this is so, the manner in which other disciples may make similar claims of their own invokes a long-standing tension in Western tradition regarding the proper character of Christian devotion. In his magisterial *Summa Theologiae*, Thomas Aquinas (1225–1274) debates the relative merits of the *vita activa* and *vita contemplativa*, arguing strongly in favor of the latter.[24] Key to his argument is the contrast between Martha and Mary, one of whom prefers to serve while the other is content simply to sit and learn at the feet of her Lord. Jesus appears to settle the matter by declaring, "'Mary has chosen what is better, and it will not be taken away from her'" (Luke 10:42 NIV). Thomas's argument in favor of the contemplative life captures the outlook of the Western church prior to the Reformation. Yet a clear preference for Christian activism is self-evident in almost every aspect of life within churches of the modern West. Citing Hannah Arendt, Jennifer Summit observes that "the inversion of the traditional hierarchy of contemplative life over active life has been called the defining paradigm shift of modernity itself."[25] In our day, as was evident from discussion both of the missional church movement and of speech act theory, we gravitate instinctively toward agency, efficacy, and technique, whether in mission and ministry generally or preaching specifically.

---

24. *Summa Theologiae* Second Part, Part Two, Questions 179–82 (esp. Q. 182: "Comparison of the Active and Contemplative Ways of Life"): see Aquinas, *Summa Theologiae 46*, esp. 67–77. For a brief introduction of the *Summa* in relation to the life of preaching, see Pasquarello, *We Speak*, 72–88.

25. Summit, "Active and Contemplative Lives," 529.

From the standpoint of a robust Christian activism, actively claiming space for Christ appears to represent a kind of territorial aggression in the spiritual realm, with human agents wielding the name and power of Christ as their instruments of conquest. As such, it bears an uncomfortably close resemblance to colonialism. In more moderate form, it is a species of theological and devotional hospitality that, like the ministry of John the Baptist, endeavors to "Prepare the way of the Lord" (Mark 1:3 and parallels), whether by means of personal repentance, moral reform, social justice initiatives, or some other missional endeavor. But on either view, the advance of God's territorial claims—God's kingdom—awaits human initiative. By contrast, the theological priority and historical anteriority of Jesus' incarnation, death, and resurrection "as the other side within this world" implies that the Third Space of interstitial Christian identity is established less on the basis of human enterprise than by unsubstitutable divine initiative. On this view, the resurrection in particular is the means by which Christ calls us out into the Third Space of wayfaring, wherein we confess that our πολίτευμα is in heaven and that we are "on the way" toward a heavenly community and "better country" that is as yet some distance away. From this perspective, making spatial claims (whether literally or figuratively) is a matter of ceding territory to divine sovereignty rather than actively appropriating territory on Christ's behalf. Likewise (notwithstanding Christian responsibility for pursuing personal holiness, corporate righteousness, and public justice alike), the counterintuitive concept of "creating space" by withdrawing from it, affirming the claims of Christ by yielding to his Lordship, seems more appropriate both to New Testament metaphors of the church as God's new temple and habitation (1 Cor 3:16; 2 Cor 6:16; 1 Pet 2:5, etc.) and to the larger trajectory of participation in Christ's death and resurrection. Especially if Weissenrieder is correct in her assertion that "the Corinthian *ekklēsía* not only possessed a space, but rather *was* this space" by virtue of remembering and thereby embodying "the humiliating death of Jesus Christ,"[26] creating space for God and the Word of God is first and foremost a gesture of humility, weakness, and defeat. Or, if it is to be an expression of triumph and (as it were) territorial conquest, any sense of victory originates with Christ in his resurrection, applying to his followers only by way of secondary association.

Whether with reference to Christian identity in principle, Christian ministry generally, or preaching in particular, finding a proper balance

---

26. Weissenrieder, "Contested Spaces in 1 Corinthians 11:17–33 and 14:30," 106.

between the Scylla of Pelagianism and the Charybdis of Quietism is a matter of considerable delicacy. Viewed in light of postcolonial theory and the concept of Third Space, the question of "making space for God" (whether in Philippi of the first century, Bonn during the 1930s, or at some other time and place) brings the relevant issues into sharp relief. All the perils of "heresy" (to use Bhabha's term) and of a hybrid identity that is largely unrecognizable in failing to conform fully either to its culture of origin or to the customs of its intended destination are fully evident. The point of balance in this liminal space is the question of response. Christians are those who follow Christ in response to his call, find new identity in being gradually conformed to his identity, and preach because we have been given words to speak that are vastly superior to any we could have chosen on our own. As Rowan Williams explains,

> We speak because we are called, invited and authorized to speak, we speak what we have been *given*, out of our new "belonging," and this is a "dependent" kind of utterance, a responsive speech. But it is not a dictated or determined utterance: revelation is addressed not so much to a will called upon to submit as to an imagination called upon to "open itself." The integrity of theological utterance, then, does not lie in its correspondence to given structures of thought, its falling into line with an authoritative communication, but in the reality of its rootedness, its belonging, in the new world constituted in the revelatory event or process.[27]

Pinpointing this delicate balance is always problematic. Its frustrations are illustrated by the paradoxical situation of Mary Magdalene in the garden on Easter morning:

> Mary stood weeping outside the tomb. As she wept, she bent over to look into the tomb; and she saw two angels in white, sitting where the body of Jesus had been lying, one at the head and the other at the feet. They said to her, "Woman, why are you weeping?" She said to them, "They have taken away my Lord, and I do not know where they have laid him." When she had said this, she turned around and saw Jesus standing there, but she did not know that it was Jesus. Jesus said to her, "Woman, why are you weeping? Whom are you looking for?" Supposing him to be the gardener, she said to him, "Sir, if you have carried him away, tell me where you have laid him, and I will take him

---

27. Williams, *On Christian Theology*, 146–47, quoted in part by Pasquarello, *We Speak*, 39.

away." Jesus said to her, "Mary!" She turned and said to him in Hebrew, "Rabbouni!" (which means Teacher). Jesus said to her, "Do not hold on to me, because I have not yet ascended to the Father. But go to my brothers and say to them, 'I am ascending to my Father and your Father, to my God and your God.'" (John 20:11–17)

Mary's first difficulty is that she doesn't recognize the risen Lord, even though she obviously loves him. Yet once the question of his identity has been resolved, Jesus himself confuses her further. She wants nothing so much as to care for him, even if means arguing with an apparent stranger over his lifeless body (20:15). But the narrative turns on his strange rebuke, "Do not hold on to me" (NRSV), perhaps better translated "Do not cling to me" (20:17 ESV, etc.) because the form of the Greek imperative "probably implies that she is already touching him and is to desist."[28] Although this answer has engendered a small library of explanations ranging from the banal to the bizarre, Brown's proposal is both simple and compelling: whereas Mary thinks that Jesus "has returned as he promised and now . . . will stay with her and his other followers, resuming former relationships," the permanent intimacy for which she longs will come only after he has departed and returned once more (so John 14:2–3, 18–19; 16:22).[29] In the meantime, it is the Holy Spirit who will remind them of his teaching (John 14:26; 16:14) and thus of his presence.

Whether for Mary Magdalene or Thomas the Twin (who is bidden to touch, rather than to refrain from touching Jesus), the situation of the disciples in the forty days between his resurrection and ascension is temporary, and as such unique. During this interval, they must reckon with the interstitial character of their resurrected Lord: Thomas (looking back) needs reassurance of Jesus' enduring humanity in the form of his scars, whereas Mary (looking forward) needs to be reminded that Jesus has not yet fulfilled his purpose by returning to the Father (John 7:33; 14:28; 16:28, etc.). But their own Third Space—the Third Space of normative Christian discipleship—will not be like this. Once Jesus has again departed (an eventuality of which John's Gospel makes no direct mention), there will be even less to hold onto: disciples will be able neither to touch his wounds nor to cling to him bodily. Instead, they will simply speak of him to all who are drawn into fellowship by such remembrance, even as

---

28. Brown, *Gospel according to John XIII–XXI*, 992.
29. Brown, *Gospel according to John XIII–XXI*, 1012; cf. 992–93.

Jesus instructs Mary, "Go to my brothers and say to them, 'I am ascending to my Father and your Father, to my God and your God'" (John 20:17). As Mechteld Jansen reminds us, for those who are between their place of origin and their desired destination, Third Space is "storied space."[30] This is the context in which we tell the story of Jesus' destination, and of how his saving trajectory draws us forward in its wake.

Observing the annual cycle of a liturgical calendar encourages celebration of every season in the Christian story: from Advent to Christmas, Epiphany, Lent, Passiontide, Easter, Ascension, and life in the power of Pentecost. But the one day that most clearly expresses the interstitial character of Christian identity is Holy Saturday, midway between the agony of Good Friday and the joy of Easter morning. Exploring its significance for preaching will require a shift from spatial to temporal metaphors.

Ever Holy Saturday

The problem with Holy Saturday is that it is the day on which the disciples truly wonder how they could have been so wrong. Or, worse, how a ministry that had begun so well could have ended so badly. For all their hesitations and imperfections, they had truly believed Jesus to be the Messiah; despite occasional bickering, they had genuinely believed themselves destined, as Jesus himself assured them, to reign with him in his kingdom. Since they, more than anyone, knew the many healings and deliverances they had witnessed to be genuine, the defeat of all their expectations would have been a crushing disappointment for the eleven surviving men and many women of Jesus' inner circle. In one of his poems, the thirteenth century Sufi mystic whom we know as Rūmī imagines Jesus fleeing, "as though a wild animal were chasing him." A disciple pursues him, badgering Jesus for an explanation until he receives the following, delivered on the run:

> *I say the Great Name over the deaf and the blind,*
> *   they are healed. Over a stony mountainside,*
> *and it tears its mantle down to the navel.*
> *   Over non-existence, and it comes into existence.*
> *But when I speak lovingly for hours, for days,*
> *   with those who take human warmth*
> *and mock it, when I say the Name to them, nothing*

---

30. Jansen, "Christian Migrants," 154–58, cited above.

> *happens. They remain rock, or turn to sand,*
> *where no plants can grow. Other diseases are ways*
> *for mercy to enter, but this non-responding*
> *breeds violence and coldness toward God.*
> *I am fleeing from that.*[31]

The problem for Jesus' disciples on Holy Saturday is not simply that they are disappointed or confused or feel betrayed; it is that the cold and darkness of pious obstinacy (or obstinate piety) appears to have defeated the one in whom they had seen God most clearly. We catch a glimpse of this turmoil in the comment of the two travelers on their way to Emmaus, "We *had hoped* that he was the one . . ." (Luke 24:21). One of several post-canonical endings to Mark's Gospel pictures the disciples as being simply overcome with grief: "Mary Magdalene . . . went out and told those who had been with him, while they were mourning and weeping. But when they heard that he was alive and had been seen by her, they would not believe it" (Mark 16:9–11). Again, the dilemma they face is not that they have been entirely mistaken, but that what (to paraphrase 1 John 1:1) they "have heard, what they have seen with their eyes, what they have looked at and touched with their hands, concerning the word of life," is once again out of reach and out of sight, having for a brief time been so tangible and close. Just when they thought their long wait over, they are back to waiting all over again. If Fitzmyer is correct, as seems likely, this is what Jesus must explain to Mary Magdalene when he tells her not to cling to him.

Of course, the grief and confusion of the original Holy Saturday is temporary, for within a few hours bright messengers will be reminding the disciples of his promised return (Mark 16:7), and within a few hours more they will see him for themselves. Further ahead, Jesus' ascension will convey humanity into the full presence of the Father and Pentecost will provide a more permanent solution to distance and the disciples' failed expectations.[32] Still, Holy Saturday provides a helpful metaphor for the situation of post-Pentecostal followers of Jesus who find themselves once more in a "revisionary time" between suffering and restoration. Ironically, far from being a denial or reversal of the resurrection, expectation of a fuller and final renewal of all things is the direct consequence

---

31. Barks, *The Essential Rumi*, 204; emphasis original.

32. In *Reconstructing Pastoral Theology* (esp. 107–26), Andrew Purves provides a compelling account of the significance of Jesus' ascension, based primarily on the theology of Athanasius, John Calvin, and Thomas F. Torrance.

of Jesus' resurrection.[33] Describing the hope of future transformation, Paul's metaphors for physical existence in 2 Corinthians—tents, homes, and houses—may seem rather forced. Regardless, the contrast he intends is between an impermanent, perishable dwelling place and one that is permanent and eternal:

> For we know that if the earthly tent we live in is destroyed, we have a building from God, a house not made with hands, eternal in the heavens. For in this tent we groan, longing to be clothed with our heavenly dwelling—if indeed, when we have taken it off we will not be found naked. For while we are still in this tent, we groan under our burden, because we wish not to be unclothed but to be further clothed, so that what is mortal may be swallowed up by life. (2 Cor 5:1–4)

It is easy to overlook the fact that Paul is referring to *bodily* transformation, in which case the precedent on which such expectation is directly based is the bodily resurrection of Jesus. According to the apostle, longing in hope and expectation is now characteristic not just of disciples who yearn for more of life and God, but characteristic also of creation as a whole:

> For the creation waits with eager longing for the revealing of the children of God; for the creation was subjected to futility, not of its own will but by the will of the one who subjected it, in hope that the creation itself will be set free from its bondage to decay and will obtain the freedom of the glory of the children of God. We know that the whole creation has been groaning in labor pains until now; and not only the creation, but we ourselves, who have the first fruits of the Spirit, groan inwardly while we wait for adoption, the redemption of our bodies. For in hope we were saved. Now hope that is seen is not hope. For who hopes for what is seen? But if we hope for what we do not see, we wait for it with patience. (Rom 8:19–25)

---

33. The metaphorical reading of Holy Saturday proposed here, which articulates the "already but not yet" nature of Christian experience while nonetheless acknowledging the reality of Good Friday and Easter alike, is in contrast to that of Purves (*Resurrection of Ministry*, 16 and passim) for whom "ministry in the mood of Holy Saturday" falls short of full confidence in Jesus' present ministry on our behalf. Yet as Purves himself acknowledges, "Ministry that moves from the mood of Holy Saturday to the mood of Easter Sunday does not cease to have to deal with ambiguity" (73; further, 114–20).

To reiterate, such hope arises in response to the temporal and metaphysical precedent of Jesus' resurrection.

Just so, and in contrast to the spatial metaphor proposed by Bhabha and postcolonial theory, Barth situates the interstitial character of Christian preaching on a temporal and eschatological axis, between the "unconditional *whence*" and the "unconditional *whither*" of the Christian life as a whole. "Whence" is the ἐφάπαξ (Heb 10:10) of Christ's accomplishment "once for all"; "whither" is the prospect of Jesus' glorious return. Accordingly,

> Preaching stands between the first advent and the second. So does the whole life of the Christian . . . This assurance is in fact a profound nonpossessing. This wealth, as we turn to the future, is total poverty and lack. But it is also expectation and hope, the prospect of what will then be given us. The Christian life is a striding from the one pole to the other, from having to not having, then to a confident reaching out for new riches. We walk by faith, not by sight (2 Cor. 5:7). Had we sight already, there would be neither a first advent nor a second, no yesterday, today, or tomorrow. But we walk by faith, i.e., in a double movement from Christ to Christ.[34]

As for Augustine also, this "double movement" of a pilgrimage oriented both to the past and to the future is marked—especially for preachers—by longing and desire for homecoming: "Preachers who set out from a fixed starting point are the very ones who must press on, who must hunger and thirst, though always with the promise that they will be satisfied."[35]

This suggests, paradoxically, that post-Easter, post-Pentecost preaching will always include an element of lamentation. Every Easter, we sing,

> The strife is o'er, the battle done!
> The victory of life is won!
> The song of triumph has begun!
> Alleluia![36]

---

34. Barth, *Homiletics*, 51–54.

35. Barth, *Homiletics*, 55.

36. Pott, *Hymns Fitted to the Order of Common Prayer*, 82 (#91). The lyrics are Pott's translation of an anonymous seventeenth century Latin hymn, "Finita iam sunt proelia."

Except that, of course, what the hymn proclaims is (in a certain sense) not entirely true. It is certainly true of Jesus, just as it is true of disciples insofar as they are made one with him. But because this longed-for union is not yet complete—not yet consummated, we might say—the strife and battle are still very much underway. Stated more finely, Easter preaching acknowledges that resurrection (as well as victory, life, and the "song of triumph") are already fully Christ's, but only in process of becoming our own. We are still in the Third Space between death and resurrection, still waiting in the experiential half-light of Easter Saturday, between promise and fulfillment, both of which are integral to the "whence" and "whither" of which Barth speaks.

More finely still, it is helpful to think of Holy Saturday as the most important Sabbath of all, which brings all work to a perfect end. The first Sabbath marks the conclusion of God's work of creation: "And on the seventh day God finished the work that he had done, and he rested on the seventh day from all the work that he had done. So God blessed the seventh day and hallowed it, because on it God rested from all the work that he had done in creation." (Gen 2:2–3) Likewise on Good Friday, Jesus declares, "It is finished" (John 19:30) and rests from his work in death, taking all creation with him. Although Christian tradition has sometimes assigned him tasks to occupy the hours prior to Easter dawn, the deathly stillness of Holy Saturday signals the finality of his achievement. It extends the "second silence" of the Word of God long enough for it to be both definitive and, as it were, deafening. Jesus rests from the work of salvation because it is now complete, inviting preachers to rest with him in the assurance that he does not need them to accomplish his finished work all over again. For those who trust in him, this is the last Sabbath, the final prelude to the first day of the new creation on which the church will henceforth celebrate new life in Christ.[37]

The point, then, of these two metaphors—Third Space and Holy Saturday—is to articulate in spatial and temporal terms not only the inescapably interstitial character of Christian existence, but more importantly the theological premise that we are drawn forward into this time and space by irreplaceable divine initiative. Far, indeed, from this kind of hybrid identity being a constructive endeavor on the part of enterprising disciples—a bold initiative that launches itself in the direction of God—we are, rather, held back only by our own reluctance to let go of

---

37. On the day of resurrection as the first day of the new creation, see Barn. 15:8–9; Justin Martyr, *1 Apol.* §67.

all that is humanly safe and familiar. Third Space and Holy Saturday are truly *terra incognita*, a "dangerous indeterminacy" that we experience as simultaneously destabilizing and profoundly hopeful. This is the territory in which, having called us to die in Christ, the Creator declares over us, "Behold, I am making [ποιῶ] all things new" (Rev 21:5). Here the verb (in the present tense, implying continuous action) is all-important, since it describes a state or process that is still ongoing.[38]

All that now remains is to summarize the implications of spiritual hybridity—the consequences of Jesus' resurrection—for the task of preaching. Without repeating all the details of previous discussion, a series of key considerations situate the sermon beyond the realm and reach of customary human discourse, not by virtue of any intrinsic linguistic or rhetorical distinctives, but in terms of its self-transcending reference in openness to the "ways of life" and God.

Preaching Resurrection

Whether we begin our summary on the near or far shore of Bunyan's "River of Death" (whether, that is, in "This World" or "That Which is to Come") makes little difference, since the most perplexing aspect of resurrection preaching is that it takes both into consideration. In practical terms, this means that Christian preaching is essentially visionary, offering a perspective on the ordinary that causes us to see our world in a new and different light. This is a key characteristic of Jesus' parables, which typically depict familiar or stock characters (lazy farmers, heartless judges, women baking bread, kings and their armies) in unfamiliar postures. Only in the stories of Jesus does a father whose son has ruined the family estate outdo the young man's disobedience by refusing to honor the command of Scripture that he be stoned to death (Deut 21:18–21). Only in the world that Jesus narrates is it possible (at least in his day) for wheat to give back a hundredfold yield. And who else would have thought that taking care of the poor, the naked, the sick, or those imprisoned for their crimes should be equivalent to caring for the One who judges on judgement day? Yet this is how things operate in the kingdom of God. For otherwise myopic disciples, it is simply a matter of seeing aright. In similar fashion, Jesus exhorts his followers:

---

38. Cf. Aune, *Revelation 17–22*, 1125; Aune notes that this wording alludes to Isa 43:19, "Behold, I am doing a new thing."

> Look at the birds of the air; they neither sow nor reap nor gather into barns, and yet your heavenly Father feeds them. Are you not of more value than they? And can any of you by worrying add a single hour to your span of life? And why do you worry about clothing? Consider the lilies of the field, how they grow; they neither toil nor spin, yet I tell you, even Solomon in all his glory was not clothed like one of these. (Matt 6:26–29)

It is such a familiar passage that we fail to notice Jesus explicitly contradicting the terms of Genesis 3:17–19, in which Adam is sentenced to wrestle his sustenance from the ground by the sweat of his brow. The parable even expands God's gracious provision of clothing for an exiled Adam and Eve (Gen 3:21) by assigning God the traditional tasks of a wife (preparing food and clothing, as in *m. Ketub.* 5:5) for the benefit of creation as a whole.[39] One way or another, Jesus is able to see beyond the grime, poverty, and injustice of his day (not least the fact that God's chosen people live under military occupation by pagan idolaters) to the beauty of his Father's abundant generosity. Indeed, such insight is itself the gift of God, one that Jesus values for his disciples as well as for himself: "At that time Jesus said, 'I thank you, Father, Lord of heaven and earth, because you have hidden these things from the wise and the intelligent and have revealed them to infants; yes, Father, for such was your gracious will'" (Matt 11:25–26/Luke 10:21). Neither in Matthew nor in Luke is it immediately clear what exactly Jesus means by "these things"; nonetheless, what he affirms in principle is insight into a divine purpose that remains otherwise wholly inscrutable.[40] Accordingly, recognition is key, in all the senses that have been discussed already. The particular characteristics of resurrection preaching begin on this point.

Life in the Shape of Cross and Resurrection

The first essential facet of an outlook oriented to resurrection concerns Jesus' understanding of life under the reign of God, initially as revealed in the Scriptures of Israel. At first, this seems to contradict all that

---

39. See further Knowles, "Consider the Lilies," 15–18.
40. Cf. Davies and Allison, *Matthew* 2:276–77; Fitzmyer, *Luke X–XXIV*, 872–73. Reference elsewhere to hiddenness and divine revelation confirms that a general principle is in view; e.g., Jesus' citation of Ps 78:2 to explain his use of parables ("I will open my mouth to speak in parables; I will proclaim what has been hidden from the foundation of the world"; Matt 13:35) or Mark 4:22/Luke 8:17.

resurrection represents, for it concedes that suffering and death are part of the human condition, even for the Messiah. Much as we are desperate to escape our fate and look to the power of his resurrection as the perfect means of doing so, Jesus reads the testimony of Israel ("the things about himself in all the Scriptures"; Luke 24:27) in a manner that embraces mortal affliction rather than denying it. Yet that he does so from the other side of death invites his followers (preachers, for instance) to find in him the point of reconciliation between our longing for life and our own flight from suffering.

However counterintuitive, the interpretation that Jesus provides encourages the infant church to view the sacred text, the cross, and their own experience in a similar light. That Jesus neither evades death nor is defeated by it represents the essence of cruciform identity; he models a disposition of radical self-abandonment to God as the sole source of life.[41] Demonstrating absolute trust in divine sufficiency, he chooses to be non-self-sustaining in the most concrete sense possible. But given this example, to interpret his and the experience of all God's people in light of the cross, and to preach accordingly, is not an end in itself. Because he does not remain dead, Jesus invites us to interpret our experience and therefore to preach in light of his resurrection also, as the reversal of all that the cross entails. Again, each implies the other, however incommensurate the two parts of this paradox may appear: such preaching fearlessly embraces death because death has been defanged by Jesus' resurrection; it humbly and gratefully embraces his gift of life in the conviction that "conformity to Christ's self-giving, life-giving death"[42] is the only avenue of access to new creation. Or, in keeping with the example of the apostles on the day of Pentecost, to preach in this manner proclaims God's "mighty works" with a Galilean twang, as ordinary people from places we recognize give voice to a grace that resolves our differences and leads us beyond ourselves.

---

41. Cruciform identity and the cruciform preaching to which it gives rise are central themes of *We Preach Not Ourselves* and *Of Seeds and the People of God*, and so need not be pursued in greater detail here.

42. Gorman, "Preaching and Living the Resurrection Today," 7.

Liturgy and the Life of the Community

If Christian preachers are bidden, first, to read the history of God's people—both that of ancient Israel and their own—in terms of Jesus' death and resurrection, their preaching is appropriately situated, second, in the context of liturgy and worship. Just as cross and resurrection themselves are mutually illuminating, so our celebration of Jesus' self-offering (in the Lord's Supper) and our proclamation of its definitive acceptance by God (in preaching) serve to interpret each other as reciprocal sources of identity in Christ. As Rowan Williams reminds us, "Where there is salvation, its name is Jesus; its grammar is the cross and the resurrection."[43] Accordingly, cross and resurrection furnish the "grammar" of Christian identity, of worship, and of preaching alike.[44] Remembering Jesus' execution when we gather for worship reminds us that this form of identification is our only point of entry into his life or that of a suffering world. Remembering his exaltation reminds us that to join Jesus in his death is to be drawn into the trajectory of his new life, and of new creation. Resurrection preaching is therefore theologically committed to hope, even (especially!) in the face of death: again, not because of its innate power to persuade but because God restored the Word to life when that life and his voice had fallen silent. Preaching oriented to Jesus' resurrection will therefore be marked by wonder, amazement, and hope. Conscious of the pessimism and spiritual ennui that often characterize Western society, post-resurrection preaching acknowledges that although we do not yet experience "all things in subjection to God," we nonetheless "see Jesus . . . crowned with honor and glory" (Heb 2:8–9), as the basis of profound confidence for the future of God's creation.

More particularly, to set preaching within the context of eucharistic celebration is to invite comparison between them as parallel responses to grace. According to Paul, in sharing bread and wine we "*proclaim the Lord's death until he comes*" (1 Cor 11:26). His use of the verb καταγγέλλειν (to announce, proclaim) makes this action analogous to, perhaps even an enacted form of, preaching itself.[45] But by the same

---

43. Williams, *Resurrection*, 72.

44. "Because the language of preaching is inseparable from the language of worship, our thinking and speaking are most truthful when ordered by a 'grammar' that leads to union with Christ in love for God, as God, and loving neighbours in God" (Pasquarello, *We Speak*, 57).

45. Compare 1 Cor 2:1; 9:14; Phil 1:17–18; Col 1:28, etc., and, more fully,

token he indicates that both are temporary gestures ("until he comes"), simply anticipations of a fuller and more permanent spiritual experience as yet unrevealed. In this sense, preaching and the Lord's Supper share a similar theological obscurity or ambiguity. Commenting on the same verse in his "Explanation of the Small Catechism," Luther observes that "by the power of His word, Christ gives His body and blood *in, with, and under* the consecrated (blessed) bread and wine" (*LW* 37:306, §291). This seems an equally fitting explanation of the power, life, and authority of Christ that may be in, with, and under the words of the sermon, but are never coterminous with those words. The weak words of the preacher and the powerful words of Christ may overlap, but always invisibly so. The same will be true of the preacher herself, who knows only too well that her life is, as Paul says, "*hidden* with Christ in God" (Col 3:3). She therefore preaches and administers the elements in the posture of one who requires, rather than dispenses grace. As those who break bread and pour out wine for them to serve as tokens of Jesus' body and blood, we confess our own complicity in bringing about his death, much as we preach from the position of those who have nothing to say for ourselves other than to call on Christ. To borrow once more from Rowan Williams, "the Eucharist is a reminder to the whole Church of its liability to desert and betray: the eucharistic church 'locates' itself in Gethsemane before it finds itself finally in and with the risen Jesus."[46]

Always Preaching to Ourselves

Accordingly, third, preaching resurrection can never be disembodied or disinterested: it is always intensely personal because affliction and death ensnare preachers also, together with everyone they love. While Jesus speaks of suffering from the far shore of resurrection, we speak of new life from the near shore of unavoidable mortality. Just so, in his vastly entertaining account of resurrection preaching, Blount likens preachers and their hearers to zombies, who are the waking, walking, living dead: "What, then, are we? Some degree of dead. Distant from God. In direct proximity to the animate power that John calls Death and Hades."[47] As distinct from the fully concrete, physical manner in which Thomas

---

Schniewind, s.v. ἀγγελία, κτλ., *TDNT* 1:71–72.

46. Williams, *Resurrection*, 58.

47. Blount, *Invasion of the Dead*, 16.

touches Jesus' hands and side, our own grasp of his scars may be largely metaphorical, but we too are hungry for proof that death no longer has the last word. The plain fact of the matter is that even the most altruistic of preachers are also in it for themselves: preaching is not simply about salvation, compassion, and justice for everyone else (however much we love them), but for our own lives and futures as well. For preachers whose sermons are heavy with named injustice and the imperatives of righteous action, Jesus' healed scars are assurances of ultimate victory; for those whose preaching tends toward triumphalism or other-worldliness, the marks on Jesus's body remind us that the road to life always goes by way of death and solidarity with the afflicted.

With respect to preaching itself, to proclaim Jesus' resurrection will always require of preachers the same trust in God that the sermon asks of its hearers. Preaching does not simply invite religious trust; it enacts trust by casting itself on the power of God to grant a hearing for its words among those who listen. Resurrection is personal because apart from God's gift of new life we are simply exhorting folks to live better lives in this world without helping them to accomplish even this much. Apart from resurrection and the reality of a life-giving God, the congregation will just have to take our word for what we say, and most preachers know themselves too well to consider this a wise course of action.

Preaching with God in View

For our sermons to speak well of divine life will require them to be expressly theological, invoking the identity, character, and agency of God, to whom resurrection testifies, and on whom those who offer and receive that testimony directly rely. At least as classically understood, the death of Jesus is a consequence of divine justice, as well as evidence of the extent to which God's own people reject the emissaries and purposes of their Lord. If, that is, Christ died "on behalf of the ungodly" (Rom 5:6, 8), "the righteous on behalf of the unrighteous" (1 Pet 3:18), that death is the greatest of all transgressions that this same death overcomes. Yet Jesus' resurrection reverses even the enormity of his rejection. All this puts the enterprising preacher in an awkward position, for the theological character of crucifixion and of resurrection, respectively, go hand in hand. If Christ has not been put to death as sin and on account of sin, then there is nothing for God to reverse: it is simply a garden-variety execution for which there is ample precedent in Roman Palestine of the day. A postmortem vision or two is all that grieving disciples will require to encourage them on their way. But if we claim to take sin, injustice, oppression, and unrighteousness with the seriousness that they deserve, then the gravity of Jesus' crucifixion—as the ultimate expression of human sin—is such that only grace and the power of God can possibly remedy it. The theological implications of cross and resurrection are thus equivalent: each implies the other. We cannot preach about sin, justice, or solidarity without acknowledging that we ourselves are victimizers as much as victims, in which case we are in no position to take over as agents or instruments of God's purpose.

On either count, only God can vindicate the Son; by extension, God alone is the guarantor of any words that speak about him. Here, a theological reading of speech act theory comes to the fore: however appropriate this model may be for language that names a newborn child or terminates an employee, it fails to account sufficiently for utterances that refer to God. That is to say, the "extra-linguistic" conditions necessary for validation of speech concerning God necessarily involve its divine Subject, both as to divine fidelity as the guarantee of God's promissory speech and with regard to divine power that is sufficient to raise the dead.

Looking to Jesus

Self-evidently, therefore, resurrection preaching will be unremittingly Christofocal. It has sometimes been observed that throughout its lengthy history, the church has tended to focus either on Jesus' death (with concomitant emphasis on life as a "Vale of Misery")[48] or on his resurrection (thus affirming all the positive and other-worldly dimensions of the life of faith). Yet focusing on either to the exclusion of the other fails to do justice to the full dimensions of his work. Because Jesus' incarnation ("fully God and fully human") is unique and unrepeatable, Chalcedonian metaphysics do not provide the best framework for understanding Christian speech. Rather, Holy Saturday (in the experience of the disciples) and the weeks between Easter and Ascension (in the biography of Jesus) provide more accessible analogies for the life of Christian faith and the ministry that such an orientation entails. Both are more appropriately

---

48. This is Miles Coverdale's translation of Ps 84:6, first published in 1535 and popularized by inclusion of his Psalter in the English *Book of Common Prayer*.

interstitial and hybrid, poised in the Third Space between mortality and the eternal, or between apparent divine absence and life in the fullness of God's presence.

Somewhat unexpectedly, the initial point of contact between the incarnate Word and Christian preaching, as between discipleship and Christology in principle, is not triumphant proclamation but chastened silence. For just as incarnation and crucifixion are essential antecedents to resurrection, so keeping silence and listening are necessary in order for us to have words worth speaking. In similar measure, words that concern resurrection (as well as words concerning other dimensions of Christian faith) will rely on divine power for their message to convey God's gift of new life. The paradox of language that speaks of Christ and in the name of Christ is not that it is intrinsically powerless (which is only to be expected since human speakers are not God). The paradox is that knowing its own incapacity, such speech may find itself embraced by a power not its own; by participating existentially and linguistically in the conditions of crucifixion, it yields to the divine prerogative of resurrection. It is under this category that we will understand descriptions of Jesus "opening" the Scriptures or the minds of disciples (Luke 24:32, 45, etc.), or holding "the keys of Death and Hades" (Rev 1:18).

Power and the Spirit of God

For the same reason, the resurrection of preaching and of preachers (regardless of their subject matter) necessitates a robust theology of the Holy Spirit. In this regard the expectations of a Western congregation in the theological tradition of cessationism will differ markedly from those of, say, an African Independent Church or Chilean Pentecostals. But all Christians agree that the power of God's Spirit is essential for the life of the church. Luke, for one, is convinced that "signs and wonders" normally attend preaching of the Christian message (Acts 4:33; 14:3); Paul is of the same mind (Rom 15:18-19; 2 Cor 12:12, etc.), as is the writer of the Letter to the Hebrews (Heb 2:3-4).[49] In response to fractious congregants who doubt his qualifications for preaching (indeed for congregational ministry generally), Paul responds, "My speech and my proclamation were not with plausible words of wisdom, but with a demonstration [ἀποδείξει] of the Spirit and of power, so that your faith might

---

49. Further, Knowles, *Of Seeds and the People of God*, 113–14, 167–69, 173–75.

rest not on human wisdom but on the power of God" (1 Cor 2:4–5). The apostle's choice of language is significant: although "a *hapax legomenon* in the New Testament," ἀπόδειξις "occurs frequently as a technical term in rhetoric which means a demonstration or cogent proof of argument from commonly agreed premises."[50] Thus, even though some of his own converts accuse Paul of failing miserably in rhetorical skill, "He asserts that his word and his preaching are based upon a demonstration, not of the rhetorical kind, but of the Spirit and of power. This demonstration does not consist of arguments from generally accepted truths, but upon the divine conviction of the Spirit and power (cf. 1 Cor. 4:20)."[51] Sometimes the confirmation of the Spirit is wholly interior, as in Paul's explanation that "when we cry, 'Abba! Father!' is that very Spirit bearing witness with our spirit that we are children of God" (Rom 8:15–16). Whatever form such confirmation may take, a clear pattern emerges in response to testimony that God has raised the Messiah from death to life. As the church and its preachers bear verbal witness to Christ, God confirms their word, sometimes by means of "works of power" but also more unobtrusively by simply drawing hearers to himself, confirming the veracity of what has been said. Far from despairing that mere words can communicate divine truth, preachers are encouraged in their task by the manner in which the Holy Spirit validates faithful proclamation in the experience of those who receive it.

To set such claims within their proper theological context, Paul understands the power of the Holy Spirit, the power of God manifest in Jesus' resurrection, the power that sustains discipleship, and the power of preaching to be one and the same. This explains why he uses similar language for each. His declarations of the power of the Gospel in the opening chapters of Romans and 1 Corinthians, respectively, are perhaps best known:

> For I am not ashamed of the gospel; it is the power of God for salvation to everyone who has faith, to the Jew first and also to the Greek. (Rom 1:16)

> For the word of the cross is foolishness to those who are perishing, but to us who are being saved it is the power of God. (1 Cor 1:18)

---

50. Lim, "'Not in Persuasive Words of Wisdom,'" 147.
51. Lim, "'Not in Persuasive Words of Wisdom,'" 147.

But the fullest account of the divine power that links resurrection, the Spirit of God, discipleship, and ministry appears throughout the Letter to the Ephesians, more than once in the context of prayer. Thus Paul prays that God will grant the believers "a spirit of wisdom and revelation" so that they will know "what is the immeasurable greatness of his power for us who believe, according to the working of his great power." This, he says, is the power of Jesus' resurrection: "God put this power to work in Christ when he raised him from the dead and seated him at his right hand in the heavenly places" (Eph 1:17–20; cf. 3:20). The same divine power undergirds apostolic ministry: "Of this gospel I have become a servant according to the gift of God's grace that was given me by the working of his power" (Eph 3:7; cf. Col 1:29). To the saints at Thessalonica, Paul explains the effectiveness of his ministry in equivalent terms: "For we know, brothers and sisters beloved by God, that he has chosen you, because our gospel came to you not in word only, but also in power and in the Holy Spirit and with full conviction" (1 Thess 1:4–5; cf. 2:13).

Preachers without exception want to preach powerful and effective sermons. Doing so, according to Paul, depends on the power of the Holy Spirit that attends the message of God's vindication of Jesus, which is a message of divine power in the face of death. Efficacious preaching, resurrection, and the agency of God's Spirit are inextricably linked.

Resurrection Preaching as Premature Death

The sticking point is how much this sort of preaching will cost us. Paul's own example (cited earlier) is hardly alluring: "We have become like the rubbish of the world, the dregs of all things, to this very day" (1 Cor 4:13). As we have seen, however, our precedent in this regard is not the apostle himself, but the humiliation of the incarnate Word. As with the life of Christian discipleship generally, the prerequisite for participation in resurrected, resurrectional preaching is participation in Jesus' prior silence and defeat. Paul states the matter with characteristic bluntness:

> We have this treasure in clay jars, so that it may be made clear that this extraordinary power belongs to God and does not come from us. We are afflicted in every way, but not crushed; perplexed, but not driven to despair; persecuted, but not forsaken; struck down, but not destroyed; always carrying in the body the death of Jesus, so that the life of Jesus may also be made visible in our bodies. (2 Cor 4:7–10)

Here it seems appropriate to recall again Barth's comment on the nature of Christian proclamation: "Preaching is not a neutral activity. It is not an action involving two equal partners. It can mean only Lordship on God's side and obedience on ours."[52] Yielding to this Lordship, in its distinctively cruciform manifestation, implies preaching that is not only noncoercive but non-agential and thus nonconstructive. Paul illustrates this stance with a simple, yet compelling agricultural metaphor:

> What then is Apollos? What is Paul? Servants through whom you came to believe, as the Lord assigned to each. I planted, Apollos watered, but God gave the growth. So neither the one who plants nor the one who waters is anything, but only God who gives the growth. (1 Cor 3:5–7)

This is precisely the sense of Luther's multilingual comment, noted earlier, that "wir haben wohl *ius verbi* aber nicht *executionem* [We have the right to speak but not the power to accomplish]."[53] In the terms proposed by speech act theory, preachers are responsible for locution and illocution, but when it comes to matters so momentous as forgiveness, new life in Christ, and the renewal of creation, perlocutionary force belongs to God alone.

This being the case, resurrection preaching must categorically exclude any measure of triumphalism, since yielding to the power and authority of Christ implies acknowledgment that these are not ours to wield. Stated succinctly, to proclaim Jesus' glorious resurrection is to declare our need of it, not our possession of it or our power over it. Like the disciples who saw him face to face in the days following the first Easter, we will always greet the Risen One with a measure of incredulity, awe, and outright terror. Or, to choose a different metaphor, we will always meet a scarred Jesus with scars of our own. Resurrection preaching will always be the foolish testimony of those who are themselves frail and foolish in the eyes of others who know better (which is exactly how Paul explains his own ministry; 1 Cor 1:18—2:5).

Despite all this, however, the converse will be equally true.

---

52. Barth, *Homiletic*, 50.
53. *LW* 51:76; *WA* 10:15.

Preaching and the "Word of Life"

On the one hand, Paul exhorts the saints of ancient Philippi, gathered in sacred space (perhaps *as* sacred space) within Roman walls, to work out their salvation "with fear and trembling" (Phil 2:12). Yet he goes on immediately to declare that the very power of God is at work within them, indeed that they already "shine as lights in the world, holding fast the word of life" (2:15–16 RSV). Ralph Martin explains the key phrase λόγον ζωῆς ("word of life") as "a synonym for the gospel as the word which brings the life of God into the lives of people wherever its message is received and obeyed."[54] The reference, in other words, is to its life-giving function in their midst. At the same time, he proposes, "This is more [than] likely a personal reference to Christ as 'the Word of life' (as in 1 Jn. 1:1)."[55] In other words, given the broad semantic range of the term λόγος (L&N §33.98–100), Paul envisages the resurrected Jesus, the message of the Gospel, and the identity of the saints themselves as each fully characterized by "life" that comes from God. Despite persecution and suffering (Phil 1:27–30; cf. 4:5–7), the saints at Philippi are living embodiments of the Gospel.

But there is considerable debate as to the meaning of Paul's participle (ἐπέχοντες), in particular whether he envisages the saints "holding *onto*" the word of life (as a matter of faith and piety; so ESV, NASB, NIV, NRSV) or "holding *forth* the word of life" (KJV) in the sense of offering it to others (so also NEB, NJB).[56] In fact, the Greek word can mean either, in which case "The two meanings of the verb happily dovetail. Only as we firmly 'hold fast' to the gospel truth can we effectively 'hold it out.'"[57] Given that Paul is discussing the importance of living blameless lives and shining "as lights in the world," perhaps a missionary sense is thus to the fore: "the Philippians are exhorted to 'hold forth the word of life.' This is how they shine as luminaries in the midst of a dark and twisted world."[58]

Debate over Paul's intent does not simply concern accurate exegesis: it poses the challenge for preachers and their communities of living as

---

54. Martin, *Philippians*, 121; similarly Reumann, *Philippians*, 413: "the gospel that brings life in contrast to a world of death around them that faces *destruction* (1:28)" (emphasis original).
55. Martin, *Philippians*, 121.
56. Cf. Reumann, *Philippians*, 393–95.
57. Martin, *Philippians*, 121–22.
58. Cousar, *Philippians and Philemon*, 60.

well as speaking in a manner that is suffused with resurrection life—living and speaking, that is, by a power that is not their own. As with the earlier discussion of preaching that accords with God's "ways of life" (Acts 2:28), the prospect of bearing the "word of life" in a manner consistent with God's own gift implies genuine authority that is nonetheless generous, invitatory, and empowering. In essence, it joyfully promises life rather than threatening death. Thus, to preach the "word of life" is to preach a message that is itself life-giving, offered in the same manner that God grants us life in the person of Jesus. Such preaching will be both powerful and authoritative, although neither quality will reside in or derive from the one who preaches. Notwithstanding postmodern anxieties on this point, it is therefore no contradiction or denial of divine authority for Paul to speak of what Christ has accomplished in him "by word and deed, by the power of signs and wonders, by the power of the Spirit of God" (Rom 15:18–19), or to remind the Corinthians that his "speech and . . . proclamation" came to them not as mere words, but "with a demonstration of the Spirit and of power" (1 Cor 2:4). He speaks of having authority because he knows full well that such authority has been delegated to him only for "for building up and not for tearing down" (2 Cor 10:8; 13:10, citing Jer 24:6), as befits the "word of life."

If resurrection preaching is intrinsically life-giving, the same will be true of the individuals and communities whom such preaching calls forth: they will be characterized by their other-worldly oddness, their journey with Jesus, their commitment to reconciliation, their love of righteousness, and their resistance to evil.[59] Paradoxically, communities of resurrection will likely be small, obscure, and far from centers of power. They will lack the normal trappings of security or success. In a word, they will be cruciform. Paul describes them perfectly in 2 Corinthians, "as unknown, and yet . . . well known; as dying, and see—we are alive; as punished, and yet not killed; sorrowful, yet always rejoicing; as poor, yet making many rich; as having nothing, and yet possessing everything" (2 Cor 6:9–10). The quirky "in-between-ness" that Paul describes is not only joyful, but also deeply committed to ministries of justice and compassion.[60] Life enacted and enabled by the life of Jesus implies commit-

---

59. Emphasis on resistance to evil as characteristic of trust in Jesus' resurrection derives from Purves, *Resurrection of Ministry*, 104–6.

60. Just so, in his address to the 2002 Annual Meeting of the Academy of Homiletics ("Turning the World Upside Down: Preaching Resurrection"), Richard Hays contends that proclaiming resurrection in practical terms consists of practices such as

ment to embodiment and the created order because in Jesus' incarnation and resurrection alike, God embraces creation rather than condemning or abandoning it. Indeed, as we have noted already, by ascending to the Father in fulfilment of all that resurrection signifies, Jesus brings humanity and the created order into the very presence of God. That is the source of the hope that undergirds the life of faith to which resurrection preaching bears witness.

Resurrection Preaching as the Confession of Hope

Most readers—most preachers—who pick up a book about "the resurrection of preaching" do so because they would love to know what makes new life happen (if only in the form of life-giving sermons). As should be amply evident by now, readers of the present volume will only find here what they already knew to be true. Resurrection relies on the promises of God alone, because the only power capable of accomplishing resurrection belongs to God, as demonstrated, first, in the biography of Jesus and, second, in our own partial and proleptic experience of new life in union with him. We do not preach as if hoping to arrive at resurrection, because the only points of departure that lead in such a direction take us well beyond ourselves. Much less may we hope to make resurrection happen in our hearers, because it does not lie within our abilities to do so. In this regard, Barth's well known comment that "one can *not* speak of God simply by speaking of man in a loud voice," seems particularly apt.[61] Neither, therefore, is it our task to rhetorically browbeat our audience into intellectual submission, as though acquiescence either to the idea or to the experience of resurrection might result from clever and persuasive argumentation. Although wholly rational and reasonable on its own terms, resurrection is only dimly perceived from within the bounds (intellectual and otherwise) of the old creation. Rather, we preach in the assurance (even if we stumble a little over certain details) that Christ himself is risen. That is our point of departure. In this regard, preaching itself must be considered an etiological rather than a teleological activity. It is not causative so much as caused: it relies on grace, and is undertaken solely in response to the prior (and ongoing) activity of God.

---

peacemaking, sharing possessions, reconciliation in the form of table fellowship, and Sabbath-keeping.

61. Barth, *The Word of God and the Word of Man*, 196.

We must expect to be mocked and misunderstood on this point, even by some within the church. The offer of new life (whether manifest in the person of Jesus or as God's gift to humanity as a whole) will only appeal to those whose own lives are tenuous, inadequate, or unbearable: only the dying and the dead have any substantial interest in resurrection. That is why they set out on pilgrimage in the first place, into the unknown, ill-defined territory that lies between them and the "better country" that is "the city of the living God" (Heb 11:16; 12:22). In this Third Space, having left home behind but with our destination still in the distance, we tell stories of the Resurrected One while he retells our own stories back to us in such a way that they lead to new life, rather than ending in death. Christian pilgrimage is thus a journey through storied space, a place of hybrid identity shaped by the life narrative of Jesus. To preach in a manner that is governed by Jesus' resurrection and encouraged by the prospect of our own is to preach in a Third Voice, one that articulates a narrative and theological arc that, for the time being, is fully visible only in him. To preach in a Third Voice is thus to speak with hope and expectation of "What no eye has seen, nor ear heard, nor the human heart conceived, what God has prepared for those who love him" (1 Cor 2:9), all on the basis of what we have nonetheless glimpsed already in the life of Christ.

As has been evident throughout this study, my concern with much contemporary homiletical theory is that it is irrepressibly activist and in large measure self-referential, even while intending to speak of Christ. This is not to deny that Christ commissions an active and activist community of faith, but to insist on the unique character of specifically Christomorphic action and of specifically Christofocal speech. The humanly unaccountable trajectory of death and resurrection implies that the dynamics and characteristics of God's reign emerge in the context of abject human failure to act in obedience to (much less on behalf of) God. Yet the opposite is equally true: the ability to act in obedience to (sometimes on behalf of) God comes as a result of having first waited upon God, both in the temporal and soteriological sense of having waited for Christ to act in our place and therefore also in the sense of now serving God first. For preachers, this existential trajectory begins with the moral, theological, and practical necessity of falling silent with the absolute silence of Christ in order to hear a new and foreign word that speaks of resurrection, a word that comes from the "far country" of God's reign and draws us in that direction. We discover, perhaps to our surprise, that this word is more solid and sustaining than any we could have come up with on our own, and so we learn to articulate its message instead. This is a matter of spirituality, identity, and existential orientation more than of language, method, or homiletical technique alone. That such an apprenticeship is both arduous and lifelong goes without saying, especially for those of us in the homiletical guild who love nothing quite so much as the sound of our own voices.

In short, the resurrection of preaching requires the resurrection of dead preachers, even though resurrection is something that, by definition, the dead are unable to accomplish for themselves. In this consists our hope, both for preaching itself and for the congregations in our care. To preach of resurrection, sustained by Jesus' resurrection, is to preach of trust in God who raises the dead and to trust God in the process of doing so. Barth concludes his essay on "The Need and Promise of Christian Preaching," originally an address to pastors from July of 1922, on a similar note. Rather than rely on his own theology, Barth turns to Calvin, just as Calvin, rather than relying on *his* own theology, turns to consider resurrection. Knowing the difficulty of preaching, Barth invites his audience to view their ministry not in the context of their own capacities, but in light of the life-giving power of God:

> I should like to close with a confession of *hope*. It consists of a few sentences taken from Calvin's commentary on Micah 4:6 ("In that day, saith the Lord, will I assemble her that halteth, and I will gather her that is driven out, and her that I have afflicted"). "Although the church," Calvin comments, "is at the present time hardly to be distinguished from a dead or at best a sick man, there is no reason for despair, for the Lord raises up his own suddenly, as he waked the dead from the grave. This we must clearly remember, lest, when the church fails to shine forth, we conclude too quickly that her light has died utterly away. But the church in the world is so preserved that *she* rises *suddenly* from the dead. Her very preservation through the days is due to a succession of such miracles. Let us cling to the remembrance that she is not without her resurrection, or rather, not without her many resurrections. '*Tenendum est, ecclesiae vitam non esse absque resurrectione, imo absque multis resurrectionibus*.'"[62]

---

62. Barth, *The Word of God and the Word of Man*, 134. Strictly speaking, Calvin's Latin text (which Barth is partly paraphrasing) specifies that "the *life of the church* is not without its resurrection . . ."

In many traditions, it is customary for Christians to greet one another on Easter morning with the acclamation (here in its traditional Greek form), Χριστὸς ἀνέστη! ("Christ is risen!"), and to answer by affirming, Ἀληθῶς ἀνέστη! ("Truly He is risen!" or "He is risen indeed!"). Although the initial acclamation is hardly a sermon in itself, it represents the essence of preaching in a Third Voice. It is simply a response, a verbal declaration of what God has already done for us in the person of Jesus. The response to this response is equally apt, for it joyfully concurs that what was first true for Jesus now refashions our manner of speaking, our identity, and our experience of God in the present moment. Indeed, this simple exchange redefines our relationship to each other, thereby constituting us as a church. It turns out, therefore, that "Show me your resurrection" is not a *kōan* after all, nor is it a demand that we may make of one another. Rather, it is the humble prayer of preachers and their congregations who look to the Risen Lord for life. It is a prayer that he has already answered.

Bibliography

Allen, O. Wesley. "Mark 16:1-8: A Case Study of Resurrection Revised." *Homiletic* 28.2 (2003) 7–15.

Allison, Dale C., Jr. *Resurrecting Jesus: The Earliest Christian Tradition and Its Interpreters*. New York: T. & T. Clark, 2005.

Althaus, Paul. *The Theology of Martin Luther*. Translated by Robert C. Schultz. Philadelphia: Fortress, 1966.

Andrewes, Lancelot. *Seventeen Sermons on the Nativity*. London: Griffith, Farran, Okenden, & Welsh, 1887.

Aquinas, Saint Thomas. *Summa Theologiae*. Vol. 46, *Action and Contemplation (2a2æ. 179–182) Latin Text: English Translation, Introduction, Notes, Appendices & Glossary*. Edited and translated Jordan Aumann. Cambridge: Cambridge University Press, 1966.

The Archaeological Receipts Fund. *Archaeological Site of Philippi*. Athens: Hellenic Republic—Ministry of Culture and Sports, 2015.

Augustine, Saint. *Homilies on the First Epistle of John (Tractates in Epistolam Joannis ad Pathos)*. Translated by Boniface Ramsey. The Works of Saint Augustine: A Translation for the 21st Century I/14. Hyde Park, NY: New City, 2008.

———. *Sermons for Christmas and Epiphany*. Translated by Thomas Comerford Lalor. Ancient Christian Writers 15. New York: Newman, 1952.

Aune, David E. *Prophecy in Early Christianity and the Ancient Mediterranean World*. Grand Rapids: Eerdmans, 1983.

———. *Revelation 1–5*. Word Biblical Commentary 52A. Nashville: Thomas Nelson, 1997.

———. *Revelation 17–22*. Word Biblical Commentary 52C. Nashville: Thomas Nelson, 1998.

Austin, J. L. *How To Do Things with Words: The William James Lectures delivered at Harvard University in 1955*. 2nd ed. Edited by J. O. Urmson and Marina Sbisá. London: Oxford University Press, 1976.

———. *Philosophical Papers*. 3rd ed. Edited by J. O. Urmson and G. J. Warnock. Oxford: Oxford University Press, 1979.

Baker, Christopher. *The Hybrid Church in the City*. Aldershot: Ashgate, 2007.

Bakirtzis, Charalambos, and Helmut Koester, eds. *Philippi at the Time of Paul and after His Death*. Harrisburg, PA: Trinity Press International, 1998.

Balch, David L., and Annette Weissenrieder, eds. *Contested Spaces: Houses and Temples in Roman Antiquity and the New Testament*. Wissenschaftliche Untersuchungen zum Neuen Testament 285. Tübingen: Mohr Siebeck, 2012.
Barks, Coleman, et al., trans. *The Essential Rumi*. New expanded edition. New York: HarperOne, 2004.
Barth, Karl. *Church Dogmatics*. Vol. 4, pt. 1, *The Doctrine of Reconciliation*. Edited by G. W. Bromiley and T. F. Torrance. Translated by G. W. Bromiley. Edinburgh: T. & T. Clark, 1956.
———. *The Epistle to the Romans*. Translated by Edwyn C. Hoskyns. Oxford: Oxford University Press, 1933.
———. *Homiletics*. Translated by Geoffrey W. Bromiley and Donald E. Daniels. Louisville: Westminster John Knox, 1991.
———. *Homiletik. Wesen und Vorbereitung der Predigt*. Zürich: EVZ, 1966.
———. *The Word of God and the Word of Man*. Translated by Douglas Horton. Boston: Pilgrim, 1928. Reprint, New York: Harper, 1957.
Barton, Stephen C. *The Spirituality of the Gospels*. Eugene, OR: Wipf & Stock, 2005 [1992].
Barton, Stephen C., and Graham Stanton, eds. *Resurrection: Essays in Honour of Leslie Houlden*. London: SPCK, 1994.
Bauckham, Richard. *The Climax of Prophecy: Studies on the Book of Revelation*. London: Continuum/T. & T. Clark, 1993.
Baudrillard, Jean. *Simulacra and Simulation*. Translated by Sheila Faria Glaser. The Body, In Theory: Histories of Cultural Materialism. Ann Arbor: University of Michigan Press, 1994.
Baumgärtel, Friedrich, and Johannes Behm. "καρδία, καρδιογνώστης, σκληροκαρδία." In *TDNT* 3:605–14.
Bayne, Paul. *An Entire Commentary Upon the Whole Epistle of the Apostle Paul to the Ephesians* [etc.]. London: Samuel Gellibrand, 1647.
Beasley-Murray, George R. *Preaching the Gospel from the Gospels*. Peabody, MA: Hendrickson, 1996.
Beaudean, Jr., John William. *Paul's Theology of Preaching*. National Association of Baptist Professors of Religion Dissertation Series 6. Macon: Mercer University Press, 1988.
Behm, Johannes, and Ernst Würthwein, "Νοέω, Νοῦς, Νόημα, Ἀνόητος, κτλ." In *TDNT* 4:948–1022.
Berry, C. Everett. "Speech-Act Theory as a Corollary for Describing the Communicative Dynamics of Biblical Revelation: Some Recommendations and Reservations." *Criswell Theological Review*, n.s., 7.1 (2009) 81–100.
Bhabha, Homi K. "Culture's In Between." In *Multicultural States: Rethinking Difference and Identity*, edited by David Bennett, 29–36. London: Routledge, 1998.
———. "Editor's Introduction: Minority Maneuvers and Unsettled Negotiations." *Critical Inquiry* 23.33, "Front Lines/Border Posts" (1997) 431–59.
———. "Frontlines/Borderposts." In *Displacements: Cultural Identities in Question*, edited by Angelika Bammer, 269–72. Bloomington: Indiana University Press, 1994.
———. *The Location of Culture*. London: Routledge, 1994.

———. "The Third Space: Interview with Homi K. Bhabha." In *Identity: Community, Culture, Difference*, edited by Jonathan Rutherford, 207–21. London: Lawrence & Wishart, 1990.
Blount, Brian K. *Invasion of the Dead: Preaching Resurrection*. Louisville: Westminster John Knox, 2014.
Bonhoeffer, Dietrich. *The Cost of Discipleship*. Translated by Reginald Fuller. Revised by Irmgard Booth. New York: Macmillan, 1977.
———. *Ethics*. Edited by Clifford J. Green et al. Translated by Reinhard Krauss et al. Dietrich Bonhoeffer Works 6. Minneapolis: Fortress, 2005.
Bosch, David. *Transforming Mission: Paradigm Shifts in Theology of Mission*. American Society of Missiology Series 16. Maryknoll: Orbis, 1991.
———. *Witness to the World: The Christian Mission in Theological Perspective*. Atlanta: John Knox, 1980.
Botha, Eugene. "Speech Act Theory and Biblical Interpretation." *Neotestamenica* 41.2 (2007) 274–94.
Boyer, Ernest. *A Way in the World: A Family Life as Spiritual Discipline*. San Francisco: Harper & Row, 1984.
Braaten, Carl E. "The Resurrection Debate Revisited." *Pro Ecclesia* 8.2 (1999) 147–58.
Brown, Raymond E. *The Gospel according to John XIII–XXI: A New Translation with Introduction and Commentary*. Anchor Bible 29A. Garden City, NY: Doubleday, 1981.
Brueggemann, Walter. *Cadences of Home: Preaching among Exiles*. Louisville: Westminster John Knox, 1997.
Buechner, Frederick. *Telling the Truth: The Gospel as Tragedy, Comedy, and Fairy Tale*. San Francisco: HarperSanFrancisco, 1977.
Bultmann, Rudolf, et al. *Kerygma and Myth: A Theological Debate*. Edited by Hans Werner Bortsch. Translated by Reginald H. Fuller. New York: Harper, 1961.
Bunyan, John. *The Pilgrim's Progress*. Edited by W. R. Owens. Oxford World's Classics. Oxford: Oxford University Press, 2003.
———. *The Pilgrim's Progress from This World to That Which Is to Come* [etc.]. London: [Nathaniel] Ponder, 1678.
Burnaby, John, trans. *Augustine: Later Works*. Library of Christian Classics 8. Philadelphia: Westminster, 1955.
Burton-Christie, Douglas. "Living Between Two Worlds: Home, Journey and the Quest for Sacred Place." *Anglican Theological Review* 79 (1997) 413–32.
Büttgen, Philippe. "Luther et l'objet de la predication." *Revue des sciences philosophiques et théologiques* 98.3 (2014) 563–80.
Buttrick, David G. "Easter Preaching." *Interpretation* 65.1 (2011) 56–67.
———. *Homiletic: Moves and Structures*. Philadelphia: Fortress, 1987.
———. "Preaching on the Resurrection." *Religion in Life* 45.3 (1976) 278–95.
Calvin, John. *Commentaries on the Catholic Epistles*. Translated by John Owen. Edinburgh: Calvin Translation Society, 1855.
———. *The Epistle of Paul the Apostle to the Hebrews and the First and Second Epistles of St Peter*. Translated by William B. Johnston. Edited by Thomas F. Torrance and David W. Torrance. Calvin's New Testament Commentaries 12. Grand Rapids: Eerdmans, 1994.

———. *Institutes of the Christian Religion*. 2 vols. Translated by Ford Lewis Battles. Edited by John T. McNeill. Library of Christian Classics 20, 21; London: SCM; Philadelphia: Westminster, 1960.

———. *Institutes of the Christian Religion: 1541 French Edition*. Translated by Elsie Anne McKee. Grand Rapids: Eerdmans, 2009.

———. *Ioannis Calvini Opera Quae Supersunt Omnia*. Vol. 55. Edited by Edouard Cunitz et al. Corpus Reformatorum 83. Brunsvigae [Braunschweig]: Schwetschke, 1863.

Campbell, Charles L. *Preaching Jesus: New Directions for Homiletics in Hans Frei's Postliberal Theology*. Grand Rapids: Eerdmans, 1997.

Campbell, Constantine J. *Paul and Union with Christ: An Exegetical and Theological Study*. Grand Rapids: Zondervan, 2012.

Carnley, Peter. *The Structure of Resurrection Belief*. Oxford: Clarendon, 1987.

Chadwick, Henry, trans. *Origen: Contra Celsum; Translated, with an Introduction and Notes*. Cambridge: Cambridge University Press, 1953.

Chan, Sam. *Preaching as the Word of God: Answering an Old Question with Speech-Act Theory*. Eugene, OR: Pickwick, 2016.

Childers, Jana, ed. *Purposes of Preaching*. St. Louis: Chalice, 2004.

Cohen, Leonard. *Parasites of Heaven*. Toronto: McClelland and Stewart, 1966.

Cohn, Haim Hermann, and Yuval Sinai. "Witness." In *EncJud* 21:115–25.

Coffin, William Sloan. "Easter and Forgiveness." *The Living Pulpit* 7.1 (1998) 8–9.

Coupland, Douglas. *Life After God*. New York: Pocket Books, 1994.

Cousar, Charles B. *Philippians and Philemon: A Commentary*. Louisville: Westminster John Knox, 2009.

Craddock, Fred B. *As One Without Authority: Fourth Edition Revised and with New Sermons*. St. Louis: Chalice, 2001.

Cranfield, C. E. B. *A Critical and Exegetical Commentary on the Epistle to the Romans*. 2 vols. International Critical Commentary. Edinburgh: T. & T. Clark, 1975, 1979.

Crossan, John Dominic. *Jesus: A Revolutionary Biography*. San Francisco: HarperCollins, 1994.

———. "The Life of a Mediterranean Jewish Peasant." *The Christian Century* 108.37 (1991) 1194–200.

Davies, W. D., and Dale C. Allison. *The Gospel according to Saint Matthew*. 3 vols. International Critical Commentary. Edinburgh: T. & T. Clark, 1988–1997.

Dickens, Charles. *A Christmas Carol in Prose: Being a Ghost Story of Christmas*. London: Chapman and Hall, 1843.

Draper, Marilyn. "Lived Doxology: A Spiritual Theology for the Church in Mission." PhD diss., McMaster Divinity College, 2016.

Dykstra, Craig R. *Growing in the Life of Faith: Education and Christian Practices*. 2nd ed. Louisville: Westminster John Knox, 2005.

Eliot, T. S. *Collected Poems 1909–1962*. London: Faber & Faber, 1963.

———. *Notes towards the Definition of Culture*. New York: Harcourt Brace, 1949.

Ellul, Jacques. "Témoignage et Société Technicienne." In *Le Témoignage; actes du colloque organisé par le Centre international d'études humanistes et par l'Institut d'études philosophiques de Rome, Rome, 5–11 janvier 1972*, edited by Enrico Castelli, 441–55. Paris: Aubier, 1972.

———. *The Technological Society*. Translated by John Wilkinson. New York: Knopf, 1965.

Epstein, Isidore, ed. *The Babylonian Talmud, Translated into English with Notes, Glossary and Indices*. 35 vols. London: Soncino, 1935–1952.

Evans, Donald. *The Logic of Self-Involvement: A Philosophical Study of Everyday Language with Special Reference to the Christian Use of Language about God as Creator*. Library of Philosophy and Theology. London: SCM, 1963.

Fee, Gordon D. *The First Epistle to the Corinthians*. New International Commentary on the New Testament. Grand Rapids: Eerdmans, 1987.

Feldman, Louis H., and Meyer Reinhold, eds. *Jewish Life and Thought among Greeks and Romans: Primary Readings*. Minneapolis: Fortress, 1996.

Ferry, Patrick. "Martin Luther on Preaching: Promises and Problems of the Sermon as a Source of Reformation History and as an Instrument of the Reformation." *Concordia Theological Quarterly* 54 (1990) 265–80.

Finegan, Jack. *The Archeology of the New Testament: The Mediterranean World of the Early Christian Apostles*. Boulder, CO: Westview, 1981.

Fish, Stanley. *Is There a Text in this Class? The Authority of Interpretive Communities*. Cambridge, MA: Harvard University Press, 1980.

Fitzmyer, Joseph A. *The Gospel according to Luke I–IX: Introduction, Translation, and Notes*. Anchor Bible 28. Garden City, NY: Doubleday, 1981.

———. *The Gospel according to Luke X–XXIV: A New Translation with Introduction and Commentary*. Anchor Bible 28A. Garden City, NY: Doubleday, 1986.

———. *Romans: A New Translation with Introduction and Commentary*. Anchor Bible 33. New York: Doubleday, 1993.

Freyne, Seán. *The Jesus Movement and Its Expansion: Meaning and Mission*. Grand Rapids: Eerdmans, 2014.

Gaarden, Marianne. *The Third Room of Preaching: The Sermon, the Listener, and the Creation of Meaning*. Westminster Homiletics Monograph Series 1. Louisville: Westminster John Knox, 2017.

Geyer, Hans-Georg. "The Resurrection of Jesus Christ: A Survey of the Debate in Present Day Theology." Translated by R. A. Wilson. In *The Significance of the Message of the Resurrection for Faith in Jesus Christ*, edited by C. F. D. Moule, 105–35. Studies in Biblical Theology 2.8. London: SCM; Naperville: Allenson, 1968.

Al-Ghazālī. *The Ninety-Nine Beautiful Names of God: al-Maqṣad al-asnā fī sharḥ asmā' Allāh al-ḥusnā*. Translated by David B. Burrell and Nazih Daher. Cambridge: Islamic Texts Society, 1992.

Gilroy, Paul. *The Black Atlantic: Modernity and Double Consciousness*. London: Verso, 1993.

González, Justo L. "Standing at the Púlpito." In *Púlpito: An Introduction to Hispanic Preaching*, edited by Justo L. González and Pablo A. Jiménez, 57–69. Nashville, TN: Abingdon, 2005.

Goodman, Elizabeth R. "Preaching the Easter Texts." *Journal for Preachers* 35.3 (2012) 3–12.

Gorman, Michael J. *Cruciformity: Paul's Narrative Spirituality of the Cross*. Grand Rapids: Eerdmans, 2001.

———. "Preaching and Living the Resurrection Today." *The Living Pulpit* 21.2 (2012) 4–8.

Graham, Keith. *J. L. Austin: A Critique of Ordinary Language Philosophy*. Harvester Studies in Philosophy 1. Hassocks, Sussex: Harvester, 1977.

Greidanus, Sidney. *The Modern Preacher and the Ancient Text: Interpreting and Preaching Biblical Literature.* Grand Rapids: Eerdmans, 1988.

Grewendorf, Gunther, and Georg Meggle, eds. *Speech Acts, Mind, and Social Reality.* Studies in Linguistics and Philosophy 79. Dordrecht: Kluwer Academic, 2002.

Guder, Darrell, ed. *Missional Church: A Vision for the Sending of the Church in North America.* Grand Rapids: Eerdmans, 1998.

Harstine, Stan. "Un-Doubting Thomas: Recognition Scenes in the Ancient World." *Perspectives in Religious Studies* 33.4 (2006) 435–47.

Hays, Richard B. "Turning the World Upside Down: Preaching Resurrection." Address to the Annual Meeting of the Academy of Homiletics, Boston, December 5, 2002.

Heinemann, Joseph. "The Background of Jesus' Prayer in the Jewish Liturgical Tradition." In *The Lord's Prayer and Jewish Liturgy*, edited by Jakob J. Petuchowski and Michael Brocke, 81–89. New York: Seabury, 1978.

Hemingway, Ernest. "A Clean Well-Lighted Place." *Scribner's Magazine* 93.3 (March 1933) 149–50.

Hengel, Martin. *Crucifixion in the Ancient World and the Folly of the Message of the Cross.* Translated by John Bowden. Philadelphia: Fortress, 1977.

Hilkert, Mary Catherine. "Preachers of Grace, Witnesses to the Resurrection." *Worship* 77.4 (2003) 293–307.

Holmes, Michael W., ed. *The Greek New Testament: SBL Edition.* Bellingham, WA: Lexham; Atlanta: Society of Biblical Literature, 2011–2013.

Homer. *The Odyssey.* Translated by Rodney Merrill. Ann Arbor: University of Michigan Press, 2002.

Hooker, Richard. *Of the Laws of Ecclesiastical Polity, Book I.* Oxford: Clarendon, 1888.

Huddart, David. *Homi K. Bhabha.* Routledge Critical Thinkers. London: Routledge, 2006.

Hughes, Graham. *Worship as Meaning: A Liturgical Theology for Late Modernity.* Cambridge: Cambridge University Press, 2003.

Ilan, Tal. "Gender Issues and Daily Life." In *The Oxford Handbook of Jewish Daily Life in Roman Palestine*, edited by Catherine Hezser, 48–68. Oxford: Oxford University Press, 2010. DOI: http://dx.doi.org/10.1093/oxfordhb/9780199216437.013.0004.

Inge, John. *A Christian Theology of Place.* Aldershot: Ashgate, 2003.

Instone-Brewer, David. *Feasts and Sabbaths: Passover and Atonement.* Traditions of the Rabbis from the Era of the New Testament 2A. Grand Rapids: Eerdmans, 2011.

Isaac, Benjamin. "The Babatha Archive: A Review Article." *Israel Exploration Journal* 42.1/2 (1992) 62–75.

Jacobs, Alan. "Naming of the Animals." In *A Dictionary of Biblical Tradition in English Literature*, edited by David L. Jeffrey, 537–38. Grand Rapids: Eerdmans, 1992.

Jacobsen, David Schnasa, ed. *Homiletical Theology in Action: The Unfinished Theological Task of Preaching.* Promise of Homiletical Theology 2. Eugene, OR: Cascade, 2015.

———. *Toward a Homiletical Theology of Promise.* Promise of Homiletical Theology 4. Eugene, OR: Wipf & Stock, 2018.

Jansen, Mechteld. "Christian Migrants and the Theology of Space and Place." In *Contested Spaces, Common Ground: Space and Power Structures in Contemporary Multireligious Societies*, edited by Ulrich Winkler et al., 147–61. Currents of Encounter 50. Leiden: Brill, 2017.

Jiménez, Pablo A. "If You Just Close Your Eyes: Postcolonial Perspectives on Preaching from the Caribbean." *Homiletic* 40.1 (2015) 21–27.

———. "Toward a Postcolonial Homiletic: Justo L. González's Contribution to Hispanic Preaching." In *Hispanic Christian Thought at the Dawn of the 21st Century: Apuntes in Honor of Justo L. Gonzalez*, edited by Alvin Padilla et al., 159–67. Nashville: Abingdon, 2005.

———. "The Troublemaker's Friend: From Text to Sermon in a Postcolonial Context." *Apuntes* 34.3 (2014) 84–90.

Johnson, Stephen. *Late Roman Fortifications*. London: Batsford, 1983.

Jones, Joe R. *A Grammar of Christian Faith: Systematic Explorations in Christian Life and Doctrine*. Vol. 1. Lanham, MD: Rowman and Littlefield, 2002.

Josephus, Flavius. *Jewish Antiquities. Books I–III*. Translated by H. St. J. Thackeray. Loeb Classical Library 242. Cambridge, MA: Harvard University Press, 1930 [1998].

Kay, James F. "The Word of the Cross at the Turn of the Ages." *Interpretation* 53.1 (1999) 44–56.

Keener, Craig. *Acts: An Exegetical Commentary*. Vol. 1, *Introduction and 1:1—2:47*. Grand Rapids: Baker Academic, 2012.

Kim, Duk Hyun. "An Alternative Pneumatological Epistemology and Its Praxis in a Text-Driven Preaching Based on the Speech Act Theory (SAT)." *Journal of Youngsan Theology* 37 (2016) 159–81.

———. "The Homiletical Appropriation of Biblical Passages in the Light of Speech Act Theory: Preaching as a Performance of the Biblical Text." PhD diss., University of Stellenbosch, 2014. Online: http://scholar.sun.ac.za/handle/10019.1/96016.

———. "Reframing the Hermeneutical Question as Part of Its Homiletical Responsibility: Making Extensive use of the Speech Act Theory." *Journal of the Evangelical Homiletics Society* 16.1 (2016) 30–46.

Kim, Eunjoo Mary. *Christian Preaching and Worship in Multicultural Contexts: A Practical Theological Approach*. Collegeville, MN: Liturgical, 2017.

———. *Preaching in an Age of Globalization*. Louisville: Westminster John Knox, 2010.

———. *Preaching the Presence of God: A Homiletic from an Asian American Perspective*. Valley Forge, PA: Judson, 1999.

Kim, Matthew D. "Possible Selves: A Homiletic for Second Generation Korean American Churches." *Homiletic* 32.1 (2007) 1–17.

———. *Preaching to Second Generation Korean Americans: Towards a Possible Selves Contextual Homiletic*. American University Studies. New York: Peter Lang, 2007.

Knowles, Michael P. "Consider the Lilies: A Hermeneutic of the New Creation." In *Inaugurations: Inaugural Lectures Delivered at McMaster Divinity College*, edited by Stanley E. Porter, 13–29. McMaster Divinity College General Studies Series 9. Eugene, OR: Pickwick, 2017.

———. "Cross-Cultural Preaching: Proclaiming a Global Faith." In *The Globalization of Christianity: Implications for Christian Ministry and Theology*, edited by Gordon L. Heath and Steven M. Studebaker, 69–84. McMaster Divinity College Theological Studies Series 6. Eugene, OR: Pickwick, 2015.

———. *Jeremiah in Matthew's Gospel: The Rejected-Prophet Motif in Matthaean Redaction*. Journal for the Study of the New Testament Supplement Series 68. Sheffield: JSOT, 1993. Reprint, Bloomsbury Academic Collections. London: Bloomsbury, 2015.

———. "Mark, Matthew, and Mission: Faith, Failure, and the Fidelity of Jesus." In *Christian Mission: Old Testament Foundations and New Testament Developments*, edited by Stanley E. Porter and Cynthia Long Westfall, 64–92. McMaster New Testament Study Series 9. Eugene, OR: Pickwick, 2010.

———. *Of Seeds and the People of God: Preaching as Parable, Crucifixion, and Testimony.* Eugene, OR: Wipf & Stock, 2015.

———. *The Unfolding Mystery of the Divine Name: The God of Sinai in Our Midst.* Downers Grove: IVP Academic, 2012.

———. *We Preach Not Ourselves: Paul on Proclamation.* Grand Rapids: Brazos, 2008.

———. "'Wide Is the Gate and Spacious the Road That Leads to Destruction': Matthew 7:13 in Light of Archaeological Evidence." *Journal of Greco-Roman Christianity and Judaism* 1 (2000) 176–213.

Koch, Klaus. "דֶּרֶךְ *derekh** [etc.]." In *TDOT* 3:270–93.

Kraemer, David. *The Meanings of Death in Rabbinic Judaism.* London: Routledge, 2000.

Kwok, Pui-lan. *Postcolonial Imagination and Feminist Theology.* Louisville: Westminster John Knox, 2005.

———. "Postcolonial Preaching in Intercultural Contexts." *Homiletic* 40.1 (2015) 8–21, http://www.homiletic.net/index.php/homiletic/article/view/4117.

L'Engle, Madeleine. *The Irrational Season.* Crosswicks Journal 3. New York: HarperSanFrancisco, 1977.

Larsen, Kasper Bro. *Recognizing the Stranger: Recognition Scenes in the Gospel of John.* Biblical Interpretation 93. Leiden: Brill, 2008.

Lash, Nicholas. *Theology on the Way to Emmaus.* London: SCM, 1986.

Lee, Sang Hyun. *From a Liminal Place: An Asian American Theology.* Minneapolis: Fortress, 2010.

———. "Pilgrimage and Home in the Wilderness of Marginality: Symbols and Context in Asian American Theology." *Princeton Seminary Bulletin* 16.1 (1995) 49–64.

Lim, Timothy H. "'Not in Persuasive Words of Wisdom, but in the Demonstration of the Spirit and Power.'" *Novum Testamentum* 29.2 (1987) 137–49.

Lischer, Richard. "'Resurrexit': Something to Preach." *The Christian Century* 97.12 (1980) 371–74.

Long, Thomas G. "Preaching Easter at Old First Gnostic." *Journal for Preachers* 35.3 (2012) 13–25.

———. "Preaching the Gospel of Resurrection." In *Preaching Gospel: Essays in Honor of Richard Lischer*, edited by Charles L. Campbell et al., 71–87. Lloyd John Ogilvie Institute of Preaching 9. Eugene, OR: Cascade, 2016.

Longenecker, Richard N. *The Epistle to the Romans.* New International Greek Testament Commentary. Grand Rapids: Eerdmans, 2016.

———. "The Messianic Secret in the Light of Recent Discoveries." *Evangelical Quarterly* 41.4 (1969) 207–15.

Lose, David J. *Confessing Jesus Christ: Preaching in a Postmodern World.* Grand Rapids: Eerdmans, 2003.

Lüdemann, Gerd, with Alf Özen. *What Really Happened to Jesus: A Historical Approach to the Resurrection.* Translated by John Bowden. Louisville: Westminster John Knox, 1995.

Lukaszewski, Albert L., et al. *The Lexham Syntactic Greek New Testament, SBL Edition: Expansions and Annotations.* Bellingham, WA: Lexham, 2011.

Maan, Ajit K. *Internarrative Identity.* Lanham, MD: University Press of America, 1999.

MacArthur, John. "The Authority of the Preacher." https://www.gty.org/library/sermons-library/80-133/the-authority-of-the-preacher.

Macaskill, Grant. *Union with Christ in the New Testament*. Oxford: Oxford University Press, 2013.
Marcus, Joel. *Mark 1–8: A New Translation with Introduction and Commentary*. Anchor Bible 27. New Haven, CT: Yale University Press, 2000.
———. *Mark 8–16: A New Translation with Introduction and Commentary*. Anchor Bible 27A. New Haven: Yale University Press, 2009.
Martin, Ralph P. *The Epistle of Paul to the Philippians: An Introduction and Commentary*. 2nd ed. Tyndale New Testament Commentaries 11. Leicester: InterVarsity; Grand Rapids: Eerdmans, 1987.
Matsuoka, Fumitaka. *Out of Silence: Emerging Themes in Asian American Churches*. Eugene, OR: Wipf & Stock, 2009.
Meconi, David Vincent. "Silence Proceeding." *Logos: A Journal of Catholic Thought and Culture* 5.2 (2002) 59–75.
Metzger, Bruce M. *A Textual Commentary on the Greek New Testament, Second Edition. A Companion Volume to the United Bible Societies' Greek New Testament (Fourth Revised Edition)*. Stuttgart: Deutsche Bibelgesellschaft, 1994.
Michaelis, Wilhelm. "ὁράω, κτλ." *TDNT* 5:315–82.
Moltmann, Jürgen. *Theology of Hope: On the Ground and the Implications of a Christian Eschatology*. Translated by James W. Leitch. Minneapolis: Fortress, 1993.
Muraoka, Takamitsu. "Prophetic Perfect." In *EHLL* 3:279b–80a.
Neusner, Jacob, et al., ed. and trans. *The Babylonian Talmud: A Translation and Commentary*. 22 vols. Peabody, MA: Hendrickson, 2011.
———, et al., ed. and trans. *The Jerusalem Talmud: A Translation and Commentary*. Peabody, MA: Hendrickson, 2008.
———, trans. *The Mishnah: A New Translation*. New Haven: Yale University Press, 1988.
———, trans. *The Tosefta: Translated from the Hebrew with a New Introduction*. 2 vols. Peabody, MA: Hendrickson, 2002.
Newbigin, Lesslie. *The Gospel in a Pluralist Society*. Grand Rapids: Eerdmans, 1989.
———. *The Open Secret: An Introduction to the Theology of Mission*. Rev. ed. Grand Rapids: Eerdmans, 1995.
Niebuhr, H. Richard. *Christ and Culture*. New York: Harper, 1951.
———. *The Meaning of Revelation*. New York: Macmillan, 1962.
Packer, J. I. *Knowing God*. London: Hodder and Stoughton, 1973.
Pasquarello, Michael, III. *We Speak Because We Have First Been Spoken: A Grammar of the Preaching Life*. Grand Rapids: Eerdmans, 2009.
Pearce, Sarah J. K. *The Words of Moses: Studies in the Reception of Deuteronomy in the Second Temple Period*. Texts and Studies in Ancient Judaism/Texte und Studien zum antiken Judentum 152. Tübingen: Mohr Siebeck, 2013.
Peterson, Eugene. *Working the Angles: The Shape Of Pastoral Integrity*. Grand Rapids: Eerdmans, 1987.
Picard, Charles. "Un texte nouveau de la correspondance entre Abgar d'Osroène et Jésus-Christ, gravé sur une porte de ville, à Philippes (Macédoine)." *Bulletin de correspondance hellénique* 44 (1920) 41–69.
Plato. *Plato: With an English Translation*. Vol. 8, *Statesman, Philebus, Ion*. Translated by Harold N. Fowler and W. R. M. Lamb. Loeb Classical Library 164. Cambridge, MA: Harvard University Press; London: Heinemann, 1925.

Pott, Francis. *Hymns Fitted to the Order of Common Prayer, and Administration of the Sacraments, and Other Rites and Ceremonies of the Church, according to the Use of the Church of England* [etc.]. London: Hamilton, Adams, 1861.

Poythress, Vern S. "Canon and Speech Act: Limitations in Speech-Act Theory, with Implications for a Putative Theory of Canonical Speech Acts." *Westminster Theological Journal* 70.2 (2008) 337–54.

Presa, Neal D. *Ascension Theology and Habakkuk: A Reformed Ecclesiology in Filipino American Perspective*. Asian Christianity in the Diaspora. Cham: Palgrave Macmillan, 2018.

Purves, Andrew. *Reconstructing Pastoral Theology: A Christological Foundation*. Louisville: Westminster John Knox, 2004.

———. *The Resurrection of Ministry: Serving in the Hope of the Risen Lord*. Downers Grove: InterVarsity, 2010.

Ramachandra, Vinoth. *Subverting Global Myths: Theology and the Public Issues Shaping Our World*. Downers Grove: IVP Academic, 2008.

Rambo, Shelley. *Resurrecting Wounds: Living in the Afterlife of Trauma*. Waco, TX: Baylor University Press, 2017.

Reumann, John. *Philippians: A New Translation with Introduction and Commentary*. Anchor Yale Bible 33B. New Haven: Yale University Press, 2008.

Richmond, I. A. "Commemorative Arches and City Gates in the Augustan Age." *Journal of Roman Studies* 23.2 (1933) 149–74.

Ricoeur, Paul. *Essays on Biblical Interpretation*. Edited by Lewis S. Mudge. Philadelphia: Fortress, 1980.

Roger, J. "L'enceinte basse de Philippes." *Bulletin de correspondance hellénique* 62 (1938) 20–41.

Rossetti, Christina. *Goblin Market and Other Poems*. London: Macmillan, 1862.

Rottman, John M. "Performative Language and the Limits of Performance in Preaching." In *Performance in Preaching: Bringing the Sermon to Life*, edited by Jana Childers and Clayton J. Schmidt, 67–86. Grand Rapids: Baker Academic, 2008.

Rudrum, Alan. "T. S. Eliot on Lancelot Andrewes's 'Word Within A Word.'" *ANQ: A Quarterly Journal of Short Articles, Notes and Reviews* 9.4 (1996) 43–44.

Runions, Erin. *Changing Subjects: Gender, Nation and Future in Micah*. Playing the Texts 7. London: Sheffield Academic, 2001.

Rupp, E. Gordon. *The Righteousness of God: Luther Studies*. London: Hodder and Stoughton, 1953.

Rushdie, Salman. *Imaginary Homelands: Essays and Criticism 1981–1991*. London: Granta, 1991.

———. *The Satanic Verses*. London: Viking Penguin, 1988.

Sancken, Joni S. *Stumbling Over the Cross: Preaching the Cross and Resurrection Today*. Lloyd John Ogilvie Institute of Preaching Series 8. Eugene, OR: Cascade, 2016.

Sanneh, Lamin. *Translating the Message: The Missionary Impact on Culture*. 2nd ed., revised and expanded. American Society of Missiology 42. Maryknoll, NY: Orbis, 2009.

———. *Whose Religion Is Christianity? The Gospel Beyond the West*. Grand Rapids: Eerdmans, 2003.

Schaff, Philip, ed. *The Creeds of Christendom, with a History and Critical Notes*. Vol. 2, *The Greek and Latin Creeds, with Translations*. New York: Harper, 1877.

Schlafer, David J. "Anticipating Unpredictable Resurrection: Preaching in the Hope of a God-Engendered Future." In *The Future of Preaching*, edited by Geoffrey Stevenson, 206–14. London: SCM, 2010.

Schlütter, Morten. "Kōan." In *EncBudd* 1:426–29.

Schniewind, Julius. "ἀγγελία, ἀγγέλλω, κτλ." In *TDNT* 1:56–73.

Schrenk, Gottlob. "διαλέγομαι, διαλογίζομαι, διαλογισμός." In *TDNT* 2:93–98.

Seamands, Stephen A. *Give Them Christ: Preaching His Incarnation, Crucifixion, Resurrection, Ascension, and Return*. Downers Grove: InterVarsity, 2012.

Searle, John R. "A Classification of Illocutionary Acts." *Language in Society* 5.1 (1976) 1–23.

———. *Expression and Meaning: Studies in the Theory of Speech Acts*. Cambridge: Cambridge University Press, 1979.

———. "A Taxonomy of Illocutionary Acts." In *Language, Mind, and Knowledge*, edited by Keith Gunderson, 344–69. Minnesota Studies in the Philosophy of Science 7. Minneapolis: University of Minnesota Press, 1975.

Searle, John R., and Daniel Vanderveken. *Foundations of Illocutionary Logic*. Cambridge: Cambridge University Press, 1985.

Seybold, Klaus. "*הֶבֶל* hebhel;* *הָבַל* hābhal." *TDOT* 3:312–20.

Smith, Christian, and Melinda Lundquist Denton. *Soul Searching: The Religious and Spiritual Lives of American Teenagers*. New York: Oxford University Press, 2005.

Sophocles. *The Three Theban Plays: Antigone; Oedipus the King; Oedipus at Colonus*. Translated by Robert Fagles. Introductions and Notes by Bernard Knox. New York: Penguin, 1984.

Spong, John Shelby. *Resurrection: Myth or Reality?* New York: HarperCollins, 1994.

Strack, H. L., and Günter Stemberger. *Introduction to the Talmud and Midrash*. 2nd ed. Translated and edited by Markus Bockmuehl. Minneapolis: Fortress, 1996.

Strathmann, Hermann. "Πόλις, Πολίτης, Πολιτεύομαι, Πολιτεία, Πολίτευμα." In *TDNT* 6:516–35.

Summit, Jennifer. "Active and Contemplative Lives." In *Cultural Reformations: Medieval and Renaissance in Literary History*, edited by James Simpson and Brian Cummings, 527–53. Oxford Twenty-First Century Approaches to Literature. Oxford: Oxford University Press, 2010.

Tappenden, Fred. *Resurrection in Paul: Cognition, Metaphor, and Transformation*. Early Christianity and Its Literature 19. Atlanta: SBL, 2016.

Taylor, Barbara Brown. "The Easter Sermon." *Journal for Preachers* 18.3 (1995) 10–14.

Taylor, John. "Recognition Scenes in the Odyssey and the Gospels." In *The Bible and Hellenism: Greek Influence on Jewish and Early Christian Literature*, edited by Thomas L. Thompson and Philippe Wajdenbaum, 247–57. London: Routledge, 2014.

Thane, Markus. "Speech-Act Theory to Enhance Karl Barth's Homiletical Postulation of A Sermon's 'Revelatory Compliance.'" *Scottish Journal of Theology* 68.2 (2015) 187–200.

Thate, Michael J., Kevin J. Vanhoozer, and Constantine R. Campbell, eds. *"In Christ" in Paul: Explorations in Paul's Theology of Union and Participation*. Wissenschaftliche Untersuchungen zum Neuen Testament 2.384. Tübingen: Mohr Siebeck, 2014; Grand Rapids: Eerdmans, 2018.

Travis, Sarah. *Decolonizing Preaching: The Pulpit as Postcolonial Space*. Lloyd John Ogilvie Institute of Preaching Series 6. Eugene, OR: Cascade, 2014.

———. "Troubled Gospel: Postcolonial Preaching for the Colonized, Colonizer, and Everyone in Between." *Homiletic* 40.1 (2015) 46–54.
Turner, Victor, and Edith Turner. *Image and Pilgrimage in Christian Culture: Anthropological Perspectives*. Lectures on the History of Religions, n.s., 11. New York: Columbia University Press, 1978.
Updike, John. "Seven Stanzas at Easter." *The Christian Century* 78.8 (1961) 236.
Valle-Ruiz, Lis. "Toward Postcolonial Liturgical Preaching: Drawing on the Pre-Columbian Caribbean Religion of the Taínos." *Homiletic* 40.1 (2015) 28–37.
Van Gelder, Craig, and Dwight Zscheile. *The Missional Church in Perspective: Mapping Trends and Shaping the Conversation*. Grand Rapids: Baker Academic, 2011.
Vanhoozer, Kevin J. *Is There a Meaning in This Text? The Bible, the Reader, and the Morality of Literary Knowledge*. Grand Rapids: Zondervan, 1998.
———. *Remythologizing Theology: Divine Action, Passion, and Authorship*. Cambridge: Cambridge University Press, 2010.
Van Toorn, Penelope. *Rudy Wiebe and the Historicity of the Word*. Edmonton: University of Alberta Press, 1995.
Vorgrimler, Herbert. *Understanding Karl Rahner: An Introduction to His Life and Thought*. Translated by John Bowden. London: SCM, 1986.
Wan, Sze-kar. "'To the Jew First and Also to the Greek': Reading Romans as Ethnic Construction." In *Prejudice and Christian Beginnings: Investigating Race, Gender, and Ethnicity in Early Christian Studies*, edited by Laura Nasrallah and Elisabeth Schüssler Fiorenza, 129–55. Minneapolis: Fortress, 2009.
Warnock, G. J., ed. *Essays on J. L. Austin*. Oxford: Clarendon, 1973.
Watts, Isaac. *Hymns and Spiritual Songs: In Three Volumes*. London: John Lawrence, 1707.
Webster, John. *Barth*. Outstanding Christian Thinkers. London: Continuum, 2000.
Wells, Samuel. "The Challenge and Opportunity of Easter Preaching." *Journal for Preachers* 35.3 (2012) 26–32.
Wengert, Timothy J. "'Peace, Peace . . . Cross, Cross': Reflections on How Martin Luther Relates the Theology of the Cross to Suffering." *Theology Today* 59.2 (2002) 190–205.
Wengert, Timothy J., ed. *The Roots of Reform*. Volume 1 of *The Annotated Luther*, edited by Hans J. Hillerbrand et al. Minneapolis: Fortress, 2015.
Wiebe, Rudy. *The Blue Mountains of China*. Toronto: McClelland and Stewart, 1970.
Williams, Rowan. *On Christian Theology*. Challenges in Contemporary Theology. Oxford: Blackwell, 2000.
———. *Resurrection: Interpreting the Easter Gospel*. Harrisburg, PA: Morehouse, 1994.
Willimon, William H. "Preaching After Easter." *Journal for Preachers* 34.3 (2011) 38–41.
———. "Preaching as Demonstration of Resurrection." *Journal For Preachers* 37.3 (2014) 13–17.
———. "Preaching as Demonstration of Resurrection." *Journal For Preachers* 38.3 (2015) 6–10.
———. *Proclamation and Theology*. Horizons in Theology. Nashville: Abingdon, 2005.
Wilson, Paul Scott. *The Four Pages of the Sermon: A Guide to Biblical Preaching*. Rev. ed. Nashville: Abingdon, 2018.
———. "New Homiletic." In *The New Interpreter's Handbook of Preaching*, edited by Paul Scott Wilson et al., 398–401. Nashville: Abingdon, 2008.

Wolters, Albert M. *Creation Regained: Biblical Basics for a Reformational Worldview.* 2nd ed. Grand Rapids: Eerdmans, 2005.

Wolterstorff, Nicholas. *Divine Discourse: Philosophical Reflections on the Claim That God Speaks.* Cambridge: Cambridge University Press, 1995.

Wood, Arthur Skevington. *Captive to the Word: Martin Luther; Doctor of Sacred Scripture.* Grand Rapids: Eerdmans, 1969.

Wright, Christopher. *The Mission of God: Unlocking the Bible's Grand Narrative.* Downers Grove: IVP Academic, 2006.

Wright, N. T. *Paul and the Faithfulness of God.* Minneapolis: Fortress, 2013.

———. *The Resurrection and the Son of God.* Volume 3 of *Christian Origins and the Question of God.* Minneapolis: Fortress, 2003.

Yamada, Frank M. "The View From 2040: The Futures of Theological Education," [n.p.], online: https://mccormickpresident.wordpress.com/2012/02/15/the-inaugural-address-the-view-from-2040-the-futures-of-theological-education/.

Yang, Sunggu. "The Promised Land: A Postcolonial Homiletic of Promise in the Asian American Context." In *Toward a Homiletical Theology of Promise*, edited by David Schnasa Jacobsen, 9–27. Promise of Homiletical Theology 4. Eugene, OR: Wipf & Stock, 2018.

Index of Modern Authors

Allen, O. Wesley, 6–7, 233
Allison, Dale C., Jr., 3, 106, 167, 217, 233, 236
Althaus, Paul, 47, 233
Andrewes, Lancelot, 81, 233
Aquinas, Saint Thomas, 207, 233
Archaeological Receipts Fund, 157, 233
Aumann, Jordan, 233
Aune, David E., 45, 93–95, 135, 216, 233
Austin, J. L., 51–55, 57, 64, 66, 75, 78, 155, 190, 233, 237, 244

Baker, Christopher, 185, 233
Bakirtzis, Charalambos, 157, 233
Balch, David L., 159, 234
Bammer, Angelika, 234
Barks, Coleman, 1, 212, 234
Barth, Karl, xv, 5, 19, 21–22, 45–49, 79, 92, 99, 151–53, 155, 161, 202–6, 214–15, 226, 229, 231, 234, 243, 244
Barton, Stephen C., 4, 19, 21, 22, 102, 104, 136, 142, 171, 234
Battles, Ford Lewis, 236
Bauckham, Richard, 83, 234
Baudrillard, Jean, 7, 234
Baumgärtel, Friedrich, 135, 234
Bayne, Paul, 35–36, 234
Beasley-Murray, George R., 145, 234
Beaudean, Jr., John William, 13, 234
Behm, Johannes, 134, 135, 234
Bennett, David, 234

Berenbaum, Michael, xv
Berry, C. Everett, 51, 52, 234
Bertram, Martin H., 154
Bhabha, Homi K., 29–30, 155, 160–69, 171–73, 179–80, 185, 188, 193, 206, 209, 214, 234–35, 238
Blount, Brian K., 11, 20, 27, 44, 91, 220–21, 235
Bockmuehl, Markus, 243
Bonhoeffer, Dietrich, 24–25, 190, 235
Bortsch, Hans Werner, 235
Bosch, David, 41–43, 45, 235
Botha, Eugene, 51, 235
Botterweck, G. Johannes, xvi
Bowden, John, 238, 240, 244
Boyer, Ernest, 200, 235
Braaten, Carl E., 3, 4, 235
Brocke, Michael, 238
Bromiley, Geoffrey W., xvi, 234
Brown, Raymond E., 210, 235
Brueggemann, Walter, 65, 235
Buechner, Frederick, 83, 235
Bultmann, Rudolf, 3, 5, 65, 235
Bunyan, John, 160, 175, 181, 216, 235
Burnaby, John, 201, 235
Burrell, David B., 237
Burton-Christie, Douglas, 170, 235
Buswell, Robert E., xv
Büttgen, Philippe, 47, 235
Buttrick, David G., 7, 8, 11, 58–61, 82, 90, 134, 235

INDEX OF MODERN AUTHORS

Calvin, John, 34–35, 47–48, 92, 204, 212, 231, 235–36
Campbell, Charles L., 5, 40, 236, 240
Campbell, Constantine J., 43, 236, 243
Carnley, Peter, 3, 7–8, 236
Castelli, Enrico, 236
Chadwick, Henry, 104, 236
Chan, Sam, 71, 236
Childers, Jana, 36, 90, 236, 242
Cohen, Leonard, vii, 58, 85, 236
Cohn, Haim Hermann, 100, 236
Coffin, William Sloan, 6, 236
Coupland, Douglas, 87, 89, 236
Cousar, Charles B., 227, 236
Craddock, Fred B., 80, 236
Cranfield, C. E. B., 88, 236
Crossan, John Dominic, 8, 11, 236
Cummings, Brian, 243
Cunitz, Edouard, 236

Daher, Nazih, 237
Daniels, Donald E., 234
Davies, W. D., 106, 167, 217, 236
Denton, Melinda Lundquist, 13, 243
Dickens, Charles, 145, 236
Draper, Marilyn, 41–45, 236
Dykstra, Craig R., 205, 236

Eliot, T. S., 33, 81, 99, 163, 199, 236, 242
Ellul, Jacques, 45, 90, 236
Epstein, Isidore, xvi, xvii, 237
Evans, Donald, 64, 66, 69–70, 237

Fabry, Heinz-Josef, xvi
Fagles, Robert, 243
Fee, Gordon D., 107, 176, 237
Feldman, Louis H., 102, 237
Ferry, Patrick, 47, 237
Finegan, Jack, 159, 237
Fiorenza, Elizabeth Schüssler, 244
Fish, Stanley, 56, 237
Fitzmyer, Joseph A., 17, 88, 107, 142, 146, 184, 212, 217, 237
Fowler, Harold N., 241
Freyne, Seán, 183, 237

Friedrich, Gerhard, xvi
Fuller, Reginald, 235

Gaarden, Marianne, 40, 204, 237
Geyer, Hans-Georg, 3, 237
Gilroy, Paul, 179, 237
Glaser, Sheila Faria, 234
González, Justo L., 188, 237, 239
Goodman, Elizabeth R., 6, 144–45, 237
Gorman, Michael J., 125, 153, 218, 237
Goulder, Michael, 4, 104
Graham, Keith, 52, 54–55, 59, 237
Green, Clifford J., 235
Green, David E., xvi
Greidanus, Sidney, 35, 238
Grewendorf, Gunter, 55–56, 238
Guder, Darrell, 42, 238

Harstine, Stan, 144, 238
Hays, Richard B., 228, 238
Heinemann, Joseph, 15, 238
Hemingway, Ernest, 86–87, 89, 238
Hengel, Martin, 100, 238
Hezser, Catherine, 238
Hickling, Colin, 136, 142
Hilkert, Mary Catherine, 7–8, 238
Hillerbrand, Hans J., 244
Holmes, Michael W., xvii, 238
Hooker, Richard, 11–12, 21, 238
Hoskyns, Edwyn C., 234
Huddart, David, 161, 163, 165, 168, 172, 179, 238
Hughes, Graham, 62, 238

Ilan, Tal, 101–2, 238
Inge, John, 181, 238
Instone-Brewer, David, 129, 238
Isaac, Benjamin, 102, 238

Jacobs, Alan, 60, 238
Jacobsen, David Schnasa, 65, 66, 71, 238, 245
Jansen, Mechteld, 172–74, 181, 211, 238
Jeffrey, David L., 238

Index of Modern Authors

Jiménez, Pablo A., 188–89, 237, 238
Johnson, Stephen, 157, 239
Jones, Henry Stuart, xv
Jones, Joe R., 61, 239

Kay, James F., 28, 65–66, 71, 239
Keener, Craig, 148, 239
Khan, Geoffrey, xv
Kim, Duk Hyun, 71–73
Kim, Eunjoo Mary, 188–89
Kim, Matthew D., 188–89
Kittel, Gerhard, xvi
Knowles, Michael P., 13, 24, 45, 62, 77, 95, 118, 127, 136, 153, 157, 175, 183, 217, 223, 239
Knox, Bernard, 243
Koch, Klaus, 148, 240
Koester, Helmut, 157, 233
Kraemer, David, 129, 240
Krauss, Reinhard, 235
Kwok, Pui-lan, 185, 189–91, 193, 240

L'Engle, Madeleine, 12, 240
Lalor, Thomas Comerford, 233
Lamb, W. R. M., 120, 241
Larsen, Kasper Bro, 139, 240
Lash, Nicholas, 22, 240
Lee, Sang Hyun, 192–94, 240
Lehmann, Helmut T., xv
Leitch, James W., 241
Liddell, Henry George, xv
Lieu, Judith, 102
Lim, Timothy H., 224, 240
Lischer, Richard, 91, 240
Long, Thomas G., 5, 19, 240
Longenecker, Richard N., 63, 88, 135, 240
Lose, David J., 69, 240
Louw, Johannes P., xv, 116
Lüdemann, Gerd, 3–4, 240
Lukaszewski, Albert L., 63, 240
Luther, Martin, xv, xvi, 29, 35, 47–49, 62, 79–80, 92, 95–96, 151–54, 220, 226, 233, 235, 237, 242, 244, 245

Maan, Ajit K., 173, 240
MacArthur, John, 36–37, 240
Macaskill, Grant, 43, 241
Marcus, Joel, 106, 167, 241
Martin, Ralph P., 227, 241
Matsuoka, Fumitaka, 193, 241
McKee, Elsie Ann, 236
McNeill, John T., 236
Meconi, David Vincent, 81, 241
Meggle, Georg, 56, 238
Merrill, Rodney, 238
Metzger, Bruce M., 142, 166, 176, 241
Michaelis, Wilhelm, 16, 241
Moltmann, Jürgen, 71, 73–74, 241
Morgan, Robert, 21
Moule, C. F. D., 237
Muraoka, Takamitsu, 65, 241

Nasrallah, Laura, 244
Neusner, Jacob, xvii, 85, 241
Newbigin, Lesslie, 4–5, 41–42, 46, 241
Nida, Eugene A., xv, 116, 241
Niebuhr, H. Richard, 165, 193, 241

Owen, John R., 235
Owens, W. R., 34, 235
Özen, Alf, 240

Packer, J. I., 29, 241
Padilla, Alvin, 239
Pasquarello, III, Michael, 25, 28–29, 45, 57, 149, 207, 209, 219, 241
Pearce, Sarah J. K., 101, 241
Pelikan, Jaroslav, xv
Peterson, Eugene, xv, 92–93, 241
Petuchowski, Jakob J., 238
Picard, Charles, 160, 241
Pietersma, Albert, xvi
Porter, Stanley E., 239, 240
Pott, Francis, 214, 242
Poythress, Vern S., 57, 242
Presa, Neal D., 189, 242
Purves, Andrew, 19, 20, 44, 212, 213, 228, 242

Ramachandra, Vinoth, 25, 185–86, 242
Rambo, Shelley, 145, 242
Ramsey, Boniface, 233
Reinhold, Meyer, 102, 237
Reumann, John, 227, 242
Richmond, I. A.157, 242
Ricoeur, Paul, 5, 242
Ringgren, Helmer, xvi
Roger, J., 157, 242
Rogers, Patrick, 101, 103
Rossetti, Christina, 127, 242
Rottman, John M., 40, 45, 242
Rudrum, Alan, 81, 242
Runions, Erin, 162, 242
Rupp, E. Gordon, 96, 242
Rushdie, Salman, 163–65, 187, 242
Rutherford, Jonathan, 235

Sancken, Joni S., 27–28, 242
Sanneh, Lamin, 186–87, 242
Sbisá, Marina, 233
Schaff, Philip, 169, 242
Schlafer, David J., 105, 156, 243
Schlütter, Morten, 200, 243
Schmidt, Clayton J., 242
Schniewind, Julius, 220, 243
Schrenk, Gottlob, 142, 243
Schultz, Robert C., 233
Scott, Douglas W., xvi
Scott, Robert, xv
Seamands, Stephen A., 27, 243
Searle, John R., 52–55, 57, 64, 75, 78, 155, 190, 243
Seybold, Klaus, 88, 243
Simpson, James, 243
Sinai, Yuval, 100, 236
Skolnik, Fred, xv
Smith, Christian, 13, 243
Spong, John Shelby, 3, 243
Stanton, Graham, 4, 19, 21, 22, 102, 104, 136, 142, 234
Stemberger, Gunter, 129, 243
Stevenson, Geoffrey, 243
Strack, H. L., 129, 243
Strathmann, Hermann, 158, 243
Summit, Jennifer, 207, 243

Tappenden, Fred, 7, 243
Taylor, Barbara Brown, 12, 90–91, 199–200, 243
Taylor, John, 137, 140, 243
Thackeray, Henry St. John, 104, 239
Thane, Markus, 46, 203, 243
Thate, Michael J., 43, 243
Thomson, G. T., xv
Thompson, Thomas L., 243
Torrance, David W., 235
Torrance, Thomas F., 212, 234, 235
Travis, Sarah, 162, 189–90, 191–92, 194, 243
Turner, Mary Donovan, 36–37
Turner, Edith and Victor, 181, 244

Updike, John, 18, 21, 244
Urmson, J. O., 233

Valle-Ruiz,, Lis, 188, 244
Vanderveken, Daniel, 52, 64, 243
Van Gelder, Craig, 42, 244
Vanhoozer, Kevin J., 5, 52, 78, 243, 244
Van Toorn, Penelope, 171, 244
Vorgrimler, Herbert, 83, 96, 244

Wajdenbaum, Philippe, 243
Wan, Sze-kar, 158, 168, 192, 244
Warnock, G. J., 64, 66, 233, 244
Watson, Francis, 18–19, 20
Watts, Isaac, 30, 244
Webster, John, 202–3, 244
Weissenrieder, Annette, 159, 208, 234
Wells, Samuel, 7, 244
Wengert, Timothy J., 152, 244
Westfall, Cynthia Long, 240
Wiebe, Rudy, 169–71, 174, 244
Wilkinson, John, 236
Williams, Rowan, 4, 62, 107–10, 209, 219, 220, 244
Willimon, William H., 13, 14, 41, 90, 110, 123, 244
Wilson, Paul Scott, 45, 71, 152, 244
Wilson, R. A., 237
Winkler, Ulrich, 238

Wolters, Albert M., 88, 245
Wolterstorff, Nicholas, 75–80, 245
Wood, Arthur Skevington, 35, 245
Wright, Benjamin G., xvi
Wright, Christopher, 43, 245
Wright, N. T., 3, 168, 245
Würthwein, Ernst, 134, 234

Yamada, Frank M., 185, 245
Yang, Sunggu, 192–95, 245

Zscheile, Dwight, 42, 244

Index of Early Literature

HEBREW BIBLE

Genesis

1—2	63
1:3	64
1:3–4	67
1:9, 11, 24	67
2:2–3	215
2:7	61
2:18–23	60
2:19	59, 61
2:23	60, 61
3:9	133
3:17–19	217
3:21	217
7:10	129
17:1–3	93
27:12, 22	143
50:10	129

Exodus

3:2	16
6:3	16
20:7	15
20:8–10	128
23:12	128
31:15	128

Leviticus

5:1	100
9:24	93

Numbers

20:6	93
35:30	100

Deuteronomy

5:11	15
5:13–14	128
10:21	184
11:7	184
17:6	100
19:15	100
21:18–21	216
28:29	143

Joshua

5:14	93

Judges

13:20	93
16:26	143

1 Kings

18:39	93

2 Kings

6:17	146

1 Chronicles

21:16	93

Psalms

5:11	96
15	148
15:10	148
15:11	148
16	148
40:10	63
40:6	92
68:6	154
68:11	47
73	10
78:2	217
84:6	222
89:1–2	62
112:3	10

Proverbs

2:19	148
3:5	118
5:6	148
6:23	148
15:24	148
17:28	134

Qohelet

1:1–4, 8–9	88
2:17	88
5:2	11
12:13–14	88

Isaiah

6:9–10	91
28:21	151
30:15, 18	84
43:19	216
46:11	65
55:10–11	65
55:11	78
58	36, 38
59:10	143
61	36, 38

Jeremiah

21:8	148
24:6	228

Ezekiel

1:28	93
43:3	93

Daniel

2:46	93
8:17–18	93
10:9	93

Micah

4:6	231

Zechariah

12:10	144

NEW TESTAMENT

Matthew

3:2	24, 193
4:17	24, 193
5:3	193
5:12	116
5:39, 41	166
6:3	94
6:9	24
6:10	15
6:26–29	217
7:13–14	148
7:29	154
8:5–13	166
8:13	67
8:16	67
8:20	171
10:7	24
10:20	24
10:25	24
10:40	24
11:25–26	24, 217
12:38	81
12:40	20
13:35	217

INDEX OF EARLY LITERATURE 255

14:25–33	120	1:10	25
14:26	145	1:17	67
16:16, 22–23	120	1:22	154
16:18–19	120	1:22, 27	67
16:19	69	1:25	67
16:21	113, 114	1:41	67
17:5–6	94	2:5–12	68
17:6	93	2:14	167
17:22–23	113	3:14	182
17:23	114	3:15	24, 73
20:1–16	194	3:18	167
20:18–19	113	4:9, 23	91
20:19	114	4:10–12	91
21:33–41	194	4:22	217
21:43	50	4:26–29	50
22:37	135	4:39	67
25:29	15	5:8	67
25:33, 41	94	5:41	68
26:26–27	140	6:3	204
26:52	113	6:8–11	24
26:52–53	167	6:12–13	24, 73
26:73	183	6:49	145
26:75	73	7:34	68
27:55–56	106	8:17–18	92
27:56	114	8:29	106
27:61	114	8:31	113
27:62–66	113	8:35	104
28:1	111, 114, 131	9:18	73
28:1–7	111	9:25	67
28:3	113	9:31	113
28:4	94, 113	9:38	108
28:6	112	9:39–40	108
28:6–7	112, 114	10:32	175
28:7	112	10:33–34	113
28:7, 10	117	10:42–45	122
28:8	116	11:9–10	136
28:8–10	115	12:1–8	191
28:9	14	12:1–12	49
28:9–10	14	12:17	166
28:10	120	12:24	118
28:11	117	13:10	24
28:11–15	119	14:22–23	140
28:13	112	14:31	73, 105
28:16–20	119	14:49	82
		14:61	82
		14:65	82
		15:40–41	105–106

Mark

1:3	208
16:1	130

Mark (continued)

16:2	131
16:7	107, 112, 212
16:9–11	212

Luke

1:11	16
1:28	116
1:48	184
1:49	184
1:76	148
2:35	142
3:5	148
4	38, 39
4:14, 18–19	24
4:18–19	36, 38
4:32	154
5:22	142
6:8	142
6:13	182
6:15	167
7:1–10	166
7:14	67
7:29–34	10
7:47	109–10
8:17	217
9:1–2	38
9:2	182
9:6	182
9:22	134
9:22, 44	113
9:45	146
9:46–47	142
10:16	24, 38, 71
10:21	217
10:21–22	24
10:42	207
11:2	24
12:12	24
12:16–24	50
14:35	91
16:16	9
16:19–31	9
16:29–31	9
17:20	177
18:32–33	113
18:34	147
21:9	141
21:19	140
22:19	141
22:31–32	74
23:24	133
23:35	105, 133
23:49	106
23:54	130
23:54–56	129
23:54–24:10	107
23:56	130
24	131, 145, 147
24:1	131
24:5	141
24:10–11	103
24:11	133
24:13–16	131–32
24:16	132, 147
24:17	132
24:17–25	14
24:18	133
24:19	133
24:21	133, 212
24:22	133
24:23	112
24:25	134
24:26	136
24:27	135, 140, 218
24:30	140
24:30–31	140
24:31–32	146
24:32, 45	223
24:33–34	107
24:34	16
24:37	147
24:37, 39	120
24:38	134, 141, 142
24:39	120, 142, 143
24:41	141
24:41–43	141
24:42–43	14, 17
24:44–48	146
24:45	146

John

1:11	167
1:19–23	73

1:43	67	21:3	105
3:34	63	21:9	14, 109
3:36	167	21:13	141
4:25, 29	106	21:16, 17	109
4:32	24		
5:30	73	Acts	
6:68	82		
6:69	106	1:6	182
7:25–26, 31, 41	106	1:8	187
7:33	210	1:9–11	182
7:41–52	183	1:15–26	182
9:2	10	2:1–4	183
9:40–41	92	2:3	16
11:25	27	2:5–11	184
11:27	106	2:5–13	183
11:31	129	2:11	184
13:20	24	2:14–36	136, 183
13:21	141	2:22–24	185
14:2–3, 18–19	210	2:27, 31	148
14:26	210	2:28	148, 228
14:28	210	3:6–8	8
15:20	24, 137	3:15	82
16:14	210	3:18	147
16:22	210	3:22–26	136
16:28	210	4:11	136
18:18	109	4:30	8
18:31	133	4:33	223
18:36	180	6:8	8
19:25–27	106	7:2	16
19:26	105	7:30, 35	16
19:30	215, 83	7:31	142
19:34–37	144	9:3–9	94
19:38–40	74	9:17	16
19:38–42	130	10:4	141
20:1	131	10:40–41	17
20:11–17	209–210	10:43	136
20:14–17	115	13:10	148
20:15	112	13:30–31	16–17
20:15–17	14	13:32–41	136
20:17	145, 211	14:3	8
20:19, 21, 26	67	16:9	16
20:19, 26	17	16:12	156
20:22	14, 24	16:14	147
20:25	116	17:2–3	147
20:25–27	143	17:13	142
20:27	144	17:16	158
20:28	145	17:24–27	143
20:29	177	17:27	143

Acts (continued)

17:32	125
22:6–11	94
23	172
23:36	116
24:5	141
26:12–18	94
26:15, 17–18	147
26:22–23	147

Romans

1:4	8, 134
1:16	100, 224
1:18	167
2:5	135
3:22–23	187
5:6, 8	221
6:4	99
6:5–8	43
6:8	24
8	88
8:15–16	224
8:18–23	88
8:19–25	213
8:23	131
8:29	153
10:12	187
10:17	63, 65
12:15	84
13:4	121
13:11–12	131
13:4	149
15:18–19	223, 228
15:19	8

1 Corinthians

1:18	225
1:18—2:5	226
1:24–25	126
1:25	21
1:27–29	125
2:1	220
2:3	123
2:4	228
2:4–5	224
2:4–7	124
2:9	230
2:9–10	181
3:5–7	226
3:16	159, 208
4:4–5	153–54
4:13	86, 225
4:15	34
4:16	153
4:20	224
6:19	159
9:14	220
9:16	47
11:1	153
11:24	140
11:26	219
12:3	56
12:28	8
13	85
13:1	183
13:7	85
13:9	125, 176
13:12	176
15	3, 125
15:1–5	65
15:3–8	17, 106–107
15:6	108
15:8	108
15:9	73, 108
15:14–17	19
15:22	149
15:35–44	8
15:56	122, 130
15:57	45

2 Corinthians

1:9	155
1:20	66
1:23–24	153
2:15–16	100
3:1–3	13
3:1–6	79
3:2–3	124
3:3	72
3:5–6	124
3:18	15, 168, 175
4:5	125
4:6	175–76

Philippians

4:7	108, 125
4:7–10	226
4:8–10	26
4:16–5:2	175
4:18	177
5:1–4	213
5:2	169
5:6–8	161
5:7	214
5:11, 14	122
5:16	132–33, 176
5:17	91, 169, 177
5:20	65, 77
6:3–10	77
6:8b–10	26
6:9–10	228
6:16	159, 208
10:5	28
10:5–6	79
10:8	77, 228
10:10	123
11:6, 30	123
12:12	8, 223
13:3	65
13:3–4	124
13:10	77, 228

Galatians

1:11	34
2:19–20	23, 95
2:20	24
3:1	176
3:1, 3	134
3:5	8
3:28	168
4:19	24
6:15	168
6:25	168

Ephesians

1:17–20	225
2:11–20	168
2:17	35, 165
2:17, 19	187
3:7	225
3:20	225

Philippians

1:13	159
1:17–18	220
1:23	160
1:27–30	227
1:28	227
2:5	78
2:6	78
2:7	167
2:12	227
2:15–16	227
3:5, 8	86, 172
3:8	86
3:20	158
4:4	116
4:5–7	227
4:22	159

Colossians

1:13	169, 187
1:15	176
1:28	220
1:29	225
2:12, 20	43
2:18	112
3:1	23, 43
3:1–3	169
3:3	23, 176, 220
3:4	176

1 Thessalonians

1:4–5	225
1:7	153
2:1–2, 14–16	34
2:3–6	181
2:12	159
2:13	33, 181, 225

1 Timothy

3:16	15
4:7	134
4:11	36

Titus

2:15	36
3:3	134

Hebrews

1:1–2	63
2:3–4	223
2:4	8
2:8–9	166, 219
3:10	148
4:11	178
9:28	16
10:10	214
10:32–34	178
11:1	180
11:4	99
11:8–16	178
11:15	178
11:16	156, 230
11:35	18
12:1	179
12:1–2	178
12:18	143
12:22	230
12:22–23	178
13:3	84

James

1:1	116
5:16	67

1 Peter

1:1	158
1:17	178
1:25	34
2:5	208
2:9	158
2:11	178
2:11–12	158
2:12	158
2:17	122
2:19	158
2:20	158
3:18	221

1 John

1:1	92, 143, 144, 212, 227
1.2	16
3:2	175, 201
4:18	122

Revelation

1:2	63
1:5	63
1:16	93
1:16, 20	94
1:17	93, 94
1:17–19	94
1:18	94, 223
2:1	94
3:14	63
4:10	93
4:11	122
5:1, 7	94
5:6	145
6:10	83
7:11	93
8:1	83
11:13	141
12:11	44
15:3	148
21:5	216

CLASSICAL, INTERTESTAMENTAL, EARLY CHRISTIAN, AND ISLAMIC SOURCES

Aeschines

On the Embassy

2 §53	103

Al-Ghazālī

Ninety-Nine Beautiful Names of God

	11

INDEX OF EARLY LITERATURE

Augustine
Fourth Homily on the First
Epistle of Saint John
    201
Sermon 184 §3   81
Sermon 190 §3   81

Aristotle
Poetics
1452a–b   139
1454b–55a   139

Barnabas
15:8–9   215

1 Clement
24:1–26:3   20

Didache
1:1   148

Eusebius
Ecclesiastical History
I:13.2   160

4 Ezra
10:30   94

Hippocrates
De morbis popularibus
Epidemics 1 §4   103

Homer
Odyssey
9:416   143
19:386–93   138
19:471–75   138
23:73–77   138
24:327–35   138

Flavius Josephus
Antiquities
4:219   101
13:380–83   18

War
1:97–98   18
3:351–52   103
3:399–401   103
3:403–404   103
3:405   104

Justin Martyr
First Apology
67   215

Lucian
Saturnalia
§8   103

Origen
Contra Celsum
3:44, 49   104

Plato
Ion
534e   120

Plutarch
De garrulitate
§20   103

Sophocles
Oedipus the King
1028–33   139

Theophrastus
Characters
§28.3   103

Vita Barlaam et Joasaph

32 §295	103

※

TALMUDIC LITERATURE

Mishnah

'Abot

2:5	85
5:20	15
5:25	137

Berakot

5:5	121

Ketubbot

2:5–6	100
5:5	217
9:8	100

Makkot

1:7–9	100

Qiddušin

1:7	102
4:13	102
4:14	10

Roš Haššanah

1:8	100

Šabbat

7:2	129
23:5	129, 130

Šebuʿot

4:1	100

Soṭah

3:4	102
9:8	100
9:15	90

Yebamot

15:1–16:2	100
16:7	100

Tosefta

'Abot

9:1	94

Megillah

3:11	102

Šabbat

17:18–19	129

Sanhedrin

11:8	10

Soṭah

10:3	129

Palestinian Talmud

Berakot

2:8	129
3:1	129

Šabbat

16:8	183

Soṭah

3:4	102

Moʿed Qaṭan

3:5	129

Babylonian Talmud
'Abodah Zarah
20b   90

Sanhedrin
108b   129
113a   95

Sukkah
28a   183

Ta'anit
2a   95

www.ingramcontent.com/pod-product-compliance
Lightning Source LLC
Chambersburg PA
CBHW022003220426
43663CB00007B/933